Equality for some

Equality for some

The story of girls' education

Barry Turner

Ward Lock Educational

ISBN 0 7062 3426 X

First published 1974

Set in 11 on 13 point Imprint
by Robert MacLehose and Company Limited
Printers to the University of Glasgow
for Ward Lock Educational
116 Baker Street, London W1M 2BB
Made in Great Britain

Contents

Introduction

The female intellect is a recent educational discovery. Traditionally Western civilization has distrusted and discouraged clever women, initially because they were regarded as a threat to the spiritual well-being of the community (everyone knew how much suffering and anguish mankind might have avoided if Adam had not listened to Eve) and later because cleverness was not considered to be a high ranking quality for a good homemaker.

Even those advanced thinkers of the seventeenth and eighteenth centuries who supported education for girls – at least for the daughters of the ruling class – were careful to point out that their ideas were not aimed at changing the social status of women so much as raising the standard of intellect within the family environment. But the mildest proposals for extending the curriculum beyond the scope of domestic competence aroused strong opposition from diehards who argued that learning, particularly of a literary nature, would inflame the conceit of women and disrupt society. Supporting evidence for this view was provided by the scandalous personal history of Mary Wollstonecraft whose books, Vindication of the Rights of Women and Thoughts on the Education of Daughters gave the first hints of a feminist movement by seeking to prove that girls were the intellectual equal of boys and thus fit 'to participate in the inherent rights of mankind'.

The break with tradition for which Mary Wollstonecraft was campaigning came almost a century later with the great spurt forward in education initiated by the 1870 Act. In the elementary schools girls were often treated harshly and suffered uninspired teaching on a narrow curriculum but at least they were set on the way to equality with boys and their education, however limited, was better than nothing. But more significant in the long run was the emergence of a system of private education for middle class girls. Although in

Victorian middle class society, women were subservient as never before, economic prosperity freed them from the need to contribute to the family income. And since domestic servants were plentiful and cheap, they were blessed with unlimited leisure. A minority rebelled against idleness and worked to secure for women the right to exercise their brains. Unfortunately, beyond this stage in the argument the campaigners were unable to agree on a single philosophy and programme. There were those (chiefly associated with the Church) who wanted to enhance the domestic image, to promote women from mere homemakers to agents of humanity capable of merging a lively intellect with the essentially feminine qualities of gentleness and sensitivity. A second, more radical group, looked to the eventual achievement of sex equality when middle class girls could emerge from the domestic environment to offer their intellectual skills to the labour market and break into the male dominated professions.

The contrast in attitudes was reflected in the policies of two of the most famous of the new girls schools. At the North London Collegiate, Frances Mary Buss took a lead in proving that girls were every bit as capable as boys. She adopted the curriculum used in boys schools, introduced the prefectorial system and emphasized the virtue of competition in sport and work. On the other hand, Dorothea Beale, Principal of Cheltenham Ladies College, developed a curriculum and teaching techniques that she thought were especially appropriate to girls. She opposed competitive sport and claimed that girls had unique emotional and intellectual needs related to their future family responsibilities. The same disparity of views characterized the battle for girls higher education with Emily Davies proclaiming the need for total equality and Anne Clough defending a form of intellectual training that kept faith with the traditional interpretation of female qualities and duties.

The result was not an outright victory for one side or the other but an unsatisfactory compromise which allowed for a social blessing on single girls who used their education as a basis for a career but disapproval for those who continued to assert their intellectual and economic independence after they married. This conflict of interest has never been resolved. Despite the broadening of educational and employment opportunities for girls the pressures on them to look to marriage, family and home as their first and natural responsibility remains overwhelmingly powerful. Educationists talk favourably of the need to create equality of opportunity yet much of what they provide in the way of intellectual training runs directly counter to the principle.

But there are signs that the double think philosophy is at last in decline. Women are having fewer children, finding less to do in the home and enjoying longer lives – a combination of factors which adds up to a frustration of inactivity. The feminist solution is to break down the remaining educational and employment barriers which prevent women from fully utilizing their abilities. But if this programme is to be successful there must be an accompanying reform in our entire social perspective, not least in the interpretation of family rights and responsibilities. The purpose of this book is to describe in a historical and sociological setting the contribution of education to the continuing debate on equality and its potential as the leading agency for changing social attitudes.

Chapter one

In pursuit of virtue

'If you must play hockey,' said the Mistress of Girton College, Cambridge, when her girls started to show an enthusiasm for organized sports, 'do try to hit the ball gently.' Her commandment had no lasting impact but the advice was meant to be taken seriously. After all, she was merely translating to a new situation the popular Victorian concept of the perfect woman. It was an ideal which embraced sensitivity, modesty, gentleness and the duty to provide comfort and support for the other sex; characteristics that were thought to be less suited to man who, of course, was allowed to hit the ball as hard as he liked.

The idea of the gentle woman derived from what at the time was progressive Christian teaching. Certainly it was in advance of the pre-Victorian hard-line view that all of man's troubles originated in the Garden of Eden when Eve proved the intellectual and moral inferiority of her sex by responding to the sinful urgings of the serpent. The softer-natured exponents of Christianity argued, also from Genesis, that woman was the 'help and supplement' of man. Further, they balanced Eve's unfortunate lapse with the undoubted virtue of Mary, the Mother of God. In her were the qualities of love and self-sacrifice which were assumed to be essentially feminine. It was believed that if this side of woman's nature was properly nurtured it could affect all moral standards. 'Be good, sweet maid,' said Charles Kingsley, 'and let who will be clever.' He did not mean that woman was destined to be a passive spectator of life, but rather that by her example she should exercise a restraining and civilizing influence on the harsh and competitive male society.

It was a significant but nevertheless secondary role that she was called upon to play. The soft-liners went along with the established view that woman's place was in the home (or church) with her children – not because they thought she was too dangerous to be released, as the hard-liners argued, but because any weakening of her links with domesticity threatened the survival of the family – that sacred totem of Victorian society. One or other of these theological interpretations dominated every major stage in the development of girls' education up to the present century.

When the first Christian missionaries arrived in England they found a society in which females were regarded as marketable commodities – to be sold into marriage to the highest bidder. But the custom may not have been quite so degrading to women as some modern writers have supposed. In the absence of formalized wedding vows, the bridal payment was at least a symbol of a two-way agreement which imposed on the male some basic family responsibilities. Women were excluded from any major decision-making role but this seemed only natural to a primitive people who set great store by military prowess.

The Christians, however, emphasized the inferior status of women with a sophisticated code of ethics. St Augustine of Canterbury, who landed on the Isle of Thanet in 596 and commenced operations with the baptism of Ethelbert, king of Kent, proclaimed the doctrine of indissoluble marriage and the total submission of wives and daughters to the God-appointed rulers of their households. If Eve's defection in the Garden of Eden needed any supporting evidence of female inferiority there was always the judgement of St Paul, who ruled uncompromisingly that as Christ is the head of every man, every man is the head of every woman. But St Paul accepted that 'in Christ there is neither male nor female'; in his view women could at least share equally with men the hope of eventual salvation. This entitled them to discover and to practise the Christian religion even though they had to 'learn in silence with all subjection'. The doctrine was reinforced by Pope Gregory's missive on Pastoral Care which commanded his bishops and clergy to call together 'the people of every condition and sex, and plainly teach them who rarely hear the word of God'.

The idea of allowing both sexes to participate in the religious experience was in line with the Anglo-Saxon tradition which allowed for priestesses and holy women. Thus, some of the earliest monastic foundations not only catered for women, but often provided adjoining quarters for monks and nuns. The monasteries assumed some educational responsibilities, since the ability to read was important for proper understanding of Christian faith, while the nuns also acquired such domestic skills as sewing and embroidery and learned an elementary code of pious behaviour. Monastic teaching affected only a very small proportion of women, most of whom had negligible influence beyond their own communities. Still, it might have prefaced a really effective system of church-controlled co-education. Unfortunately, the high ideals of monasticism were not maintained. By the eighth century there were numerous examples of corrupt administration and dissolute living. The reputation of the monasteries was further damaged because many convents were expected to combine the services of a religious institution with the facilities of an open prison especially for high-born ladies who were guilty of infamous conduct.

There was also the threat of violence. The Viking invasions were frequently directed at monasteries where valuable booty could be taken. In such a disruptive society it was impossible for religious houses to thrive and by the mid-ninth century monastic life for women had practically ceased. A corresponding development was the growing influence among leading churchmen of the puritan ethic, which cast the female in the role of evil temptress to the lusts of man. At the Council of Macon woman was granted a soul by a majority of only one vote. St Augustine of Hippo described her as a temple built over a sewer; while St Benedict is said to have jumped naked into a rosebush in an attempt to seek a distraction from his sinful thoughts about woman. All pleasure was suspect, but sex was regarded as a particularly potent force on the side of the Devil. This theological argument was supported by the dubious theory that sexual immorality had caused the collapse of the Roman Empire.

Most people were not easily converted to asceticism, but they fell in with the idea that women, who were able to rely on male protection, should concentrate their efforts exclusively on domestic duties. Even among the wealthy, wives and daughters were discouraged from exercising independent thought, which excluded any form of education that went beyond the requirements of competent household management. The rare exception was the children of royalty and high nobility. King Alfred of Wessex, who achieved the first decisive victories against the Danish invaders, was also an enthusiastic seeker of knowledge who tried to revive English schools and libraries. His own early education was slight but he gathered scholars from France,

Germany and Wales as well as from Wessex, to help him translate the great religious books from Latin into English. His daughters were taught along with their brothers by court tutors. This helped Alfred's eldest child, Aethelflaed, who married Ethelred, Ealdorman of the Mercians, to rule Mercia successfully for eight years after her husband's death.

Alfred's son and successor, Eadward the Elder, appointed a court governess who taught all his children including eight daughters. But there were few great ladies in politics, and after the Norman Conquest examples of women exercising independent authority are even rarer. By this time the Church's teaching on the subjection of women was echoed in Common Law. The assertion that 'the head of the woman is the man' was transformed into the legal doctrine that all family property was at the absolute disposal of the husband. Thus a wife or widow had no automatic claim to any of her own goods or to those of her husband. Only among the poorer classes, where ancient custom was given greater respect than the law, was it at all usual for a woman to take over her husband's responsibilities. In the towns a guildsman's widow had precedence over her son in running the family business, and in the country a serf's widow was able to succeed her husband as tenant. But this was little consolation for the hard and often brutal domestic life they led while their husbands were alive.

A new element was introduced into the male–female relationship with the discovery that women could be objects of worship. The ideal of courtly love was exemplified in the songs and poems of the troubadors, who wrote of valiant knights and their daring adventures performed on behalf of innocent, chaste and well-bred maidens. In reality, the love relationship was a comfort few were able to experience. Even the most romantic of the romanticists concluded that love was only appropriate outside marriage. A wife, after all, was the possession of her husband and therefore in no position to give her love freely. But over a restricted area the romantic ideal had a civilizing influence. When, for instance, men joined in combat at the tournament, they were competing for the favour and approval of the ladies' gallery. They were thus encouraged to recognize certain refinements which became formalized in the rules of chivalry, and were less inclined to treat these encounters like a private war.

Gradually the Church came to recognize the value of the romantic ideal as an inspiration to gentle living. The Virgin Mary was offered as the personification of the good wife and girls were encouraged to emulate her qualities of modesty, compassion and self-sacrifice. The daughters of noble households were provided with the semblance of an education, which usually consisted of training in needlework and embroidery, sick-nursing and household management. More rarely, they were taught to read and write and to speak French, the language of the Court.

By the end of the fourteenth century, parents who wanted advice in giving moral instruction were able to refer to a guide compiled by a French noble, Geoffrey de La Tour-Landry. He extolled the virtues of piety and charity, warned against showy dress and alcohol, and forecast disaster for any girl who indulged in pre-marital or extra marital sex. Above all, he urged:

> . . . you must be meek and courteous, for there is none so great a virtue to get the grace of God and the love of all people; for humility and courtesy overcometh all proud hearts, as a sparrow-hawk, be he never so untamed, you may overcome him with goodly and courteous demeanour, you may make him come from the tree to your hand. And if you are rude and be cruel with him, he will fly his way and never come at you. And since that courtesy and softness may overcome a wild bird, that hath no reason, of necessity it ought to refrain the felonious proud heart of man and woman. . . . And therefore I advise you to be courteous and humble to both great and small. . . .[1]

The most common attitude towards child development was neatly summarized by the author of another instructional guide, *How the Good Wife taught her Daughter*:

> Take a smart rodde and bete (t)hem on a rowe
> Till thei crei mercy and be of (t)her hilt aknowe.[2]

There were many examples of attempts to impose much harsh discipline. The Paston Letters describe how Elizabeth Paston was treated by her mother Agnes:

> She was never in so great sorrow as she is now-a-days, for she may not speak with no man, whosoever come, ne nor may see nor speak with my man, nor with servants of her mother's but

that she beareth her on hand otherwise than she meaneth; and she hath since Easter the most part been beaten once in the week or twice, and sometimes twice a day, and her head broken in two or three places.[3]

Generally, the only escape for such girls was marriage, but husbands were inclined to use their fists as readily as parents. A few girls received an education of sorts in the convents where the nuns supplemented their meagre income by selling what little knowledge they possessed. The convents did not have the prestige enjoyed by their Anglo-Saxon predecessors but their services were of some value in a society in which any degree of learning was at a premium. Aside from such problems as the shortage of books, the convents were able to provide only a few places. Church leaders were concerned that the nuns should not sacrifice their religious duties for the sake of education. In particular, they imposed severe restrictions on the facilities allowed to boarders. In the 1430s, for instance, William Gray, Bishop of Lincoln, informed the nunnery at Burnham, Buckinghamshire, 'That you henceforth admit or suffer to be admitted and received to lodge . . . no women after they have completed the fourteenth year of their age and no males after the eighth year of their age. . . .'[4] The bishop was not being petty-minded. There were notorious cases of prioresses taking in so many paying guests that their convents were no less worldly than cheap lodging houses.

While the convent schools were much attacked for their low academic standards and slack moral discipline, there was some regret when at last the Dissolution of the Monasteries put an end to their activities. The Church historian, Thomas Fuller, referred to the nunneries as 'good Shee-schools, wherein the girles and maids of the neighbourhood were taught to read and work; and sometimes a little Latine was taught them therein'. He went on to say, '. . . if such Feminine Foundations had still continued . . . haply the weaker sex . . . might be heightened to a higher perfection than hitherto hath been obtained'.[5] Fuller was by no means biased in favour of the monasteries, which he regarded as purveyors of superstition and iniquity. But possibly his generous assessment of the quality of the convent schools was based on his more direct knowledge of the Church's early contribution to the teaching of boys. Many of the grammar schools, of which there were over three hundred at the time of the Reformation, were established by monasteries, cathedrals or individual clerics. They imparted a reasonable standard of learning and, more significantly, most of them managed to survive the religious upheavals of the Tudor dynasty.

It occurred to Fuller and other contemporary observers that society might well have benefited if comparable provision had been available for girls.

At the lower end of the medieval social scale education was almost totally vocational. Boys were apprenticed to tradesmen or craftsmen or, in a less formalized way, learnt what they could of husbandry by working with their elders on the land. The girls also acquired their knowledge by practical experience, although the range of occupations open to them was extremely limited. Rarely, girls were apprenticed to such crafts as glove-making and embroidery. Religious and moral instruction was invariably picked up by an occasional encounter with the parish priest and by familiarity with family custom. Reading and writing were not thought to be important skills – certainly they were not likely to enhance a girl's economic worth and they were of practical value to a boy only if he had ambitions to break through the class barrier by entering the Church.

Still, there were some members of the clergy who believed that literacy was a step towards godliness. The parishioner who could read and write, if only to an elementary standard, was at least able to approach a clearer understanding of biblical teaching and religious services. Thus classes were sometimes held at the back of a church, a cathedral might run a song school or choir school, or a female recluse might earn a little money by giving instruction. Girls as well as boys could attend such classes but very few ever came within travelling distance of a competent teacher.

The exclusive claim of the Church dogmatists to judge the female character and intellect was broken by the Renaissance. The re-discovery of Greek history and literature persuaded scholars that women were capable of fulfilling a more active and positive social role. It was noted that in Plato's blueprint for the reconstruction of the state, the family institution was abolished and since 'neither a man as a man, nor a woman as a woman, has any especial function, all the pursuits of man are the pursuits of women also'. It followed that they should enjoy a similar education and share the opportunities to participate in the tasks of government.[6]

It is a commonplace that the ideals of *The Republic* were a long way removed from the reality of Athenian society, although some classical historians have exaggerated the extent to which Greek women were kept in subservience. The wives and daughters of Athenian citizens were skilled in such home-crafts as spinning, weaving and embroidery; they enjoyed and contributed to a broad range of cultural activities including visits to the theatre where the dramatists portrayed women of character and intelligence; and they probably knew as much about the affairs of their city as most modern women.[7]

Spartan society, with its militaristic bias, favoured relationship between the sexes. Girls and boys lived an outdoor life, competing with each other at athletic meetings and dancing naked at festivals where, according to Plutarch, 'modesty attended them and all wantonness was excluded'. It was as much apart from post-medieval civilization as from modern society but the classical principle of equality gave Renaissance scholars the hint that the potentialities of the female imagination had yet to be tested.

Among the leading European intellectuals Erasmus was one of the strongest supporters of girls' education. While he was inclined to associate femininity with weakness of character (girls, he thought, were more crafty than boys and were far more likely to make a fuss over small matters), he advised that their minds should be filled with study not only during their adolescence but after marriage when their husbands would rejoice in the company of intelligent partners. Erasmus included several learned women among his regular correspondents. One of these, Margareta Peutinger, was so well versed in the classical languages that she was able to point out a significant error in Erasmus's translation of the New Testament.[8]

But the female mind for which he had the greatest admiration belonged to Margaret More, the most brilliant of Sir Thomas More's children, who at the age of nineteen translated into English his meditation on the Lord's Prayer. If contemporary observers can be believed, the More household at Chelsea was engaged in a continuing intellectual dialogue. Erasmus compared it to Plato's Academy, 'For there is none therein who does not study the branches of a liberal education'. Sir Thomas extended his love of learning to his son, his three daughters and to his eleven grandchildren. He could find no reason why education should not be shared by both sexes 'for by it reason is cultivated and, as a field sowed with wholesome seeds of good precept, it bringeth forth excellent fruit'. But he made a special plea on behalf of every girl who was expected to make a successful marriage:

> May she be learned if possible or at least capable of being made so, she will have courage and equanimity gained from the study of the greatest minds and thus become a more effective wife and mother, her accomplishments in music, singing, lute playing and conversation will enrich the domestic scene.

These ideas owed much to the teaching of the Spanish scholar, Ludovico Vives, a colleague and tutor of Erasmus and More who, in 1532, was summoned to England to superintend the upbringing of the seven-year-old Princess Mary.

Her mother, Catherine of Aragon, spent her adolescence in a court where ladies were encouraged to study at university, while Henry VIII, though notoriously insensitive to the claims of women, could at least boast a remarkably gifted grandmother, who founded the Lady Margaret professorships of divinity at Oxford and Cambridge colleges – Christ's and St John's – and refounded Christ's College.

Vives recorded his views on girls' education in his treatise, *The Instruction of a Christian Woman*, which was translated into English in 1540. It became the standard authority on the subject for the rest of the century. By modern standards, Vives was excessively cautious in his recommendations. He believed that the first responsibility of parents was to guard their daughters against the risk of moral contamination, which meant that they were rarely to be permitted to depart from the security of the home. 'Forth the maid must go sometimes,' he wrote, 'but I would it should be as seldom as may be for several causes. Principally because as often as a maid goeth forth among people, so often she cometh in judgement and extreme peril of her beauty, honesty, demureness, wit, shamefastness and virtue.'

He emphasized the need to ensure that girls' living standards were decently modest. This involved dressing them in simple clothes, discouraging their attendance at banquets, tournaments and dances, censoring their reading habits so that they should not inadvertently encounter 'filth and viciousness' and keeping them apart from boys. But he was at least willing to concede that girls deserved an education that went somewhat beyond the domestic arts. Indeed, he claimed that want of education 'is the only cause why all women are for the most part hard to please, studious and most willing to adorn themselves, marvellers at trifles, in prosperity proud and insolent, in adversity abject and feeble'.

In his *Plan of Studies for Girls*, written specifically for Princess Mary, he proposed the reading of classical and religious literature, including the writings of More and Erasmus, and the study of Latin which he liked to think quickened the mental processes as well as providing a good base for the learning of other languages.

Vives was too fond of moral precepts, the all-embracing answers to questions that, in fact, were too complicated to be answered by reference to a manual of rules for living the good life. The narrow framework of Mary's education may have had something to do with her incomprehension of the nature of political power, which she exercised without proper regard for arguments that happened to conflict with her own. Her half-sister Elizabeth, who was every bit as gifted, was more fortunate with her tutor. Roger Ascham, Fellow of St John's College, Cambridge, and author of *The Scholemaster*, disputed the need for harsh disciplinary techniques when it was possible to stimulate love of learning by offering praise when it was deserved and constructive encouragement when studies proved difficult. The system apparently worked well with Elizabeth for Ascham was soon able to report:

She speaks French and Italian as well as she does English and has often talked to me readily and well in Latin, moderately well in Greek. She read with me almost the whole of Cicero and a great part of Livy. From these two authors her knowledge of the Latin language has been almost exclusively derived. The beginning of the day was always devoted to the New Testament in Greek, after which she read select orations of Isocrates and the tragedies of Sophocles.

It was Ascham who developed the teaching method of double translation, presenting his pupil with a passage of Latin or Greek to be turned first into English and then translated back into the original.

Such sophisticated concepts of learning theory were tested only on the children of the nobility who often made an immense effort to provide the groundwork of literacy. Bess of Hardwick calculated that she needed at least £600 a year (by contemporary currency value) for the education of her grand-daughter, her 'dearest jewel Arbell'.[9]

Those who were unable to employ tutors on this extravagant scale could usually hire for a more modest sum a teacher who could offer instruction in reading and writing.

The grammar schools – the backbone of the education system, such as it was – were harsh and intellectually arid institutions and, in any case, were an exclusively male preserve. Charity schools were also dominated by boys.

For most girls with parents of moderate fortune the best they could hope for was to be boarded out with a sympathetic family with superior social pretensions. The custom gave children early experience of the wider world but deprived them of parental guidance at the most sensitive stage in their lives. Foreign observers thought it a cruel and unnatural practice. The author of *The Italian Relation* wrote:

> The want of affection in the English is strongly manifested towards their children, for having kept them at home till they arrive at the age of seven or nine years at the utmost, they put them out, both males and females, to hard service in the houses of other people. Few are born who are exempted from this fate, for everyone, however rich he may be, sends away his children into the houses of others, whilst he, in return, receives those of strangers into his own. On enquiring their reason for this severity, they answered that they did it in order that their children might learn better manners. But, for my part, I believe they do it because they like to enjoy all their comforts themselves, and are better served by strangers than they would be by their own children. . . . If the English sent their children away from home to learn virtue and good manners and took them back again when their apprenticeship was over, they might be excused; but they never return, for the girls are settled by their patrons, and the boys make the best marriages they can.[10]

Many children were treated like low-grade servants but the prospects of boarding out were not always as depressing as critics suggested. An intelligent girl, who possessed some talent for amusing her hosts, was likely to win opportunities for social advancement she would never otherwise have achieved. One outstanding example was Bess of Hardwick whose father, a very minor figure in county society, died when she was seven, leaving her mother with the major responsibility for raising the family and managing the estate. At the age of twelve Bess was boarded out with the London household of Lady Zouch, where she showed herself to be above average in her intellectual and domestic abilities. When a young and eligible visitor fell ill and required a nurse to care for him, it was Bess who was chosen. Robert Barlow, who was suffering from a 'chronic distemper', observed the charms of the girl who gave him his medicine and kept him occupied with cheerful conversation. Their relationship was strengthened by the coincidence that they were neighbours in Derbyshire, a fact that did not pass unnoticed by their families, who were soon discussing the prospects for a marriage. Bess could offer only a token dowry, but Robert possessed an estate that was quite large enough for both of them. By her marriage she became a woman of property. Unfortunately, her husband's illness was more serious than anyone dared to think, and within a few months she was a twelve-year-old widow of property with the consolation of knowing she was well on the way to social eminence. There were three other marriages in her long life and each of her husbands was richer and more noble than his predecessor.

But in strictly educational terms the great virtue of the Tudor period was the willingness of thinking people to concede that girls had as much right as boys to make use of their brains. Sir Edward Coke, Edward VI's tutor, taught his daughters in the evening exactly what he taught his monarch by day because he believed that the two sexes, like souls, were equal in capacity.[11] There were many like Richard Mulcaster, the first Master of Merchant Taylors' School, who thought that boys had the prior claim since they were 'more important in the body politic' but this did not preclude girls from the process of mental training. On the contrary, Mulcaster asserted that wherever possible girls should go well beyond elementary education into the realms of classical and modern languages, logic and rhetoric. He gave four reasons for his view. The first was the custom of the country, 'which allows them to learn. The second is the duty we owe to them charging us in conscience not to leave them deficient. The third is their own aptness to learn, which God would never have bestowed on them to remain idle or to be used to small purpose. The fourth is the excellent results shown in them when they have had the advantage of good upbringing'.[12] It was almost certainly such opinions rather than a practical knowledge of conditions in the country at large which persuaded foreign observers like Frederick, Duke of Württemberg, that the females of England 'have great liberty and are almost like their masters'.

With the accession of the Stuarts the intellectual mood changed abruptly. James I seemed to take his cue from the ravings of his wild countryman John Knox whose essay in mysogyny, *The First Blast of the Trumpet against the monstrous Regiment of Women,* was published in 1558. Knox, whose initiating motive had been the destruction of Queen Mary, 'that horrible monster Jezebel of England', based his philosophy on the teachings of Calvin, who held that woman's rule was 'a deviation from the original and proper order of nature [and] was to be ranked, no less than slavery, among the punishments consequent upon the fall of man'. Knox went even further with the sentiment that 'to place a woman in authority about a realm, is to pollute and prophane the royal seat'. For anyone who sympathized in the slightest with these views it was only a short step to the conclusion that women should be restricted to the homely tasks in life in case they might ever get ideas above their calling. James I believed that 'to make women learned and foxes tame had the same effect – to make them cunning'.

The early seventeenth-century feminine ideal was summed up in the preface to Gervase Markham's *The English Housewife,* which was advertised as

> containing the Inward and Outward Virtues which ought to be in a complete Woman. As her skill in Physic, Surgery, Cookery, Extraction of Oils, Banqueting Stuff, Order of Great Feasts, Preserving of all sorts of Wines, Conceited Secrets, Distillations, Perfumes, ordering of Wool, Hemp, Flax, Making Cloth and Dyeing, the knowledge of Dairies, Office of Malting, of Oats, their excellent uses in a Family of Brewing, Baking, and all other things belonging to an Household.[13]

This showed that although women were not expected to be cultured in the broadest sense, they were required to apply intelligence and knowledge in the area of work for which they were thought best suited.

While most writers on education referred to the needs of girls in dismissive terms, occasionally there was a hint that some effort was being made to broaden the scope of scholastic opportunities. The earliest record of anything approaching a public school for girls dates from 1617 when the pupils of the recently established Ladies' Hall at Deptford played a masque before Anne of Denmark and the Court of Greenwich.

In her account of seventeenth-century boarding schools, Josephine Kamm shows that Hackney, Chelsea and Putney were among the most popular centres for girls' schools.[14] There were so many of these establishments in Hackney that Samuel Pepys made a special visit 'to see the young ladies of the schools, whereof there is a great store, very pretty'. But if Pepys had given as much attention to the mental as to the physical attributes of the young ones he would probably have concluded that their education was little better than that provided by the village or dame schools dotted about the country where lower-class boys and girls learned to read and write.

When, under the Commonwealth, discrimination was a subject for debate, the concept was usually related to the differences between rich and poor, them and us. That man was, in Milton's phrase, 'the perfecter sex' was taken as axiomatic and no credence was given to the Catholic idea that 'the obedience of Mary was the cause of salvation to herself and all mankind', or to the views of dissenting minorities such as the Quakers who recognized the spiritual equality of women. But with the retreat of Puritanism in the second half of the century, and the accession in 1688 of Queen Mary as joint ruler with her husband William, the question of woman's role edged back into the area of public discussion. Books and pamphlets on the subject appeared more frequently than in any previous generation. And some of the ideas and proposals could be described as advanced even by our own standards. Fénelon's *The Education of Daughters*, though written in 1681, contains advice to parents that is as useful now as when it was first published. He urged that relationships with children should be governed by reason and friendship. 'It is most important that you should know your own faults,' he told his readers, '. . . generally, those who bring up children pardon nothing in them, though they pardon everything in themselves.' Learning was to be made a pleasant activity which meant that children should be helped with praise and encouragement. They are likely to acquire as much knowledge from the exercise of a free-ranging curiosity as from compulsory lessons and the association of failure with punishment.

Among the leading British writers on education was John Locke, whose *Thoughts Concerning Education* applied to girls and boys since 'I acknowledge no difference of sex . . . relating . . . to truth, virtue and obedience'. He recommended a broad-based curriculum with progressive teaching techniques which relied on good example and patient encouragement rather than compulsion. For girls only he suggested dancing instruction and, more curiously, the practice of 'washing their feet every night in cold water and exposing them to wet in the day. . . .'

In contrast there was Mrs Hannah Wooley, a schoolmistress who went into print indignantly protesting that it was not good enough for men to believe 'a Woman learned and wise if she can distinguish her Husband's bed from another's'.

The writings of Anna Maria á Schurman, a Dutch feminist, were well known and her most enthusiastic follower in this country, Bathsua Makin, not only composed an *Essay to Revive the Ancient Education of Gentlewomen in Religion, Manners, Arts and Tongues* but actually set up a school to put her ideas into practice. In the last years of the century a young enthusiast, Mary Astell, achieved a certain notoriety by proposing the foundation of a ladies' college to be run on monastic lines. 'One great end of this Institution,' she wrote, 'shall be to expel that cloud of ignorance which custom has involved us in, to furnish our minds with a stock of solid and useful knowledge that the souls of women may no longer be the only unadorned and neglected things.' Her ideas were treated seriously enough to win promises of financial support and there was even a rumour that Queen Anne had offered a gift of £10,000, but the project foundered because religious dogmatists detected hints of Catholicism and the threat of a return to convent education.

The trouble with so many educational ideas of the time was that so often they remained just bright ideas. The ruling class of the Restoration did not suffer the inhibitions of their lofty minded predecessors but they were no less inclined to patronize women. Those who rediscovered their enthusiasm for courtly elegance put a premium on the pleasure to be found in the admiration of female beauty. No longer regarded as a potential source of evil, women were nevertheless expected to serve as adjuncts to men, to grace their drawing-rooms, entertain their friends and when necessary play the role of gentle comforter.

Thus it was no longer fashionable for women in the upper ranks of society to concern themselves overmuch with domestic matters. It was considered more important that they should be able, when asked, to sing a little song, play a cheering tune on the piano or engage in light chatter. These social demands were reflected in school curricula which came to be dominated by the accomplishments. Even the small minority of parents who were prepared to take a more constructive view of education for girls were not easily convinced that it was right to send their daughters to school since this was a tacit confession that they could not handle the job themselves. Reverting sharply from the boarding-out philosophy, which many critics had condemned as unproductive and inhuman, there was now a strong feeling that any learning that was necessary should spring from the home – the focal point of moral influence and domestic discipline. It was a view that carried respect throughout the following century when theorists like Richard Lovell Edgeworth could quite seriously define any school as 'a general infirmary for mental disease, to which all desperate subjects are sent, as a last resource'. But this was an upper-class opinion that did not take account of the needs of the poor whose families were incapable of providing anything but the most meagre learning. Gradually it came to be accepted that for them schools were a necessary act of charity that could lead to a welcome improvement in social behaviour and a strengthening of the Christian religion.

References
1. T. Wright (Ed.), *The Book of the Knight of La Tour-Landry* (Early English Text Society, 1906), pp. 14–15.
2. Quoted in Evelyn Akworth, *The New Matriarchy* (Gollancz, 1965), p. 96.
3. J. Gairdner (Ed.), *Paston Letters*, No. 71 (Constable, 1896).
4. Quoted in D. W. Sylvester, *Educational Documents 800–1816* (Methuen, 1970), pp. 41–2.

5. Quoted in Josephine Kamm, *Hope Deferred* (Methuen, 1965), p. 21.
6. L. J. Ludovici, *The Final Inequality* (Muller, 1965), p. 108.
7. E. B. Castle, *Ancient Education and Today* (Pelican, 1961), pp. 61–2.
8. Roland H. Bainton, *Erasmus of Christendom* (Collins, 1969; Fontana edition, 1972), pp. 279–80.
9. Alison Plowden, *Mistress of Hardwick* (BBC, 1972), p. 39.
10. Ibid., pp. 11–12.
11. Ludovici, op. cit., p. 131.
12. Quoted in Kamm, op. cit., p. 48.
13. Ludovici, op. cit., p. 143.
14. Kamm, op. cit., chapter V.

Chapter two

Please the man

The first hints that education was destined to be a national and public service came with the development of the charity school movement in the early eighteenth century. The idea of introducing the poor to elementary learning was an extension of the evangelizing function of the Church, which stood to gain a higher proportion of genuine converts from a citizenry that was sufficiently literate to understand a few of the subtler interpretations of the Christian message. The religious motive was powerfully reinforced by social considerations. The theory, as explained by Bernard Mandeville in an essay published in 1724, was that children who '. . . are taught the principles of religion and can read the word of God, have a greater opportunity to improve in Virtue and good morality, and must certainly be more civilized than others, that are suffered to run at random and have nobody to look after them'.[1] Ignorant and irreligious youngsters were feared as potential troublemakers while those who were raised under the protective shield of the Church could learn about such qualities as respect, humility and obedience. It was a proposition that appealed strongly to those with wealth and authority who feared, above all, the destructive power of a rebellious mob. For them, the charity schools represented an insurance policy to which they were only too happy to subscribe.

Some critics warned against excessive optimism. Bernard Mandeville, for instance, argued that spending a few hours in school each week was unlikely to modify the behaviour of a child who suffered the attention of dishonest or vicious parents. But he did not think that education was entirely ineffective for he went on to claim that 'knowledge both enlarges and multiplies our desires', and that the labouring poor would thus become dissatisfied with their simple and often unpleasant tasks – the very opposite of what the charity school promoters hoped to achieve. Mandeville's theory may have carried some weight but not sufficient to blunt the popularity of the charity schools which, as he admitted, were so well received 'that whoever dares openly oppose them is in danger of being stoned by the rabble'. By 1760 they were catering for about 30,000 children.[2]

The educational agency of the established Church was the Society for Promoting Christian Knowledge founded in 1698 to undertake missionary work at home and abroad. But the Nonconformists and Roman Catholics were also active and in many districts the initiative for setting up a school came from wealthy individuals or from committees of local benefactors, who recognized the moral leadership of the Church but otherwise preferred to retain their independence. What they provided in the way of teaching was modest enough. Apart from religious instruction and services, which seem to have occupied a major proportion of the average school day, the pupils were supposed to acquire a basic knowledge of reading, writing and arithmetic, but, since there were few teachers who themselves could perform these skills with reasonable competence, it was possible for a child to leave school almost as ignorant as when he started. Whatever their defects, however, the charity schools were an important stimulus to girls' education. If there was any truth at all in the assertion that illiteracy was a cause of moral and social misbehaviour, it followed that girls needed to be educated just as much as boys. Indeed, it could be argued that girls actually had a stronger claim to the benefits – such as they were – of elementary learning because, as future mothers, they were likely to be in the best position to influence the next generation.

In most of the schools which accepted both sexes, some attempt was made to produce a girls' curriculum that was distinctly feminine. The SPCK instructed teachers:

As soon as the Boys can Read completely well . . . teach them to Write a fair legible Hand, with the Grounds of Arithmatic, to fit them for Services or Apprenticeships. Note the Girls learn to read etc and generally to knit their Stockings and Gloves; to Mark, Sew, Make and Mend their Cloaths: and several learn to Write, and some to Spin their Cloaths.[3]

Generally it was only the brightest girls who were taught to write and to handle simple accounts, while the boys were judged to have failed if they could not master these skills.

But otherwise there were few attempts to distinguish between the needs and capacities of the sexes. For boys and girls the scholastic routine was tough and probably very tedious. The pupils of the Welsh Girls' School, set up in Clerkenwell by a group of wealthy expatriates, gathered for prayers at 7 a.m., interrupted their studies for breakfast at 8.30, had their main meal at 1 p.m. and supper at 6 p.m.; and went to bed at 8 p.m. In winter they were sent to bed an hour earlier and were allowed the concession of starting work slightly later in the morning. It has been said that the Welsh School 'never tended towards softness or luxury' and certainly in the eighteenth century the regime was so harsh there were several reports of children who escaped to 'the Vice and Wretchedness of the streets'. But this did not deter the Trustees from exercising strong discipline which included 'allocating a place of separation or room for unmanageable and obstinate children'. For this purpose they commandeered part of the dormitory 'where a room of about eight feet square may be obtained without any inconvenience to the present arrangements . . .'.[4]

At Watford Grammar, founded in 1704 to cater for 40 boys and 20 girls between the ages of 7 and 14, there were no boarding facilities and thus fewer administrative problems but early on the Trustees were debating the familiar problem of just how much time was to be allowed to pupils for recreation and eating. The burden of their complaint was the 'great inconvenience in the children going home to breakfast from the hour of eight to nine both in summer and winter'. The remedy on which they eventually agreed was 'that for the future the children from Lady Day to Michaelmas come to school at seven in the morning and that the children have no time for breakfast after the coming to school in the morning'.[5]

Several notable girls' schools were founded in the early period of the charity movement. The Greycoat Hospital was opened at Westminster in 1699, the Burlington Girls' School in 1698, the Bishopsgate Ward School (later the Central Foundation Girls' School) in 1718 and Lady Eleanor Holles' School in 1711. By contemporary standards all were well financed. The last mentioned owed its existence to a £1,500 legacy from the will of Lady Eleanor Holles, a sum which boosted the subscription list to an extent that allowed for a purpose-built school comprising classrooms for boys, apartments for the principal master and his family, two garrets for a second master, a large schoolroom for girls, and two rooms on the ground floor for their mistress.

Whether or not financial support was readily available, however, the salaries for teachers were seldom fixed much above subsistence level. A master could not expect to earn more than £40 a year while a mistress was lucky to receive half that amount. The circumstances were best suited to a married couple, both of whom were paid teachers, but some of the schools catering for girls only insisted on employing single women. Why were the rewards of teaching so ungenerous? Trustees were inclined to believe that teachers, like their pupils, should not be encouraged to seek a higher social status than that to which they were born, but there was also a feeling that even if salaries were increased the quality of applicants would remain depressingly low. It was simply a case of the demand for good teachers outstripping the supply. Quite late in the century Watford Grammar received an application for the headship from the collector of turnpike tolls on the St Albans and South Mimms Road, and even in the Victorian period a warehouse clerk was encouraged to offer his services. He wrote: 'I feel myself quite confident to undertake the situation of schoolmaster.'[6]

Sometimes powerful pressure was exerted on behalf of the most unsuitable candidates. When the Trustees of the Welsh Girls' School advertised for a married couple they received a letter from the Prince of Wales recommending John Kenrick and his wife, '. . . having been assured . . . that they are perfectly qualified'. The Trustees were wise enough not to accept such assurances on trust and after submitting Kenrick to a knowledge test found that he was 'totally unqualified, not being able to read a Verse in the New Testament, or his own Printed Circular Letter'. It was to the credit of the Trustees that they subsequently wrote to the prince pointing out that Kenrick could not read, write or do arithmetic and 'humbly presuming to hope His Royal Highness will pardon us when we take the liberty in saying we think him an improper person to become a candidate'.[7]

One of the SPCK foundations for which detailed records survive is St Martin-in-the-Fields High School for Girls.[8] It was established in the first days of 1700 when 'The present Charity School erected in this Parish for the teaching of 50 poor boys meeting with good encouragement, it was thought that if such a One was raised for Poor

Girls there was hope it might meet with the like encouragement'. The initial finance for the project was provided by the Vicar of St Martin's, who agreed to allocate to the school the proceeds of a monthly collection. In January this amounted to £13 9s. 8½d. which, added to the individual subscriptions, was sufficient to rent a house in Castle Street, just off Leicester Square, and to invest in some essential materials. A ream of paper, pens, ink and a standish and sand box were bought, along with twelve spelling books, twelve psalters and thirty Expositions of the Church Catechism. The school opened with twenty pupils (the roll soon increased to forty) each of whom was given a gown, a petticoat and a pair of stockings (to be worn 'only on Sundays and Holy Days and on such Wednesdays as they go to Trinity Chapel to hear the Sermon'), a handkerchief, shoes and a cap and band. There was even a little left over for a few comforts that, strictly speaking, were beyond the call of charity. Ten shillings were reserved for the purchase of a grate, fender, shovel and poker and just in case a good fire could not alone stimulate learning the headmistress was given three shillings 'to distribute among the girls for their encouragement, in such manner as she shall think fit'.

The sources of income which were neatly chronicled by the Trustees ranged from the regular donations from wealthy sympathizers who usually timed their munificence to coincide with the celebration of holy days to the once only gifts from such as Mr Gill who handed over a £5 reward that he had acquired in his pursuit of law and order.

That the financial state of the school remained healthy was as much due to careful investment as to the generosity of local worthies. The accounts were soon showing evidence of profitable dealings in the stock market so that by the 1780s the Trustees were able to recommend expansion and improvements in the comforting knowledge that the school's reserves totalled nearly £4,000.

The need for larger premises was discussed soon after the school was founded. In 1718 a lease was taken on 'the whole upper floors of Hungerford Market House' which allowed for an agreement with the Poor Law Guardians to take on the responsibility for accommodating thirty 'poor unhappy Orphans'. In the 1750s one notion was to lease property in St Martin's Lane belonging to Lord Salisbury, a proposal that was greeted with such enthusiasm that 'in order to defray the additional rent and expense of removal, the Trustees . . . came to a resolution to double their subscriptions'. But the negotiations came to nothing because local residents advised Lord Salisbury that 'any such School would be attended with great inconvenience to the Neighbourhood'. The search for a suitable house in an area where the school would not be regarded as a social blight continued until 1783, when a lease was taken on a section of York Buildings, George Street, the property of the Adam brothers. After twelve years another move was suggested, this time to purpose-built accommodation in Heming's Row. The foundation stone was laid on 3 June 1796 and in the following year the pupils and teachers were installed in what, by the standards of the time, must have been a tolerably comfortable residence. One of the craftsmen who helped furnish the school was Chippendale, who was asked to provide 'twenty Matresses and Bolsters and twenty rugs for Children, and also a Beech Bedstead with Cotton Furniture, with Bed and Bedding for the Matron's Room'.

The Trustees held an examination every quarter but standards were not expected to be very high, at least in the early days when there was even some disagreement as to 'whether it may be proper to learn the girls to write'. Still, most of the children succeeded in memorizing the Catechism, which was the main purpose of the school, and picking up knowledge of a few simple rules of behaviour. Nevertheless, there are frequent references in the minutes to cases of indiscipline. The highest penalty for disobedience was expulsion, a threat which must have put real fear into the children who stood to lose not only the chance of gaining a basic education, which possibly did not concern them overmuch, but also the material comforts of the school which parents were in no way able to provide on their own account. But expulsion was ordered only in the most serious cases. Thus, in 1703, it was ruled that 'Elizabeth Penn be discharged from this School having been absent these two months and being Incorrigible'. The usual process was for children who were known to be constantly troublesome to have their names noted in the Doomsday Book. Any girl who committed three Doomsday offences was liable to be expelled. The rules for decent conduct even extended to parents. In 1765 Hannah Frazier was sent home 'on the misbehaviour of her mother', but was readmitted later.

The menu on which the girls were expected to nourish their bodies and their intellects was simple and unappetizing. Breakfast consisted of water gruel or broth, dinner alternated between pudding (rice, plum or suet) and boiled meat. A supper of bread and cheese was served every evening. Sunday was exceptional with the programme of church attendance getting off to a good start with a breakfast of bread and butter washed down with a mug of beer. There was a dinner of roast beef and roots, and if that was not sufficient to sustain a young appetite there was always the bread and cheese supper.

The records of St Martin's contain a menu compiled in the mid-nineteenth century. The chief difference seems to be in the quantity of food, although it is reasonable to assume that the girls were now more likely to be served with fresh milk, meat and vegetables. Beer was still regarded as an important part of the diet. Indeed, the Ladies Committee had occasion to invite the governors to test the quality of the liquor provided for the children 'which they [the ladies] think seems hardly good enough for them'.

However formal and dull the school environment happened to be, the early pupils of St Martin's were decently cared for and accommodated and were better off than they would have been in their own miserably poor homes. And while their educational attainments were minimal they had a clear advantage over the many boys and girls who received no education at all.

One of the clearest impressions that emerges from the documentary evidence is the immense care with which the Trustees exercised their responsibility to do their best for the children both while they were at school and when they were earning their own living. Prospective employers were asked detailed questions about conditions of work before they were allowed to take on apprentices from the school. In case they were unable to live up to their declarations, the Trustees reserved the right to cancel apprenticeship agreements, an option they exercised frequently enough to make clear their determination to have their rules taken seriously. In 1754 a girl was removed from her apprenticeship after a month because the Trustees were of the opinion 'that the work was too great for her strength'. Later another ex-pupil was given help in finding a more congenial occupation after a complaint that she was being required to work on Sundays. Among the employers who enjoyed the confidence of the Trustees were a shagreen casemaker, a gold and silver orrice weaver, a gingerbread baker, a peruke maker, a cork cutter, a coach carver, a mantua maker, a white knee garter maker, a snuffbox maker, a bridle cutter, a clear starcher and a silk stocking cleaner. Altogether a range of skills and occupations that compares favourably with later opportunities for girls' employment. To help them on their way the school presented each leaver with a clothing allowance of forty shillings, a Bible and a copy of *The Whole Duty of Man*.

Care was also taken with the appointment of teachers and headmistresses, though here it was often difficult to find candidates who could meet the requirements of the Trustees. The essential qualifications of the headmistress were determined when the school opened in 1700. It was agreed that she should be:

1.   ... a member ... of the Church of England and of sober life and conversation.
2.   One that has frequented the Communion once a month (at least) for some years.
3.   One that keeps good order in her family (if she have one).
4.   One that has the command of her passions.
5.   One that is of an ingenious mind, willing to learn and able to teach.
6.   ... solidly grounded in the true principles and practice of Christianity so as to give a good account thereof to the Minister of the Parish upon examination.
7.   One that is sufficiently grounded in the English tongue so as to be able to teach her scholars to read, and also one who understands knitting, writing, plane work or so as to be able to instruct her scholars in the same, in order to fit them either for service or apprenticeship.

Three candidates presented themselves for interview. The first, Mrs Grace Dobrow, had the advantage of a personal recommendation from Dr Lancaster who, as Vicar of St Martin's, was one of the more powerful trustees. Nonetheless, the report on her was not entirely favourable: 'She is of the Church of England, is a widow with two children, frequents the Communion thrice a year, has read (besides the Bible) *The Duty of Man* and Bishop Taylor's *Guide to Devotion*, understands plane work, but no knitting, can write indifferently.' The second hopeful, Mrs Jane Scatergood, who was also a widow with two children, had similar qualifications but with the added virtue of teaching experience. But both women were totally outclassed by the successful candidate:

Mrs Mary Harbin, lodging at the sign of the Coffee Mill and Sugar Loaf in St James Street came upon the same account, being recommended by Mr Gaywood. Being examined, says she is a single woman aged about 40, of the Church of England, has in her apprenticeship received the Sacrament once a month, since then once a week; has read (besides the Bible), Bishop Taylor's, Dr Scot's, Dr Horneck's, and Dr Sherlock's books; has for these twenty years past brought up several children, and has made it her chief business to instruct them in religion, so that all, but one, has received the Communion at 15 years of age; writes a very good hand, and understands knitting and plane work.

Mrs Harbin was paid £25 a year for teaching the children to spell and read and another £5 for teaching them to write, a not ungenerous salary bearing in mind the occasional bonus, such as the two guineas presented to her in 1708 'in consideration of [her] extraordinary care and diligence in teaching the girls, and making the children's linen and stockings ...'. But despite her perseverance and industry Mrs Harbin eventually fell out with 'the present happy Establishment' not because of any dispute over school administration but on a question of national politics. To the amazement of her employers she declared herself to be a Jacobite sympathizer by refusing to participate in prayers for George I. The times were too dangerous to take risks on behalf of a political dissenter and the Trustees resolved that she should go. But they were generous enough to write a testament indicating that Mrs Harbin 'was not dismist ... for any inability, or neglect ... being Admiraably Qualified and every way capacitated for her sexes instruction ...'.

Her successor was sound in politics but so poor in health that she died after a short tenure. The next headmistress was also afflicted with a weak constitution and in the end was dismissed for negligence. It is an indication of the relative status of women in eighteenth-century society that the Trustees felt bound first to inform her husband of their decision and to request him to pass on the bad news. It was perhaps the same basic attitude that led them to play safe with their next choice and appoint the wife of the headmaster of the neighbouring boys' school. She was a great success.

The girls of St Martin's were among the more fortunate of those who were taken into the charity schools. As the century progressed the critics protested louder and more often at the inadequacies of the system. Extensive publicity was given to Mrs Catherine Cappe's investigations into the administration of the Grey Coat School in York where the girls were 'sickly, remarkably low of stature, and their whole appearance . . . very unfavourable'. The cause of their distress was the selfishness of their teachers who blatantly misappropriated the funds allocated for the pupils' welfare. After suffering the deprivations of boarding school the girls were directed into apprenticeships that were notable for their total disregard for individual rights.[9] Even where pupils were decently fed and clothed, it was rare for the standards of teaching to meet the potentialities of the students. This was because the administrators were stuck with their belief that a little education was good for the social and moral health of the nation but too much education would create dissatisfaction among the masses. In most schools the curriculum was narrow, the teaching unimaginative.

Mrs Sarah Trimmer, a well-known writer of school books, described the intellectual environment experienced by the luckiest children:

> They are first taught to read in a spelling book, the lessons of which chiefly consist of sentences collected from the Scriptures . . . as soon as they can read and spell a little, they are put into the New Testament, and go through that in the same manner, without regard to anything further than improvement in the art of reading. They learn, by stated regular tasks, the columns of spelling in the spelling books, and in some schools they are taught English Grammar, writing and arithmetic.

She concluded; '. . . it must be acknowledged that the education of children brought up in the charity schools is, in general, very defective. . . .'[10] Mrs Trimmer was not opposed to religious instruction; indeed she was inclined to the view that children might profitably occupy more of their time studying the Scriptures. Her call was for livelier and more stimulating techniques of learning, an appeal which might have been taken more seriously if her own textbooks had not been so ponderously tedious.

For the poorest children who were so far sunk in ignorance that they were not even considered eligible for charity schools, Mrs Trimmer favoured schools of industry in which they could learn to spin, knit, sew or cobble shoes. With the spread of the factory system in the late eighteenth century such schools were a common feature of urban society, as were workhouse schools for destitute children. Both sexes were admitted but demand for places was limited by the needs of industry, which absorbed vast quantities of cheap, unskilled child labour. In 1804 there were nearly 200,000 children aged five to fourteen on parish relief, but of these little more than ten per cent were receiving any sort of education.[11]

In the country there were the dame schools, kept by elderly women who charged a few pence for minding the children who were too young or too sickly to work for a living. If we are to believe William Shenstone, by the mid-century the village schoolmistress was a well-established figure in rural society:

> In ev'ry village mark'd with little spire
> Embowr'd in trees and hardly known to fame,
> There dwells, in lowly shed, and mean attire,
> A matron old, whom we Schoolmistress name;
> Who boasts unruly brats with birch to tame.

For children who were sent out to work very early, the only prospect of gaining an introduction to literacy was offered by the Sunday Schools. There they were taught to read so that they could study the Bible and learn the catechism. The Sunday School movement was launched by Robert Raikes, a wealthy newspaper owner in Gloucester who helped set up schools for the children employed in the local pin factories and publicized his campaign in the *Gloucester Journal*. The Society for Establishment and Support of Sunday Schools was founded in 1785 with the cooperation of the Established Church and the Nonconformists. Within two years the Society was claiming a country-wide attendance of 250,000. The link between industry and religion, or hard work and humility, appealed to Sarah Trimmer, who opened her own Sunday Schools in Brentford, then a rural district which apparently suffered a high incidence of delinquency. Another well-publicized experiment was launched by the More sisters, Hannah and Martha, in the remote area of Cheddar in the Mendip Hills. Their plan for instructing the poor is described in one of Hannah's letters:

> They learn of week-days such coarse works as may fit them for servants. I allow of no writing. My object has not been to teach dogmas and opinions, but to form the lower class to habits of industry and virtue. I know no way of teaching morals but by infusing principles of Christianity, nor of teaching Christianity without a thorough knowledge of Scripture. . . . To make good members of society (and this can only be done by making good Christians) has been my aim. . . . Principles not opinions are what I labour to give them.[12]

While girls of the lowest class were edging towards literacy their contemporaries in the higher ranks were discovering the pleasures of relaxed gentility, an art of living which demoted the virtue of learning (too much knowledge was thought presumptuous) in favour of an acute sensitivity to the shifting patterns of fashion in dress, behaviour and drawing-room entertainment. It was far more important for a wealthy young girl to know how to play the piano, to sing prettily, to dance gracefully and to perform a supporting role at the card table than to appear erudite or even to show an interest in literary or scientific matters. The concept of woman as a social ornament was an invention of the upper-class household where most of the traditional functions of wives and mothers were performed by an army of servants. With the emergence of the industrialized community and the rise of the middle class there was an inevitable clamouring of new recruits for admission into fashionable society. The feminine ideal of the aristocracy thus became the model for middle-class aspirations.

The daughters of the ruling families received their education from private tutors but there were many schools or academies that catered for the less affluent, who were promised that their girls would learn all that was necessary to negotiate a desirable marriage. Apart from an introduction to the social graces – known collectively as 'the accomplishments' – the pupils acquired a thin veneer of culture by memorizing chunks of information from various approved texts. The practice of learning by rote was a face-saver for teachers whose fund of knowledge was scarcely greater than that of their students. This, of course, was not openly admitted; instead memory testing was justified as a morally-uplifting experience, presumably because it required a considerable act of self-discipline to put up with so much tedious repetition. It was not uncommon for pupils to learn by heart pages from a dictionary or to copy out sums together with the answers.

Among popular school books (popular with teachers if not with children) were Richmal Magnall's *Historical and Miscellaneous Questions for the Use of Young People*, which remained a best-seller well into the nineteenth century; Sarah Trimmer's *English History*; Keith's *Use of Globes* and Pinnock's *Catechisms*. Mrs Trimmer also produced a reading and spelling book which was based on the principle of splitting up words into monosyllables so that a child was 'ne-ver – al-low-ed – to – pro-nounce – two – syl-la-bles – to-ge-ther'. Most of the established textbook writers ran their own schools in which they gave practical demonstrations of their teaching techniques. It was said, for instance, that at Croften Hall in Wakefield, Miss Magnall taught with the catechism and birch-rod, which may have satisfied her sense of vocation but failed to compensate for the ignorance of her teachers. 'Our class of Geography were two hours looking for the Emperor of Persia's name,' reported one of her pupils. 'My governess told us it was Mahomet.'[13] When the girls were using Miss Magnall's own classic text they were expected to answer such exciting questions as: 'name the great events of the first century AD' and 'What learned men flourished in the first century?' Punishment and religion were twin concepts. 'Miss Ropers were sent to Coventry till they would say their Catechism. Some of the ladies had the Epistle and Gospels, twenty-eight verses, for writing on their desks.'

There were a few schools where academic standards were given a higher priority. The establishment owned by the More sisters in Bristol was distinguished by the broad scope of its curriculum which included instruction in up to four languages. Occasionally there were hints that a teacher was far too ambitious for her students. It is only possible to guess at the response of Mrs Bryan's girls at Blackheath when she launched a series of lectures encompassing 'A Compendious System of Astronomy ... also Trigonometrical and Celestial Problems, with a Key to the Ephemeris, and a Vocabulary of the Terms of Science'.[14]

Almost certainly the best girls' schools were run by the Quakers, who never had any doubt that both sexes were equally deserving of education. At the beginning of the century they controlled fifteen boarding schools. Two of them, at Warrington and Brighton, were for girls only and another two (Ramsey in Hampshire and Thornbury in Gloucestershire) were for girls and boys. Another co-educational school, Ackworth, was founded in 1779. Their next venture was at York where two eminent Quakers, Esther and William Tuke, volunteered responsibility for about two dozen girl boarders. A house was rented in Trinity Lane and the two Tuke daughters were engaged as assistant teachers although for eleven years they received no salaries.[15]

'Simplicity of manners, and a religious improvement of the minds of youth' were the principal aims of the Friends, and to achieve this they imposed strict rules of behaviour. The girls did their own housework, needlework and knitting; they wore plain dress and they were forbidden 'such literary publications as unprofitably elate the mind'. The intellectual emphasis was on the importance of patient, meticulous work. Isabel Richardson, who was at the school in 1790, used her geography lessons to make a map of England 'upon white silk in which the shape of each county was defined with exactness of outline equal to any work of an engraver'. History consisted of a succession of dates and events which the girls absorbed by listening to a teacher reading from a book while they were occupied with their sewing.

But the relationship between the children and their teachers and, for that matter, their parents seems to have been characterized by a fine sensitivity. Two of the pupils were daughters of the Coalbrookdale Darbys, the family which made a distinctive contribution to the development of the iron industry. The girls received regular letters from their relatives, one aunt writing that 'All your friends are well satisfied at the repeated accounts they have received of your agreeable deportment at school, and trust by a continuance of such conduct will be amply recompensed for their kindness in placing you under the care of such kind judicious teachers.' Her nieces were not quite so confident of achieving all that was expected of them but when they expressed their fear their mother responded with a delightful reassuring note forgiving them their sins of omission but hoping that they would at least give special attention to a scholastic art that she had sadly neglected – pen cutting.

Other pupils' letters reveal what to us is a startling precociousness, which suggests that if the teaching was excessively formal it was also effective in creating an early sense of maturity. For example:

> My dear Sister,
> . . . I must first acknowledge the receipt of Mother and Sister's truly acceptable Letters. It was very pleasing to me to hear that you continued to enjoy good health, and I doubt not but it will be equally so to you to understand that this family with myself, are well except some of them are having Colds, which are not uncommon at this Time of Year. . . .

This could have been written by a society lady but in fact was the correspondence of Phebe Day, a fifteen-year-old girl, who never had the chance to give continuing proof of her ability since she died while she was still at school.

There was a small but influential group of female intellectuals known collectively as Bluestockings. These eminent ladies, who did much to enliven mid-century society, were mostly products of upper-class home tuition and rigorous self-teaching. They preferred the art of conversation and literary pursuits to the more popular and superficial entertainments and such was their force of character that they were treated seriously even by the male intelligentsia.

Mrs Elizabeth Montagu, known as the queen of the Bluestockings, was described by Dr Johnson as the most learned woman in England. He also complimented Elizabeth Carter for her ability to make a pudding as well as translating Greek, and to sew a handkerchief as well as composing a poem. As a constructive occupation the Blue-stockings invariably turned to writing, which for some was immensely profitable. Fanny Burney received £2,000 for her novel *Camilla* and £7,000 for *The Wanderer*. Hannah More, who was one of the younger members of the group, achieved fame as the author of romantic dramas in which she promoted the cause of Christian purity and humility. The same ideal figured strongly in her writings on education, chief of which was *Strictures on Female Education*, published in 1779. In this she strongly attacked the 'phrenzy of accomplishements' which fitted middle-class daughters to make their fortunes only by marriage. But her alternative curriculum was depressingly high-minded, with recommendations for young girls to immerse themselves in such formidable works as Locke's *Essay on Human Understanding* and Bishop Butler's *Analogy*.

The Bluestockings were an exclusive sect but they had many followers and imitators in the middle class, women who desperately sought some outlet for their creative intelligence. The significance of this movement has been thoroughly explained by Virginia Woolf:

> Hundreds of women began as the eighteenth century drew on to add to their pin money, or to come to the rescue of their families by making translations or writing innumerable bad novels. . . . The extreme activity of mind which showed itself in the later eighteenth century among women – the talking, and the meeting, the writing of essays on Shakespeare, the translating of the classics – was founded on the solid fact that women could make money out of writing. Money dignifies what is frivolous if unpaid for. It might still be well to sneer at 'bluestockings with an itch for scribbling', but it could not be denied that they could put money in their purses. Thus, towards the end of the eighteenth century a change came about which, if I were rewriting history, I should describe more fully and think of greater importance than the Crusades or the Wars of the Roses. The middle-class woman began to write. For if *Pride and Prejudice* matters, and *Middlemarch* and *Villette* and *Wuthering Heights* matter, then it matters far more . . . that women generally, and not merely the lonely aristocrat shut up in her country house among her folios and her flatterers, took to writing. Without those forerunners, Jane Austen and the Brontës and George Eliot could no more have written than Shakespeare could have written without Marlowe. . . . For masterpieces are not single and solitary births; they are outcomes of many years of thinking in common, of thinking by the body of the people so that the experience of the mass is behind the single voice. Jane Austen should have laid a wreath upon the grave of Fanny Burney, and George Eliot done homage to the robust shade of Eliza Carter – the valiant old woman who tied a bell to her bedstead in order that she might wake early and learn Greek.[16]

But if hundreds of middle-class women were putting money in their pockets by writing, the greater proportion were relying on their husbands for their allowances. This is not to imply that they were necessarily idle. The leisured housewife was not much in evidence until Victorian times when the middle class had numerical strength, political influence and an extraordinary faith in the significance of the home-based wife and mother as the stabilizing factor in society and religion. In the eighteenth and early nineteenth century it was still rare for domestic administration to be so highly organized as to allow for reflective indolence – however much the wives of traders and industrialists might aspire to that distinction. The girl who did all the right things at school or at home in anticipation of a better than average marriage was still liable to end up working hard to please her husband and her family. Her poverty of academic distinction was to a great extent compensated by her rapidly acquired knowledge in the art of survival. Some idea of the diversity of tasks she was expected to perform can be judged from any of the numerous volumes of domestic hints that were kept within easy reach of the parlour shelves.

One of the best known was *The Female Instructor or Young Woman's Companion,* described as 'a guide to all the accomplishments which adorn the female character either as a useful member of society, a pleasing and instructive companion or a respectable mother of a family . . .'.[17] The author skips from social to domestic culinary to medical matters in a frenzy of encyclopaedic discourse, itemizing such topics as 'Balsam, Bathing, useful remarks on; Boiling in general; Brewing, the art of; Cold, intense, to recover from; Cramp, cures for; Ducks, how to manage; Prayer for a family; Itch, cures for; Windows, how to clean; and Rules for conversation'.

The married woman was expected to perform the functions of household manager, child raiser, family comforter and medical orderly. This last duty was strongly emphasized in *The Female Instructor,* which offers a wealth of advice on caring for the sick. There are cures for ague, cramp, stiffness of the joints ('submerge in the yoke of a new-laid egg'), dropsy, inflamed or sore eyes, bruises ('immediately apply treacle spread on brown paper; or electrify the part, which is the quickest cure of all'), coughs ('drink a pint of water lying down in bed'), the itch ('wash the parts affected with strong rum'), and rheumatism ('rub in warm treacle'). In an age when members of the medical profession were few in number and thin in knowledge, death or injury was invariably associated with negligence or ignorance. It was the mother's responsibility to deter her children from taking what were regarded as unnecessary physical risks. Thus the pleasures and benefits of strong exercise had to be balanced against the dangers of over-exertion. Swimmers, for instance, were advised that if they '. . . overheated the body, especially in the hot days of summer, it may prove instantly fatal, by inducing a state of apoplexy'.

The antidotes for the more obvious calamities resulting from swimming were itemized under the forbidding heading Drowning – Restoration of Life: 'On taking bodies out of rivers, ponds, etc the following cautions are to be used; 1) Never to be held up by the heels. 2) Not to be rolled in casks, or other rough passage.' Instead, the body was to be 'gently rubbed with flannel, sprinkled with spirits, and a heated warming-pan lightly moved over the back and spine'. To restore breathing, 'introduce the pipe of a pair of billows into one nostril; close the mouth and the other nostril, then inflate the lungs . . .'. If all else failed, 'Tobacco smoke is to be thrown gently up the fundament, with a proper instrument . . .'.

Preventive medicine for childhood ailments consisted of 'plain food, simple clothing, regular hours and abundant exercise in open air'. But there was a continuing need to watch for advanced warnings of disability. 'Great care must be taken with breeding their teeth, as many die of that painful disease.' Women were urged to give as much consideration to their own health as to that of their children and husbands. Readers of *The Female Instructor* knew the dangers associated with 'the pernicious custome of lacing too tightly' and 'worse than all the rest, the practice of bleeding' to which pregnant women were frequently submitted whether they happened to be strong or frail. To make matters worse, 'Some [pregnant] ladies are seen madly running up and down, and jumbling all the town over in the most jolting hackney-coach that could be procured'.

The emphasis on practical knowledge was not so great as to exclude all interest in academic subjects. It was accepted that 'the art of writing is exceedingly useful and is now grown so very common that the greatest part of children may attain it at an easy rate'. But in the list of female qualities literacy scored a low place following cleanliness, neatness of dress, modesty, sweetness of temper, industry, sobriety and frugality. Those who enjoyed reading and conversation were warned not to overindulge in their hobby – after all, 'wit is the most dangerous talent a female can possess'.

Most of the popular writers on education went along with the view that nature had ordained women to devote their energies to the domestic arts. Dr Gregory, whose book *A Father's Legacy to his Daughters* was published in 1774, went so far as to advise his readers, 'Be even cautious in displaying your good sense. It will be thought you assume superiority over the rest of the company. But if you happen to have any learning, keep it a profound secret, especially from the men, who generally look with a jealous and malignant eye on a woman of great parts and cultivated understanding.' Not surprisingly, perhaps, a book on electoral law, printed at about the same period, associated women with infants, idiots and lunatics, all of whom 'lie under natural incapacities and therefore cannot exercise a sound discretion, or are so much under the influence of others that they cannot have a will of their own . . .'.[18]

Even those who favoured better education for girls advocated very modest improvements. Jonathan Swift complained that 'not one gentleman's daughter in a thousand can be brought up to read or understand her own natural tongue or judge of the easiest books that are written in it', yet in his *Letter to a very young Lady on her Marriage*, he confessed 'that those who are commonly called learned women, have lost all manner of credit by their impertinent talkativeness, and conceit of themselves'. Dr Johnson enjoyed the society of intelligent women and regretted there were so many 'wretched un-idea'd girls', but even he was heard to comment that a man would 'sooner see a good dinner upon his table than hear his wife talk Greek'. The prevailing view was that respectable women should be literate but not academically pretentious, since this would distract them from their main function, which was to administer their households and support and comfort their husbands.

The philosophy was persuasively expressed by Rousseau in *Emile*, a discourse on the proper upbringing of a young man. His concern for creating an educational environment that was as close as possible to the real spirit of man inevitably led him to consider what nature had to say about the manner in which girls should be raised to maturity. He concluded that the sexes 'both pursue one common object, but not in the same manner. From their diversity in this particular, arises the first determinate difference between the moral relations of each. The one should be active and strong, the other passive and weak; it is necessary the one should have both the power and the will, and that the other should make little resistance'. It followed 'that woman is expressly formed to please the man' and therefore the education of woman 'should be always relative to man'. Her purpose, said Rousseau, is 'to please, to be useful to us, to make us love and esteem them, to educate us when young, to take care of us when grown up, to devise, to console us, to render our lives easy and agreeable'.

The theory was taken a step further by the Rev. Thomas Gisborne, who based his interpretation of the proper Duties of the Female Sex on anthropological research into the domestic habits of savage tribes. This exercise led him to agree with Rousseau that the first virtue in woman was 'in contributing daily and hourly to the comfort of husbands, of parents, of brothers and sisters, and of other relations, connections and friends . . .'. But, in Gisborne's view, her responsibility went much further than this. She had a duty 'in modelling the human mind during the early stages of its growth' and 'in forming and improving the general manners, dispositions, and conduct of the other sex, by society and example'.[19]

The idea of woman as a civilizing influence appealed greatly to Church leaders and took strong hold of Victorian middle-class imagination. But the question was then raised, if girls were to be brought up to assume such onerous duties, why should their education be counted as of less importance than that of boys? Gisborne showed that he recognized the paradox when he attacked those schools that encouraged girls to concern themselves only with fashion and display. But he seems to have been under the impression that the ideals and quality of teaching were improving so rapidly that the problem would eventually solve itself. As an example of rising standards of literacy he tried to show that 'grammatical blunders, which used to disgrace the conversation even of women in the upper and middle ranks of life . . . are already so much diminished, that in some years hence it may perhaps no longer be easy to find a young lady, who professes to be mistress of the French language, and is at the same time grossly ignorant of her own'.[20] To this limited extent Gisborne may have been right but the questions he raised and attempted to answer were in fact more provocative and far-ranging than he and most other social commentators were prepared to admit.

One of the very few critics who refused to relax in the cosiness of a moralizing philosophy was Mary Wollstonecraft, probably the most remarkable English woman of the eighteenth century, a campaigner for the liberty of her sex who produced the earliest and possibly best-reasoned charter of female independence. She came from a family that was in the twilight of the middle class – her mother a patient and intelligent woman tied to domestic drudgery, her father an incompetent businessman who, lurching from one financial disaster to another, found consolation in drunken violence, mostly committed against his wife. Mary picked up learning where she could; from a retired clergyman, for instance, who recognized her intelligence and was happy to fill his time by giving her lessons, but also from friends who had acquired a more formal education. As soon as she could escape from her family she went to work as a companion and then as a teacher and governess before taking to writing as a trade.

Her first book, *Thoughts on the Education of Daughters*, consisted of a series of essays on such topics as Moral Discipline, Fashionably Educated and left without a Fortune, Artificial Manners. It was a plea for reform based on her own unhappy experiences and those of some of her closest friends. Her aim, as she said later, was to show that if woman 'be not prepared by education to become the companion of man, she will stop the progress of knowledge and virtue; for truth must be common to all, or it will be inefficacious with respect to its influence on general practice'. It was a simple message but one that was strongly suspect in an age when the ruling sex thought that intelligence in a woman was an unattractive and even a dangerous trait. The book made its biggest impact on its publisher, Joseph Johnson, who subsequently helped Mary when she was in financial trouble, supported her in her work and introduced her to a circle of radical intellectuals. She championed the Americans in their War of Independence and was on the side of the revolutionaries in France. She was appalled by Burke's *Reflections* and produced a scathing retort to his sentimental rhetoric on behalf of the aristocracy, appealing instead for sympathy on behalf of the poor and exploited. In this book, *A Vindication of the Rights of Men*, she took particular exception to Burke's view of woman, who is, he wrote 'but an animal, and an animal not of the highest order'. 'All true, Sir,' replied Mary, 'if she is not more attentive to the duties of humanity than queens and fashionable ladies are.' And this was just the point; that most women, far from being either regal or fashionable, were hard-working wives and mothers who knew all about their duties to humanity (they were reminded of them often enough), but were totally unaware of their rights, which, argued Miss Wollstonecraft, included not being treated like second-class citizens.

Her indignation carried over into another and much better book, *The Vindication of the Rights of Women.* She began by stating that her philosophy of liberation derived from 'a profound conviction that the neglected education of my fellow creatures is the grand source of the misery I deplore'. And it was to the need for a broader-based education for both sexes that she directed her sharpest polemics. For Mary Wollstonecraft, writes her latest biographer:

Education meant access to knowledge which was the key to thought, to creativeness, to the good life. Knowledge was meant to be used and its right use was consequent upon understanding. Understanding came through experience, for which economic freedom was essential. The mind must be liberated from the shackles of prejudice, greed and financial uncertainty; only then could the human spirit achieve its fullest expression.[21]

Such views, at least when they were applied to women, put her in direct opposition to numerous philosophers of learning, including the most eminent of them all – Rousseau. But if she experienced an unnerving feeling of isolation she did not allow it to cramp her style. 'I may be accused of arrogance,' she confessed, 'still I must declare what I firmly believe, that all the writers who have written on the subject of female education and manners, from Rousseau to Dr Gregory, have contributed to render women more artificial, weak characters, than they would otherwise have been.'

Rousseau based his opinions on the concept of woman as naturally secondary to her husband. Thus, 'the first and most important qualification in a woman is good nature . . . formed to obey a being so imperfect as man . . . she ought to learn betimes even to suffer injustice, and to bear the insults of her husband without complaint'. Mary started from the opposite end of the course. 'Strengthen the female mind by enlarging it, and there will be end to blind obedience; but, as blind obedience is ever sought for by power, tyrants and sensualists are in the right when they endeavour to keep women in the dark, because the former only want slaves, and the latter a plaything.' She stopped short at the idea of equality of the sexes. 'Let it not be concluded that I wish to invert the order of things;

I [grant] that, from the constitution of their bodies, men seem to be designed by Providence to attain a greater degree of virtue.' But this was no reason to withhold a decent education from one half of humanity. ' "Educate women like men," says Rousseau, "and the more they resemble our sex the less power they will have over us." This is the very point I aim at. I do not wish them to have power over men; but over themselves.' She might have added that having power over themselves, they would also be in a position to offer greater benefits to society as a whole.

The argument was not lost on the education reformers of the nineteenth century but then religious leaders who dominated education were more sympathetic to her point of view. In her own time she was up against clerics who still blamed woman for the fall of man, a theological doctrine that she categorically denied 'though the cry of irreligion, or even atheism be raised against me'. Those who took a more charitable view of woman's state of grace, like Dr James Fordyce, whose *Sermons* were often presented to girls as an introduction to good conduct, and Dr Gregory, whose book *Legacy to his Daughters* was a best-seller, nevertheless followed Rousseau in believing that intelligence and rational thinking were qualities that should be the male prerogative.

By contrast, Mary's scheme for bringing up girls reads like the manifesto of a modern radical educationist. She wanted boys and girls to be brought up together in government-supported co-educational day schools because she believed that youngsters became silly and selfish when they were exclusively in the company of their own sex. And she was not deterred by the prospect of co-education leading to younger marriages. If marriage was approached with understanding – including a knowledge of sex and reproduction – she promised a great improvement on the prevailing system of 'legal prostitution':

> In this plan of education the constitution of boys would not be ruined by early debaucheries which now make men so selfish, or girls rendered weak and vain by indolence and frivolous pursuits. But, I presuppose that such a degree of equality should be established between the sexes as would shut out gallantry and coquetry, yet allow friendship and love to temper the heart for the discharge of higher duties.

She advocated a new style of instruction that would hold children's attention and create a love of learning. What this amounted to in practice was an emphasis on discussion instead of on the dismal routine of note-copying and memory-testing. She thought that girls and boys ought to be free to follow their interests according to their abilities, which meant that parents, particularly fathers, should not be so eager to impose their selfish wishes. 'But what have women to do in society . . . but to loiter with easy grace?' The answer was that they could study the art of healing and be physicians as well as nurses. They could also study politics and 'settle their benevolence on the broadest basis'. Then there were 'businesses of various kinds they might likewise pursue, if they were educated in a more orderly manner, which might save many from common and legal prostitution'.

If Mary Wollstonecraft had been content merely to think and to write ahead of her time, her message might have been given the critical attention it deserved. But her private life was every bit as unconventional as her social and political views and society quickly associated her reform programme with the scandal of her love affairs. The story, briefly, is that she went through a disastrous relationship with an American writer, Gilbert Imlay, who fathered her daughter. After the affair with Imlay broke up she married William Godwin, another radical author, and died in childbirth at the age of thirty-eight. Her personal history might then have been forgotten had not Godwin, with the best motives, published her love letters to Imlay, claiming that they 'may be found to contain the finest examples of the language of sentiment and passion ever presented to the world'.

The next generation of reformers was reluctant to be publicly associated with such eccentric moral precepts. But this did not stop them taking note of Mary Wollstonecraft's ideas. A strong radical element appeared in some of the writings of early nineteenth-century educationists. Sidney Smith, in his essay on *Female Education* published in 1810, asked 'Why the disproportion in knowledge between the two sexes should be so great, when the inequality in natural talents is so small; or why the understanding of women should be lavished upon trifles, when nature has made it capable of better and higher things. . . ?' It was some measure of Mary Wollstonecraft's influence that the question was no longer capable of an easy answer.

References

1. Bernard Mandeville, *The Fable of the Bees, or Private Vices, Public Benefits* (Edinburgh, 1772). Quoted in D. W. Sylvester, *Educational Documents 800–1816* (Methuen, 1970), p. 176.

2. H. C. Barnard, *A Short History of English Education* (University of London Press, 1947), p. 7.

3. *An Account of Charity Schools in Great Britain and Ireland* (Society for the Promotion of Christian Knowledge, 1711).

4. Rachel Leighton, *Rise and Progress, The Story of the Welsh Girls' School* (1950), pp. 79–83.

5. W. G. Hughes and M. Sweeney, *Watford Grammar School for Boys and Girls* (1954), p. 26.

6. Ibid., p. 23.

7. Leighton, op. cit., p. 74.

8. D. H. Thomas, *A History of St Martin-in-the-Fields High School for Girls* (1929).

9. Catharine Cappe, *Account of Two Charity Schools for the Education of Girls* (1800), pp. 17–24. Quoted in Kamm, op. cit., p. 91.

10. Sarah Trimmer, *Reflections on the Education of Children in Charity Schools* (1792), pp. 18–19.

11. *Report of Society for Bettering the Condition of the Poor* (1809), p. 307.

12. M. G. Jones, *Hannah More* (Cambridge University Press, 1952), p. 152.

13. *Diary of Elizabeth Firth*, quoted in Laurie Magnus, *The Jubilee Book of the Girls' Public Day School Trust, 1873–1923* (Cambridge University Press, 1923), pp. 1–2.

14. Kamm, op. cit., p. 141.

15. H. Winifred Sturge and Theodora Clark, *The Mount School, York* (Dent, 1931).

16. Virginia Woolf, *A Room of One's Own* (1928, Penguin Modern Classics edn.), pp. 65–6.

17. *The Female Instructor or Young Woman's Companion* (Fisher and Dixon, 1811).

18. Samuel Heywood, *Digest of the Law Respecting County Elections* (1790), p. 158.

19. Thomas Gisborne, *An Enquiry into the Duties of the Female Sex* (Cadell and Davies, 1806), pp. 12–13.
20. Ibid., pp. 62–3.
21. Edna Nixon, *Mary Wollstonecraft: Her Life and Times* (Dent, 1971), p. 86.

Chapter three

Minimum standards

Yes, indeed she's a charming woman,
And knows both Latin and Greek,
And I'm told she solved a problem
In Euclid before she could speak.
Had she been but a daughter of mine,
I'd have taught her to hem and to sew;
But I'm told that a charming woman,
Cannot think of such trifles, you know.

Popular song, late eighteenth century[1]

The latest generation of female freedom fighters seems unable to decide whether the Industrial Revolution was a good thing because it created opportunities for female employment outside the home, or a bad thing because it forced thousands of women into hard, tedious and often unhealthy work without offering any domestic compensations such as comfortable homes or a release from excessive child-bearing. On balance it was probably an advantage that so many women were able to achieve the status of independent wage earners. The spinster or the widow was freed from dependence upon relatives or upon parish relief. Even married women could find some virtue in not being totally dependent on their husbands' earning capacity, although they were nearly always excluded from the skilled and better-paid work.

The first indications of political and trade-union interest among women can be detected in the activities of the Female Reform Societies founded in the textile towns in the early years of the nineteenth century.[2] And along with growing political awareness came a boost for education. The disruption of the traditional family structure by the demand for female labour in the factories un-doubtedly encouraged Church leaders to think in terms of counter-balancing the harsh social influences of industrialization with a programme of education aimed at introducing young people – boys and girls – to the basic Christian values.

Also, there was an obvious need to prepare girls for the responsi-bilities of running a home. So many were put to work at an early age that they learned nothing of domestic work from their mothers, 'not even how to mend a stocking or boil a potato'. This comment was made by a Manchester businessman to Robert Southey, who recorded their discussion in *Letters from England* published in 1807. The employer went on to say that the demand for child labour was such that in the new manufacturing towns the only method of keeping up the supply was 'to send people round the country to get children from their parents. Women usually undertake this business; they promise the parents to provide for the children; one party is glad to be eased of a burden, and it answers well to the other to find the young ones in food, lodging and clothes. . . .'

Demands for some form of popular education – if only on a part-time basis, were stimulated by the activities of such philanthropic organizations as the Society for Bettering the Condition of the Poor, which helped to strengthen the link between charity and middle-class self-interest by pointing out the social risks of leaving a great pro-portion of the people in a state of brute ignorance. Evidence of what could be achieved by a strong reform movement was soon to be supplied by radicals like Robert Owen, who provided free schools for his workers' children between the ages of five and ten, and Samuel Wilderspin, who helped to found the London Infant School Society to cater for children aged two to six. But how could it be possible, asked the critics, to offer decent education on an appreciable scale without pushing even the most generous benefactors beyond the limit of their resources?

The answer came from Joseph Lancaster, who hit on the idea of avoiding a huge investment in the training and employment of teachers by using older pupils as staff assistants. To prove his point he opened a school in the Borough Road, London, where, as the sole adult teacher, he administered the education of five hundred children. Since the monitors were seldom more than eleven or twelve years of age and were themselves poorly educated, the instruction could hardly be said to be anything but rudimentary. The aim, however, was not to turn out learned children but to equip them with a few elementary skills. Church and social leaders were immediately attracted to the idea of experimenting with the monitorial system on a much broader basis and in 1808 the British and Foreign School Society was founded to implement schemes elsewhere in the country. But approval of Lancaster's ideas was less than unanimous. As a Quaker he favoured non-sectarian teaching, which for some was interpreted as a threat to the long-established Anglican claim to determine the shape and content of education.

A new champion had to be found whose Christian allegiance was comfortingly orthodox. The obvious candidate was Dr Andrew Bell, who had discovered the virtues of monitorial instruction while teaching in Madras. The pious Sarah Trimmer, who liked nothing better than an inter-denominational squabble, identified him as the true originator of the system and linked his name with a new organization, the National Society for Promoting the Education of the Poor in the Principles of the Established Church, soon to be known simply as the National Society.

The National Society gained a head start by taking over the charity schools run by the SPCK. Offers of financial help, although not overwhelmingly generous, were judged to be adequate. An education philosophy founded on the ideal of raising the standard of public morality and, as a consequence, maintaining social order was much favoured at times when the lower orders showed signs of disaffection, which was happening with alarming frequency. For instance, the National Society took advantage of the 1842 disturbance to launch a special appeal to help fight 'the holiest war that has ever [been] waged – a war against ignorance, vice, and infidelity'. As a result nearly £152,000 was raised to build new schools and train teachers.[3] By then some 350,000 children were receiving an elementary education in Church schools.

But the monitorial system came in for some severe criticism from the radicals, who attacked the mindless routine of rote learning that characterized the elementary schools. In order to retain some semblance of order in classes that were sometimes several hundred strong, pupils and monitors were trained to respond to a series of commands from the teacher in charge – Begin dictation! Show slates! Clean slates! and so on. Yet the instruction in the Church schools was generally superior to that provided by the dame schools, which continued to offer a popular service for fees ranging from two to seven pence a week. In the 1830s, of 123,000 children attending elementary schools in Lancashire, some 50,000 were pupils at dame or common schools. These establishments were said to be in a most deplorable condition:

> The greater part of them are kept by females, but some by old men, whose only qualification for this employment seems to be their unfitness for every other. Many of these teachers are engaged at the same time in some other employment, such as shopkeeping, sewing, washing, etc which renders any regular instruction among their scholars absolutely impossible. . . . These schools are generally found in very dirty unwholesome rooms – frequently in close damp cellars, or old dilapidated garrets. In one of these schools eleven children were found, in a small room, in which one of the children of the Mistress was lying in bed ill of the measles. Another child had died in the same room, of the same complaint a few days before; and no less than thirty of the usual scholars were then confined at home with the same disease. . . .
>
> In by far the greater number of these schools there were only two or three books among the whole number of scholars. In others there was not one; and the children depended for their instruction on the chance of some one of them bringing a book, or a part of one, from home. . . .[4]

The schools were usually mixed but in those that catered for girls only there was apparently 'a greater appearance of cleanliness, order and regularity'. This was chiefly because the pupil–teacher ratio was lower (the demand for girls' education being lower than that for boys) and because it was easier to find practical tasks to occupy the children.

In all the varying types of elementary schools it was common practice to set the girls to work on sewing or cleaning to accustom them to their future domestic role. Later in the century when the Factory Acts required children between the ages of eight and thirteen to attend school on a part-time basis, it was no surprise to inspectors to find that factory girls acquired little from their educational interludes except practice in sewing:

Mixed schools devote usually about an hour and a half, girls' schools about an hour and three quarters, to this purpose daily; and, as in a majority of cases, by a stupid arrangement, the needlework lesson is given only in the afternoon, a mill girl may, during her afternoon turn, lasting a week or a month, as the case may be, have not more than an hour a day for intellectual instruction. Indeed, in not a few private, and some public schools, needlework takes up the whole afternoon, and the girls may be left for a whole month without even having a reading lesson. . . .[5]

At least it was to the credit of the girls' schools that they had the reputation of exercising standards of discipline that were more humane than those favoured by all-male establishments. Teachers were less inclined to resort to the strap or cane and numerous girls' schools claimed never to use corporal punishment.

Education statistics for the first half of the nineteenth century are frustratingly uninformative. The Parliamentary Committee appointed in 1818 'to inquire into the Education of the lower Orders' did not even bother to distinguish between male and female pupils. A further investigation carried out in 1833 was more comprehensive but almost certainly failed to take account of many of the private schools in the larger towns.[6] But the evidence was clearly in favour of those who argued that the system was deficient and unreliable. The best estimate for the 1830s was that of every ten children of school age three went to Sunday schools only, two to dame schools or private schools, four missed out on education altogether and only one received anything like a satisfactory education, usually in one of the schools administered by the National Society.

However, whether or not to invest in a huge expansion of education to achieve a nation-wide breakthrough to literacy was the central question of a long-running controversy. On the left were a small group of radicals who argued that natural justice demanded a comprehensive system embracing all children between the ages of six and fourteen. Less ambitious reformers linked their appeal for a steady growth to the theory that education, like religion, was a social cement. 'It is not to be denied that a manufacturing population is peculiarly inflammable, and apt to be misled,' said the *Quarterly Journal of Education*, 'and the only way to secure the labourers, as well as the other classes, from the ruinous consequences that are sure to arise from their supporting any unsound or impracticable principle, is to instruct them in their real interests.'[7]

Their opponents pointed out, quite reasonably, that the converse argument made every bit as much sense; that literacy would create dissatisfaction among the working classes by encouraging them to aim for the social advantages already secured by the cultured minority. But even if the reformers could dismiss the élitist theories of the opposition, there was still the unnerving prospect of trying to raise enough capital to finance their schemes. The obvious candidate for chief sponsor was the government. So far the state had helped the British and Foreign School Society and the National Society indirectly; for instance, by providing free postage for fund-raising campaigns. But the suggestion of direct government involvement in education led to interminable debates that centred on the deep-rooted aversion to state interference in matters of social conscience and the fear of sectarian entanglements.

At the beginning of the century Samuel Whitbread introduced a Parochial Schools Bill into the House of Commons. It provided for two years of free education for children between the ages of seven and fourteen whose parents could not afford school fees. The Bill failed. In the House of Lords, the Archbishop of Canterbury said that 'it would go to subvert the first principles of education in this country, which had hitherto been, and should continue to be, under the control and auspices of the Establishment'.[8] In the second decade the campaign was taken up by Henry Brougham, who managed to persuade the government to gather some basic statistics, and in 1820 followed up this success with a proposal for financing new schools with contributions from manufacturers, support from the rates and fees from parents who were able to pay. But in the face of opposition from the Established Church, the Roman Catholics and the Non-conformists, the Parish Schools Bill was withdrawn.

Thirteen years later John Arthur Rowbuck advocated a centrally-controlled system of infant schools, schools of industry and evening schools to provide for all children from six to twelve years of age. Rowbuck could hardly have expected to win a Parliamentary majority for such an all-embracing project but he prepared the way for a major concession – an Exchequer grant to the two education societies of £20,000. The grant was renewed annually without too much bother until 1838 when it was realized that further expenditure of public money could only be justified if there was a closer check on the way it was being spent.

Initially, the societies were given the job of inspecting progress in the new schools, but reports were slow in coming in and since there were many unofficial claims of maladministration, Parliament naturally became impatient for a reckoning. Pressure on the government to take the initiative increased with the publication of a select committee investigation into the Education of the Poorer Classes, which revealed, not unexpectedly, that schooling for working-class children was miserably deficient. Measures were needed, said the report, to bring daily education within reach of at least an eighth of the population.

The first government reaction was to set up a Committee of the Privy Council 'for the consideration of all matters affecting the Education of the People'. This, in turn, led to a decision to make a start on establishing a corps of inspectors who could travel the country advising and encouraging teachers who were well intentioned but probably unsophisticated in the way of instructing, and (although this was not explicitly stated) chastise the unashamedly incompetent and the blatantly dishonest.

At this point the National Society decided that government intervention in educational administration was an attempt to undermine the proper influence of the Established Church. The principle of inspection was not in question; the quarrel was about the power to appoint and control inspectors which the National Society wanted to keep for itself. In the end Church and State agreed to share the responsibility. Inspectors had to be vetted by an archbishop before they could be empowered to enter Anglican schools; the Church retained complete control over religious instruction while the Board of Education, in the person of its first secretary, Sir James Kay-Shuttleworth, conceded that 'no plan of education ought to be encouraged in which intellectual instruction is not subordinate to the regulation of the thoughts and habits of the children by the doctrine and precepts of revealed religion'.[9]

This concession to the National Society helped to preserve and even strengthen the distinctions between boys' and girls' education. Theological doctrine ruled that girls should be trained primarily for home duties and though Church educationists realized as clearly as anyone that the majority of working-class females were destined to support themselves for at least half their working lives, this did not deter them from the formidable task of promoting the universal application of the domestic ideal. So strong was the propaganda that even the small group of working women who revealed some political awareness were preoccupied with their status as housewives. E. P. Thompson, in his classic account of *The Making of the English Working Class*, notes: 'The new independence, in the mill or full-time at the loom, which made new claims possible, was felt simultaneously as a loss in status and personal independence. Women became more dependent upon the employer or labour market, and they looked back to a "golden" past in which home earnings from spinning, poultry, and the like, could be gained from around their own door.'[10] The romantic image of cosy rural domesticity, contrasted with the harsh monotony of factory routine, certainly helps to explain the two-way stretch of loyalties, but it is unlikely that the pull of nostalgia (which, after all, was built more on imagination than on reality) would have been quite so strong had not so much effort been put into the educational campaign for reminding women of their natural duties.

Between 1839 and 1862 (the year the Revised Code came into operation) the Board of Education distributed grants totalling about £5 million. By contemporary levels of government expenditure this was a reasonably generous allocation but it was hardly enough to hold out a promise of an early solution to the massive problem of working-class illiteracy. The 1851 Census estimated (very roughly indeed, according to modern statisticians) that about 24 per cent of the male population under twenty and 20 per cent of the girls in the same age-group were enrolled for public or private day schools. Attendance figures for both sexes were about 4 per cent down on enrolment. Another qualifying factor was the average period of time spent in school, which for boys and girls was not much more than a single year out of their entire lives. Even when it is taken into account that about 19 per cent of each sex attended Sunday schools, it is a fair assumption that a clear majority of children never received an education of any sort.

Ironically, it was at the lowest levels of society that discrimination between children of different sex disappeared almost entirely. These pathetic creatures shared a single dominating purpose – to survive; and to do this they were compelled to support themselves almost as soon as they had progressed beyond infancy. To take one example, Mayhew found that the life of coster-girls was every bit as severe as that of the boys:

> Between four and five in the morning they have to leave home for the markets, and sell in the streets until about nine. Those that have more kindly parents, return then to breakfast, but many are obliged to earn the morning's meal for themselves. After breakfast, they generally remain in the streets until about ten o'clock at night; many having nothing during all that time but one meal of bread and butter and coffee, to enable them to support the fatigue of walking from street to street with the heavy basket on their heads. In the course of a day, some girls eat as much as a pound of bread, and very seldom get any meat, unless it be on a Sunday.[11]

Some of those children who enjoyed a brief acquaintance with education were not much better off. Until 1842 girls were recruited to do some of the most backbreaking work in the pits. Conditions were no better in cotton or metal or in any of the other industries that made use of female labour. Thomas Hood's *The Song of the Shirt*, which was written for *Punch* in 1843 when he found that seamstresses earned only five farthings for sewing a shirt, was a fair reflection of conditions in the sweated trade.

Despite the efforts of the Board of Education to lay down standards of building that related in some way to the learning needs of the pupils, local school managers were averse to offering accommodation that might cause children and parents to become dissatisfied with their miserable home environments and their future work prospects. Thus in searching for an example of an existing type of building that might serve as a guide to school architects, one reverend gentleman offered the thought that 'a barn furnishes no bad model; and a good one may be easily converted into a school'. No wonder that recommendations for special facilities for girls, such as needlework rooms, laundries and kitchens, were seldom, if ever, implemented. Rooms were cramped, ill-lit and badly ventilated. Fairly typically, an inspector in Wales reported that one school contained 'thirty boys and twenty girls huddled together in a low dark room' which smelt like a ship's engines.[12]

Books and other teaching materials were in short supply, though the situation improved after 1847 when the Department introduced a special equipment and book-buying grant. Available texts were overwhelmingly biased towards religious instruction. By far the most popular reader was the Bible, which may have had an elevating influence on the pupils but was not the easiest introduction to the rudiments of language. At a school in Birmingham, 'Fifty girls were present. . . . The books in use were those of the National School Society. The writing was bad. The mistress said she thought girls should not learn beyond compound addition in arithmetic, and she taught them no farther. Eighteen of the best readers then read to the monitor, making various mistakes which were noticed by the monitor or mistress. . . .'[13]

The extent of the deficiencies of elementary education became apparent to the wider public when the Newcastle Report was published in 1861. The Royal Commission, appointed to discover the 'present state of popular education', based its conclusions on investigations into a sample of schools in ten contrasting areas. On the credit side the government system of aid and inspection had 'given a powerful stimulus to the building of schools, and has created a class of schoolmasters and pupil-teachers of a superior character to any previously known in this country'. It was estimated that about one in eight citizens attended school at some time in their lives as against one in twenty-one at the beginning of the century:

On the other hand we have exposed great and growing defects in its tendency to indefinite expense, in its ability to assist poorer districts, in the partial inadequacy of its teaching, and in the complicated business which encumbers the central office of the Committee of Council; and these defects have led us to believe that any attempt to extend it unaltered into a national system would fail. We have therefore proposed, while retaining the leading principles of the present system and simplifying its working, to combine with it a supplementary and local system which may diffuse a wider interest in education, may distribute its burdens more equally, and may enable every school in the country to participate in its benefits.[14]

63

Since annual government expenditure on education was running at no more than £1 million, the Newcastle Commission's fear of 'a tendency to indefinite expense' was somewhat premature, but the other criticisms were undoubtedly justified. What they added up to was a proposal to replace the various grants by a single allocation to schools that earned a satisfactory report from a government inspector. A supplementary grant from borough and county rates was to be based on the students' attainments in reading, writing and arithmetic. In this way was introduced the infamous system of 'payment by results', which Robert Lowe, Vice-President of the Education Department, justified on the principle that 'If it is not cheap, it shall be efficient; if it is not efficient, it shall be cheap'.

As it turned out 'payment by results' was cheap (annual expenditure fell by nearly a quarter) and, in the narrowest possible sense, it was also efficient. School attendance increased to beyond one million in 1866 and teachers were compelled by self-interest to advance these pupils to a state of literacy that was calculated to produce favourable reports from the inspectors. But instead of encouraging genuine education, the system promoted rote learning, the recitation of set pieces by children lacking understanding or interest, which remained the prevailing evil of classroom teaching well into the twentieth century.

But even if the system had allowed for creative education, there was still the problem of finding teachers who possessed the competence and imagination to take advantage of the opportunities. Early on in the century the monitorial system was recognized as a stop-gap measure which could not possibly satisfy the demand for skilled staff.

In 1841 the National Society made one of the first positive moves towards finding a remedy by establishing St Mark's training college in Chelsea. The following year a women's college was founded close by at Whitelands. By 1845 there were thirteen training colleges, six of them for women, most of which were run by the Church of England.

The average course for women lasted no longer than a year and was heavily biased towards domestic economy. The curriculum was justified by the emphasis on practical work in the schools and by the fact that many of the student teachers would themselves end up caring for their own homes and families, but there was also a strong suspicion that colleges favoured practical lessons as a cheap method of disposing of the housework. At Salisbury such uncharitable criticisms were dismissed with the argument that 'such work as scrubbing, cleaning shoes, etc. has a beneficial tendency in correcting faults of vanity, indolence, etc., and in giving a practical lesson in humility'.[15] Even at Whitelands, which had one of the best academic reputations, the strongest emphasis was on the ability to undertake needlework, knitting and darning.

The standard of accommodation was far removed from the academic cloisters of higher learning. At Salisbury, where the college moved into a house on the Cathedral close, there were just twelve small bedrooms for thirty-two pupils and since there was no infirmary, teenage diseases accounted for a high casualty rate. Whitelands consisted of two houses connected by a range of long, low buildings, which faced the Kings Road in Chelsea. The rooms were said to be 'ill-lighted and insufficiently ventilated' and the laundry and scullery were 'overrun with rats'. Another college refused to instal baths on the grounds that it would not be a good idea to give teachers a taste of luxury which they would never again be able to afford.[16] Men students were invariably better off; many of them were able to take up residence in brand new colleges which might have been described as purpose-built had not their mock Gothic facades suggested that more attention had been paid to architectural whimsey than to the actual needs of the students.

Probably the most successful women's college was also the oldest and least pretentious. Emerging from Samuel Widderspin's efforts to educate the infants of the London poor, the Home and Colonial Infant School Society was set up in 1836 to provide training for teachers. The College, which was in Gray's Inn Road, offered an intensive twenty-week course for a total of thirty-six students. When they arrived most of the girls were as ignorant as it was possible to be without being totally illiterate but, by common consent, the College somehow managed to transform this unpromising material into an effective teaching force.

Overall, however, the shortage of good teachers was so great that even the National Society came to realize that it could not handle the crisis unaided.

Everyone knew that what was needed was more of the taxpayers' money to finance suitable training schemes. But this implied tighter government control, which the National Society was bound to resist. A solution was negotiated by Kay-Shuttleworth, who had long been occupied with plans for expanding the teaching force. He proposed a new set of grants to back up a system of training pupil teachers within the schools. The conditions under which this scheme was to operate were markedly different to those that characterized monitorial education. Only the best schools were to be allowed to participate. They had to be well equipped with books and apparatus and organized to take account of the needs of different age groups. Another prerequisite was the presence of a teacher who was capable of passing the skills of instruction on to his apprentices. The trainees (minimum age, thirteen) were to sit a preliminary examination and then, if successful, pursue a five-year course of study approved and regulated by the Education Department.

After a year of negotiations the approval of the National Society was won in return for assurances that there was 'no intention of diluting the 'two great principles' of education: '. . . that religion pervade the whole teaching of a school and that the main direction of education should be left in the care of those who would be prompted to approach and handle it from a care for the immortal souls of children. . . .'[17] The pupil-teacher scheme came into operation in 1846, and within two years Kay-Shuttleworth was able to report that over two thousand apprentices were in training and that demand for places was such that standards of entry could be raised.

The development of the pupil-teacher system was accompanied by an improvement and expansion of training college facilities. By 1858 there were fifteen men's colleges catering for about 750 students, thirteen women's colleges with over 800 students and five mixed colleges with 500 students. At least eighty per cent were previously pupil-teachers who had qualified for Queen's scholarships, worth about £20 to £25, which enabled them to augment their training with a year at college. But it was some time before the more traditional establishments were able to adapt themselves to the demands of the new scheme. Examinations were now tougher, which meant that the standard of college teaching had to be much improved. At one women's college 'They were not only alarmed on account of the great importance which they attached to success, but they were, unfortunately, not prepared for an examination in writing.'[18]

Even at the better places there were many students who failed to qualify, but this was seldom their fault. They were expected to work hard but too often at the wrong subjects. General domestic activities were still claimed to be great character builders. At Stockwell, dusting and scrubbing were recommended as 'affording a healthful change and comparative recreation amid their ordinary studies'. And at Lincoln the college laundry was kept going by students, who were expected to take it in turns to wind the mangle in what was called their 'recreation hour'.

Information was fed into the students like corn into a thresher but unlike the machine their minds did not possess the facility for distinguishing wheat from chaff. They departed from college with a most curious collection of intellectual snippets learned by heart for the benefit of the examiners. In an attempt to raise academic standards, textbooks were designed to extract high-flown generalizations from an amalgam of disjointed facts and assertions. Samuel Warren, who was apparently much distinguished in the Inner Temple, was persuaded to produce a text 'for the use of schools and young persons' based on *Select Extracts from Blackstone's Commentaries*, while James Cornwell, Principal of the Borough Road College, found some peculiar fulfilment in turning out a best-seller geography text containing a mass of irrelevant but greatly detailed information, climaxed by such brain teasing questions as: 'Describe England as compared with the rest of Great Britain.' The answer, which students were expected to repeat word for word was: 'England is the largest, wealthiest, and in every way the most important part of Great Britain.' No wonder that when this sort of information was retailed to the schools, critics asked what possible significance it could have for developing young minds. 'To what generation of labourers' children,' wrote a member of the Education Department, 'will it ever be expedient to discourse on the Schism of the Papacy, the Council of Basle, the Pragmatic Sanction, or the Wars of the Hussites?'

Perhaps the quality of the school books would have been less important if more imagination had been applied to the techniques of teaching. Unfortunately, college students were not given much opportunity to develop their own style of class management. According to the Department of Education Minutes for 1850–1, the woman student is 'made to observe an entire course of lessons in every elementary subject. She takes notes of all she observes. She has to state how far the method of teaching agrees with that she has learned as a pupil-teacher, or in what respects it may differ from it'. All this took from three to six months.

Nevertheless, whatever the defects of the system, it created the first really decent career structure for women from working-class and lower-middle-class families. It was an opportunity they were quick to spot and since for some time it offered the only escape from the depressing routine of low-status employment they competed strongly with their male rivals. In 1850 there were about 1,500 certificated teachers of whom one-third were women. A decade later the total had increased to 12,500 but now the proportion of women had increased to over three-quarters. Moreover, the 1861 figures for recruitment of first-year teacher apprentices showed the girls to be in a clear majority, and this despite the claim that inspectors were much stricter in their selection of female candidates, who were required to supply evidence that their homes were decent and respectable and their parents moral and responsible citizens.

A schoolmistress lived in a rent-free house and could earn around £60 a year while her male colleague was able to command a salary approaching £100. But she was almost certainly better off than her parents and way ahead of most of her contemporaries. The profession even attracted recruits from the middle class, where, ironically, job opportunities were generally less attractive.

In the first half of the century it was still the custom for the upper social groups to educate their daughters and younger sons at home. To assist them in this task they employed governesses, young ladies from respectable families who had acquired a veneer of learning and who, for one reason or another, needed to provide their own income. The tragedy of these women was the disparity between the material and social expectations that they were encouraged to adopt by their upbringing and the manner in which they were treated by their employers. A governess was a servant; her worth was calculated according to her rating on the labour market, which put a higher premium on a good cook and only a slightly lower value on a competent housemaid.

Many and many a young governess has been soured, her love turned into dislike, her kindly feelings into gall, by the treatment she has undergone. Not necessarily rudeness or positive neglect, but a chilling indifference, a well-bred surprise manifested at any self assertion or contrary opinion. . . . Of what use is it to hold forth seriously to one's children on the duty of being obedient, kind, and respectful to their governess, when that lady is quizzed and laughed at, however good temperedly, behind her back; when elder brothers march into the room before her; when elder sisters satirize her manners if she be a foreigner; and, worse of all, when the mother says, with a gentle, contemptous pity, 'Poor good soul! she meant to do well; but you had better refer everything to me, my dear'?[19]

The qualities that were expected of a governess were extremely varied and prospective employers were not at all inhibited from filling the job section of *The Times* with carefully composed advertisements offering minimum rewards for the best candidates:

Governess Wanted – A lady belonging to the Church of England, competent to undertake the education of a young lady nearly sixteen years of age. She must be a person of cultivated mind, of great steadiness of character, sound good sense, and cheerful temper. She is required to be proficient in the French, Italian, and German languages, to be a good musician and capable of teaching the piano and singing well. A proficiency in drawing and water colour is particularly to be desired.[20]

In this case a 'liberal salary' was promised but this probably meant an offer of no more than £50 a year with accommodation. A nursery governess was lucky to get half this amount. More for the sake of the children than the teacher, employers insisted on fairly generous holidays – a week or two at Christmas, two weeks at Easter and five or six weeks in the summer – but these periods of relaxation were often dreaded by the governess, who, as likely as not, had nowhere to go to enjoy her recuperation. Unless she was very fortunate she certainly needed a regular opportunity to restock her energy since at any time the relationship between parents, teacher and children was likely to develop into a war of nerves.

Anne Brontë, the youngest of the Brontë sisters, recorded her experiences as a governess in her semi-autobiographical novel, *Agnes Grey*:

My task of instruction and surveillance, instead of becoming easier as my charges and I got better accustomed to each other, became more arduous as their characters unfolded. The name of governess, I soon found, was a mere mockery as applied to me, my pupils had no more notion of obedience than a wild unbroken colt.

The habitual fear of their father's peevish temper, and the dread of the punishments he was wont to inflict when irritated, kept them generally within bounds in his immediate presence. The girls, too, had some fear of their mother's anger, and the boy might occasionally be bribed to do as she bid him by the hope of reward: but I had no rewards to offer, and as for punishments, I was given to understand, the parents reserved that privilege to themselves; and yet they expected me to keep my pupils in order. Other children might be guided by fear of anger, and the desire of approbation; but neither the one nor the other had any effect upon these.

Master Tom, not content with refusing to be ruled, must needs set up as a ruler, and manifested a determination to keep, not only his sisters, but his governess in order, by violent manual and pedal applications; and, as he was a tall, strong boy for his years, this occasioned no trifling inconvenience. . . .

To the difficulty of preventing him from doing what he ought not, was added that of forcing him to do what he ought. Often he would positively refuse to learn, or to repeat his lessons, or even to look at his book. Here, again, a good birch rod might have been serviceable: but as my powers were so limited, I must make the best use of what I had. . . .

The task of instruction was as arduous for the body as for the mind. I had to run after my pupils to catch them, to carry or drag them to the table, and often forcibly to hold them there till the lesson was done. . . .

Yet Tom was by no means the most unmanageable of my pupils: sometimes, to my great joy, he would have the sense to see that his wisest policy was to finish his tasks, and go out and amuse himself till I and his sisters came to join him; which frequently was not at all, for Mary Ann seldom followed his example in this particular: she apparently preferred rolling on the floor to any other amusement. . . .

Often she would stubbornly refuse to pronounce some particular word in her lesson, and now I regret the lost labour I have had in striving to conquer her obstinacy. If I had passed it over as a matter of no consequence it would have been better for both parties, than vainly striving to overcome it, as I did, but I thought it my absolute duty to crush this vicious tendency in the bud, and so it was, if I could have done it, and had my powers been less limited, I might have enforced obedience; but, as it was, it was a trial of strength between her and me, in which she generally came off victorious; and every victory served to encourage and strengthen her for a future contest. . . .

Another of my trials was the dressing in the morning: at one time she would not be washed; at another she would not be dressed, unless she might wear some particular frock, that I knew her mother would not like her to have; at another she would scream and run away if I attempted to touch her hair. So that, frequently, when after much trouble and toil, I had, at length, succeeded in bringing her down, the breakfast was nearly half over; and black looks from 'mamma', and testy observations from 'papa', spoken at me, if not to me, were sure to be my need; for few things irritated the latter so much as want of punctuality at meal times.

Then, among the minor annoyances, was my inability to satisfy Mrs Bloomfield with her daughter's dress; and the child's hair 'was never fit to be seen'. Sometimes, as a powerful reproach to me, she would perform the office of tire-woman herself, and then complain bitterly of the trouble it gave her.

When little Fanny came into the schoolroom, I hoped she would be mild and inoffensive, at least; but a few days, if not a few hours, sufficed to destroy the illusion. . . . As she, generally, was pretty quiet in her parents' presence, and they were impressed with the notion of her being a remarkably gentle child, her falsehoods were readily believed, and her loud uproars led them to suspect harsh and injudicious treatment on my part; and when, at length, her bad disposition became manifest even to their prejudiced eyes, I felt that the whole was attributed to me.

Few households were able to acquire a governess of the intellectual calibre of Anne Brontë, and there were homes where the teacher was of such limited talent and enthusiasm that there was some excuse for ill temper and even rough treatment. It might be said that employers who were badly served should have improved their conditions to attract better-qualified candidates but the entire system of middle-class education was so poor that few teachers of real ability were ever available. 'What salery oeght I expect as nersury governess?' asked one of hundreds of the readers of the *Girls' Own Paper* who wrote asking for career advice. 'My duties will be to wash and dress 3 small gurls, teach them reading, riting and speling, and atend to there close.' Not surprisingly the *GOP* urged her to give up any idea of teaching and added, somewhat harshly, 'try nursing, less will be expected of you'.[21]

But what of those parents who were sufficiently enlightened or, alternatively, desperate enough to consider sending their daughters to private schools? They enjoyed a reasonably wide choice of establishments, particularly if they lived in a fashionable area or were prepared to pay high fees for boarding. Brighton, for instance, could boast more than one hundred girls' schools. Few of these charged less than £120 or £130 a year, excluding extras like dancing and music, yet all of them emphasized the accomplishments before any sort of intellectual activity.[22] It was apparently thought sufficient that middle-class girls should pick up a few broad concepts that might come in useful if they ever felt inclined to take up reading as a hobby or were compelled to show the men that they at least understood the content of their conversation.

Texts were produced that managed to cover several diverse courses in a single volume, which was not so difficult as one might imagine when topics like the French Revolution were dismissed in a short sentence: '. . . the whole country was covered with guillotenes; and the streets of every town ran red with blood of those whose sole crimes were their innocence, and their horror of the scenes which were daily acting.'[23]

The full measure of the unhappiness that an intelligent and sensitive girl could suffer in one of these ladies' academies can be judged from the memoirs of Frances Power Cobbe, who spent two years in a Brighton school:

The din of our large double schoolrooms was something frightful.

Sitting in either of them, four pianos might be heard going at once in rooms above and around us, while at numerous tables scattered about the rooms were girls reading aloud to the governesses and reciting lessons in English, French, German and Italian. This hideous clatter continued the entire day till we went to bed at night, there being no time whatever allowed for recreation, unless the dreary hour of walking with our teachers (when we recited our verbs), could be so described by a fantastic imagination. In the midst of the uproar we were obliged to write our exercises, to compose our themes, and to commit to memory whole pages of prose. On Saturday afternoons, instead of play, there was a terrible ordeal generally known as the 'Judgement Day'. The two schoolmistresses sat side by side, solemn and stern, at the head of the long table. Behind them sat all the governesses as Assessors. On the table were the books wherein our evil deeds of the week were recorded; and round the room against the wall, seated on stools of penitential discomfort, we sat, five-and-twenty 'damosels', anything but 'Blessed', expecting our sentences according to our ill-deserts. It must be explained that the fiendish ingenuity of some teacher had invented for our torment a system of imaginary 'cards', which we were supposed to 'lose' (though we never gained any) whenever we had not finished all our various lessons and practisings every night before bed-time, or whenever we had been given the mark for 'stooping' or had been impertinent, or had been 'turned' in our lessons, or had been marked 'P' by the music master, or had been convicted of 'disorder' (e.g. having our long shoe-strings untied), or, lastly, had told lies!

Any one crime in this heterogeneous list entailed the same penalty, namely, the sentence, 'You have lost your card, Miss So-and-so, for such and such a thing', and when Saturday came round, if three cards had been lost in the week, the law wreaked its justice on the unhappy sinner's head! Her confession having been wrung from her at the awful judgement-seat above described, and the books having been consulted, she was solemnly scolded and told to sit in the corner for the rest of the evening! Anything more ridiculous than the scene which followed can hardly be conceived. I have seen (after a week in which a sort of feminine barring-out had taken place) no less than nine young ladies obliged to sit for hours in the angles of the three rooms, like naughty babies, with their faces to the wall; half of them being quite of marriageable age, and all dressed, as was *de rigueur* with us every day, in full evening attire of silk or muslin, with gloves and kid slippers. Naturally, Saturday evenings, instead of affording some relief to the incessant over-strain of the week, were looked upon with terror as the worst time of all. Those who escaped the fell destiny of the corner were allowed, if they chose, to write to their parents, but our letters were perforce committed at night to the schoolmistress to seal, and were not, as may be imagined, exactly the natural outpouring of our sentiments as regarded those ladies and their school. . . .

But all this fine human material was deplorably wasted. Nobody dreamed that any one of us could in later life be more or less than an 'Ornament of Society'. That a pupil in that school should ever become an artist, or authoress, would have been looked upon by both Miss Runciman and Miss Roberts as a deplorable dereliction.

Not that which was good in itself or useful to the community, or even that which would be delightful to ourselves, but that which would make us admired in society, was the *raison d'être* of each acquirement. Everything was taught us in the inverse ratio of its true importance. At the bottom of the scale were Morals and Religion, and at the top were Music and Dancing; miserably poor music, too, of the Italian school then in vogue, and generally performed in a showy and tasteless manner on harp or piano. . . .

Next to music in importance in our curriculum came dancing. The famous old Madame Michaud and her husband both attended us constantly, and we danced to their direction in our large play-room (*lucus a non lucendo*), till we had learned not only all the dances in use in England in that ante-polka epoch, but almost every national dance in Europe, the Minuet, the Gavotte, the Cachucha, the Bolero, the Mazurka, and the Tarantella. . . .

Next to Music and Dancing and Deportment, came Drawing, but that was not a sufficiently voyant accomplishment, and no great attention was paid to it; the instruction also being of a second-rate kind, except that it included lessons in perspective which have been useful to me ever since. Then followed Modern Languages. No Greek or Latin were heard of at the school, but French, Italian and German were chattered all day long, our tongues being only set at liberty at six o'clock to speak English. Such French, such Italian, and such German as we actually spoke may be more easily imagined than described. . . .

Beyond all this, our English studies embraced one long, awful lesson each week to be repeated to the schoolmistress herself by a class, in history one week, in geography the week following. Our first class, I remember, had once to commit to memory – Heaven alone knows how – no less than thirteen pages of Woodhouse-lee's Universal History!

Lastly, as I have said, in point of importance, came our religious instruction. Our well-meaning schoolmistresses thought it was obligatory on them to teach us something of the kind, but, being very obviously altogether worldly women themselves, they were puzzled how to carry out their intentions. They marched us to church every Sunday when it did not rain, and they made us on Sunday mornings repeat the Collect and Catechism; but beyond these exercises of body and mind, it was hard for them to see what to do for our spiritual welfare. One Ash Wednesday, I remember, they provided us with a dish of salt-fish, and when this was removed to make room for the roast mutton, they addressed us in a short discourse, setting forth the merits of fasting, and ending by the remark that they left us free to take meat or not as we pleased, but that they hoped we should fast; 'it would be good for our souls and our figures!' . . .

It is almost needless to add, in concluding these reminiscences, that the heterogeneous studies pursued in this helter-skelter fashion were of the smallest possible utility in later life; each acquirement being of the shallowest and most imperfect kind, and all real education worthy of the name having to be begun on our return home, after we had been pronounced 'finished'. Meanwhile the strain on our mental powers of getting through daily, for six months at a time, this mass of ill-arranged and miscellaneous lessons, was extremely great and trying.[24]

But if any hint of this academic chaos ever reached the parents, it did not deter them from maintaining their patronage. It seemed that a woman of secure reputation such as the author Mrs Sherwood, had only to announce her willingness 'to undertake the education of a few young ladies at one hundred guineas a year' and eager mothers fell over themselves to take advantage of her services. For those who could not afford extravagant fees (Frances Power Cobbe estimated that her two years' schooling cost her parents over £1,000) there were a few schools that received part of their expenses from charitable trusts. Loughborough High School, for instance, started as an offshoot of the Burton Trustees who administered three elementary schools. The fees were 1/6d a week.

There was a strong practical bias to the teaching. The grandson of one of the first pupils said, 'She was there for three and a half years and all that time she was engaged in making a nightdress, which she never finished, as her school career ended abruptly owing to rheumatic fever'. But, he added, 'I think she must have been well taught as even at ninety she could repeat some of the French she had learnt.'[25]

One of the best-known charity schools catering for middle-class girls was the Clergy Daughters' School at Casterton. It had many admirers, among whom was one eminent cleric who confessed that he 'would rather have built this school and church than Blenheim or Burleigh . . .'.[26]

But the reputation of Casterton suffered badly when it was known that Charlotte Brontë was relating her experience there as a teacher when she described in *Jane Eyre* the miserable pupils of Lowood Institution and the tyrannical and petty-minded Mr Brocklehurst, who exercised his power of administration like a prison governor. Another teacher at Casterton who achieved distinction in her profession was Dorothea Beale, later head of Cheltenham Ladies College. She found that she was expected to instruct the daughters of the Clergy in almost every subject in the curriculum. Not feeling herself properly equipped to impart a love of scripture, arithmetic, mathematics, ancient history, modern history, church history, geography, English, French, German, Latin and Italian, at least not in rapid succession, her residence at the school was short-lived.

But Casterton had at least one admirer who was so impressed by what he saw that he promptly went off to set up his own charity school. In 1832 the Rev. Henry Venn Elliott, first minister of

St Mary's Chapel in Brighton, issued a prospectus for what he described as a 'nursery for governesses for the higher and middle classes'. His clients were the daughters of clergymen of limited means who were expected to contribute £20 a year towards the education, accommodation and clothing of their children. Elliott was an inspired fund-raiser who managed to collect £16,000, chiefly from aristocratic acquaintances.

By 1839 there were one hundred pupils and a lengthy waiting list. Applicants were expected to be able to spell and read with some degree of fluency and to be versed in the first four rules of arithmetic. Possibly of greater concern to parents was the list of essential possessions that girls were supposed to bring with them to school, among them a silver dessert spoon, tea spoon and fork.

St Mary's Hall seems to have been altogether a more attractive establishment than Casterton but both shared a conviction that girls were unlikely to apply their brains unless they were strictly disciplined. Punishments for quite minor sins were varied and frequently administered: '. . . hours spent lying flat on the back on the Nursery floor, guarded by the Elliott scholar as she sat in grim silence mending her white stockings; days spent sitting on the lockers which lined a large schoolroom, hemming dusters; solitary meals eaten at a side table in the dining-room; or being sent to bed frequently throughout the day, and then as frequently being obliged to get up and dress . . .'.[27]

The parents who cared most about girls' education and who were best provided with facilities for shaping their daughters' intellects were the Quakers, although even this remarkable sect tolerated some curious notions about the way in which schools should be administered. At the Friends' School in Croydon, the attempt to merge individuals into a single unit was carried to the lengths of identifying children not by names but by numbers. But in other Quaker schools personalities were generally allowed the freedom to develop their own distinctive traits. The Mount School in York was forced to close in the early years of the century but was revived in 1831, chiefly as a result of the efforts of Joseph Rowntree and Samuel Tuke, the grandson of the original founder. Fees were fixed at £30 a year, and Hannah Brady, a young teacher from Ackworth, was appointed head.

The scholastic routine was quite strenuous. The girls had to be out of bed at six and ready to start lessons at seven. Studies accounted for seven hours in a full day, quite apart from a silent hour in the evening for reading and writing and a Bible talk last thing at night. But judging by their correspondence the pupils were encouraged to take pleasure in their academic work and there was an enthusiasm for intellectual pursuits that was extremely rare in other schools. 'Your letter says "If thou incline to learn Greek, I would entirely object to it",' wrote Anne White to her father, 'but S. Tuke thought you forgot to put "not" between "would" and "entirely" and so did I. It is therefore settled for me to learn it. . . .'[28]

An ex-pupil could recall only one occasion when punishment was administered and that was the time when a girl invited a Punch and Judy man to put on his show outside the school. 'Of course, instantly, the windows of the cloakroom and playroom, all facing the street, were crowded, tier above tier, and we were enjoying the performance, when dear Hannah Brady made her appearance in the street, and was hardly able to gain admittance to the house. . . . We were all severely reprimanded for our low taste, and I think had bread and water for our dinner. . . .' But there were constant reminders that life beyond the school could be harsh and brutal. The Assizes were held at the Castle close by and the forecourt was the arena for public hangings: '. . . the earliest wagon-loads of people arriving from the country to be in time for the sad spectacle, and the hurrying of many feet as the hours passed by, prevented us from sleeping. Our thoughts were sad and solemn, and when the tolling of the bell told us the time had come, we could hardly restrain our tears.'[29]

Because there was some difficulty in finding qualified teachers, a training section was opened for pupils who wanted to stay on as junior staff. There were also visiting teachers from nearby boys' schools but they were not very confident with female pupils and were easily taken in by pranks that they would never have tolerated from boys. For instance, the French master's technique for encouraging conversation was to invite questions for him to answer. An ex-pupil recalled, '. . . we hit upon one which served as a model for all the rest: "Avez vous jamais été à . . . ?" and then added first one town and then another; and as he spent a very long time in describing each town, the lesson got beautifully filled up and over, without any more trouble on our part.'[30] As the century progressed, Mount School acquired a reputation for a more rigid system of discipline. From 1866 the headmistress was Lydia Rous, a woman who shielded beauty and fine intellect with 'an armour of Victorian repression and Quaker discipline'. Nevertheless, she was greatly loved by the pupils and her school retained its enthusiasm for academic studies at the expense of the fashionable accomplishments.

That there were not many girls' schools offering an education of such quality was a source of indignation among intelligent women who were themselves sufficiently educated to appreciate the intellectual potentialities of their sex. Even the author of *The Complete Governess*, who could not be described as a radical reformer, complained that 'girls are not educated as if they are one day to be women, but as if they are always to remain girls'.

But the plea for a more rational attitude to women was most vividly expressed by Charlotte Brontë's heroine, Jane Eyre:

> Nobody knows how many rebellions besides political rebellions ferment in the masses of life which people live on earth. Women are supposed to be very calm generally; but women feel just as men feel; they need exercise for their faculties, and a field for their efforts as much as their brothers do; they suffer from too rigid a restraint, too absolute a stagnation, precisely as men would suffer; and it is narrow-minded in their more privileged fellow creatures to say that they ought to confine themselves to making puddings and knitting stockings, to playing on the piano and embroidering bags. It is thoughtless to condemn them or laugh at them if they seek to do more or learn more than custom has pronounced necessary for their sex.

References
1. Quoted by Mrs G. S. Reaney, *English Girls; Their Place and Power* (Kegan Paul, 1879).
2. E. P. Thompson, *The Making of the English Working Class* (Gollancz, 1963, Penguin edn.), p. 454.
3. John Hurt, *Education in Evolution* (Rupert Hart-Davis, 1971), p. 25.
4. J. M. Goldstrom, *Elementary Education 1780–1900* (David and Charles, 1972), p. 25.
5. P. H. J. H. Gosden, *How They Were Taught* (Blackwell, 1969), p. 25.

6. E. A. Wrigley, *Nineteenth Century Society* (Cambridge University Press, 1972), p. 398.
7. *Quarterly Journal of Education*, Vol. I, 1831, p. 214.
8. Barnard, op. cit., p. 65.
9. Hurt, op. cit., p. 37.
10. Thompson, op. cit., p. 455.
11. Peter Quennell (Ed.), *Mayhew's London* (Spring Books), pp. 91–2.
12. Mary Sturt, *The Education of the People* (Routledge and Kegan Paul, 1967), p. 118.
13. Ibid., pp. 118–19.
14. *Report of the Committee of Council on Education, 1862–63.*
15. Sturt, op. cit., p. 148.
16. Trevor Lloyd, *Suffragettes International* (BPC, 1971), p. 22.
17. Hurt, op. cit., p. 92.
18. Sturt, op. cit., p. 189.
19. *Girls' Own Paper*, 3 October 1885.
20. *The Times*, 13 November 1843.
21. *Girls' Own Paper*, 17 May 1884.
22. *The Life of Frances Power Cobbe as told by Herself* (Swan Sonnenschein, 1904), p. 60.
23. *The Complete Governess, A Course of Mental Instruction for Ladies* (Knight and Lacey, 1826), p. 132.
24. Cobbe, op. cit., pp. 60–9.
25. *Loughborough High School Magazine*, Jubilee Issue, June 1930.
26. Eileen E. Meades, *A Brief History of St Mary's Hall Brighton*, p. 7.
27. Ibid., pp. 9, 12.
28. Sturge and Clark, op. cit., p. 42.
29. Ibid., pp. 50, 52.
30. Ibid., p. 60.

Chapter four

Feminine ideals

Never give in, girls,
Though oft you are fain,
When hopes fade before you
And labour seems vain;
Strive onward, keep doing –
Somewhat they must win
Who keep the straight pathway,
And never give in.

Girls' Own Paper, 16 April 1892

The Victorians appointed woman as the conscience of man. Socially and economically she was ready for the part. The Church, which had long since given up the belief that the fall of man was directly attributable to the nefarious character of woman, now emphasized her vital role as dedicated and self-sacrificing mother and home maker. It was a short step from this idea to the conclusion that she should also take responsibility for exercising a civilizing influence on humanity.

Despite the awful pomposity and holy arrogance of many Church dignitaries, they were not quite so thick-skinned and socially myopic as historians have suggested. However prudish the Victorians were to become in the later years of the century, they had few illusions about man's capacity for harsh and intolerant behaviour. They were at least aware of the immorality of much commercial dealing, the appalling casualties of industrial expansion and evils like alcoholism and prostitution which thrived on mass poverty. But unable to comprehend a realistic material remedy they concentrated on promoting standards of decent behaviour to which all social ranks might eventually aspire. Naturally, the functions of gentle women were central to this policy.

'. . . she is qualified by nature,' said William Thayer, 'for ministrations of love and kindness to the unfortunate and suffering members of the human family. The female sex are universally acknowledged to be better suited to perform errands of mercy than males. Their tenderness, sensibility, and fervent sympathies and affection, adapt them to such merciful errands.'

The traveller, Ledyard, remarks: 'Women do not hesitate, like men, to perform a hospitable or generous action; not haughty, nor arrogant, nor supercilious, but full of courtesy, and fond of society; . . . I never addressed myself in the language of decency and friendship to a woman, whether civilized or savage, without receiving a friendly answer. With man, it has often been otherwise.'[1]

Working-class girls were introduced to the ideal in the Church schools but most of them were only there for a very short time before they went out to join the men in the factories or were pitched into a job of family administration that was more closely associated with the sheer practical task of survival than with considerations of moral or theological philosophy. But middle-class women had different prospects. Commercial expansion created a highly prosperous and politically influential group of manufacturers, traders and professional advisers. With their financial capacity to set up comfortable homes and hire great numbers of servants to perform essential domestic work, the scene was set for the emergence of a category of leisured women who, if they wanted it, had all the time in the world to reflect and act upon their social duties. '. . . from her very constitution and nature,' wrote the Rev. John Todd, 'from her peculiar sensibilities and tenderness, it seems to me that the great mission of woman is to take the world . . . and lay the foundations of human character . . . she can make it, shape it, mould it and stamp it just as she pleases.'[2]

Since it was not until late in the century that the middle class came round to the idea that decent schools might contribute as much to the upbringing of their daughters as to their sons, the feminine ideal was a cultural phenomenon that relied on cooperation between Church and family. Parents and parsons joined forces to urge each generation of daughters to 'resist the little temptations, to do the little duties, to overcome the little difficulties of everyday life',[3] so that they might grow up to exercise a civilizing influence on society in general and men in particular. For those who genuinely believed in giving some practical shape to the feminine ideal the responsibilities were immense:

> To us women and girls is allotted the rule and government of the homes of the land. We are the companions of fathers, brothers and husbands, and it is our privilege to influence them, often to work with and for them, and not rarely to comfort and sustain them. If we keep these homes of ours pure, refined and virtuous, we wage war against decay, and occupy the proud place of helping to build up the country, and strengthen the hands of the State. Loving, moral and religious, must be the character of the women and girls of the country if the homes over which they preside are to be pure, restful, attractive and refined. Wherever the homes of the land fall below this standard, statistics prove that the strength, life and progress of that country is sapped, notwithstanding its armies, its laws and its institutions.[4]

To prepare for this solemn task it was thought necessary for girls to be protected against influences that might destroy their faith before it could reach full bloom. 'Would that I could induce you to abjure fiction of the present mode altogether,' wrote a contributor to a girls' magazine, '... But if be vain asking on my part, at least let me implore – yes, girls, *implore* of you this much wise self-restriction – 1st, that you will never touch a novel before luncheon, and secondly that you will only read such as your mother, or motherly elder sister, approves and permits!'[5]

This prescription did not cover all works of fiction. The novels of Sir Walter Scott, for example, were thought to be relatively harmless. As for non-fiction, books receiving the seal of moral approval included such stimulating titles as *The Home Naturalist*, *The Girls Indoor and Outdoor Books*, the *History of Bible Plants* and *Restful Work for Youthful Hands*. The precise nature of the moral risk encountered by literary pleasure-seekers was spelt out by the Rev. Thomas Gisborne at the beginning of the century when he published his *Enquiry into the Duties of the Female Sex*. Novels, he said, 'commonly turn on the vicissitudes and effects of a passion the most powerful of all those which agitate the human heart. Hence the study of them frequently creates a susceptibility of impression, and a premature warmth of tender emotions, which . . . have been known to betray young women into a sudden attachment to persons unworthy of their affection, and thus to hurry them into marriages terminating in unhappiness.'[6]

But the association of unhappiness with passion implied more than a careful choice of reading material. It also assumed a denial of the pleasures of sex. The feminine ideal required a lady to retain control over her emotions so that she might, in turn, exercise some restraint on the sensual nature of man. Any woman, it was argued, who admitted openly to enjoying sexual relations or for that matter any physical contact that was not kept strictly within the limits of conventional symbols of affection, was liable to set loose the devil's nature in man. The consequent danger to the family ethic – the lynchpin of the Victorian social structure – was generally thought to be too obvious and unpleasant to be stated openly.

The scandal of prostitution, wife-beating, child-molesting and other well-documented leisure pursuits of the time, which social historians now interpret as the consequence of emotional repression, were then regarded as the products of a moral code that was too liberal in its application. Thus, as the century progressed, the frustration of the sex urge was taken to its ludicrous conclusion with medical authorities solemnly asserting that sexual enjoyment could be a detriment to health, women going to great lengths – literally – to dress in a way that camouflaged every alluring feature of their bodies, children kept in appalling ignorance of the reproductive processes and the self-appointed guardians of the laws of etiquette setting out a code of behaviour strict enough to threaten the propagation of the species.

'Folly wishes to know,' wrote the Editor of the *Girls' Own Paper* advice column, 'whether, if the harness of her carriage were put in order by a gentleman who happened to be passing . . . meeting him afterwards she should "move towards him". Do not on any account do that. It might be alarming should he have sensitive nerves. . . . A slight bow in passing would be quite sufficient.'[7] And of another girl: 'As to her receiving letters from a man with whom she is not even acquainted . . . it is utterly disgraceful, not to say undutiful. The man who could dare to compromise a girl in such a way, unknown to her parents, deserves the horsewhip.'[8]

Single girls were closely chaperoned. ('It would be utterly unseemly, and as much as your reputation is worth, to walk out at night with any man but your father or brother.')[9] At social functions they were expected to adopt the affected mannerisms of a coy virgin, a style of social gamesmanship that subtly matured into graceful aloofness once they had assented to the marriage vows. 'It is an unspeakable privilege enjoyed by the women of England,' said Mrs Ellis, author of several best-selling guides to social behaviour, 'that in the middle ranks of life a married woman, however youthful and attractive, if her own manners are unexceptionable, is seldom or never exposed to the attentions of men so as to lead her affections out of the proper channel.'[10]

Supporters of the middle-class ethic also took comfort from the medical pundits who managed to transform social rules into natural laws. William Acton, who advised on the Functions and Disorders of the Reproductive Organs, was widely applauded for his conclusion that 'the majority of women (happily for them) are not very much troubled by sexual feeling of any kind'. But if this reassurance proved unhelpful there were always the standard Victorian remedies for banishing dark thoughts – 'take plenty of exercise' and 'commend yourself to the care of your Heavenly Father'.

The married woman was expected to dedicate herself to the support and comfort of her husband, to become, in Mrs Ellis's phrase, 'a companion who will raise the tone of his mind . . . from low anxieties and vulgar cares'. She was also expected to personify goodness. She could achieve this by always setting an example whether it was in the quality of inter-family relationships or in something as fundamental as good table manners: 'Never use both hands to carry anything to your mouth,' urged a book of manners, vintage 1855. 'Wipe your nose if needful but never blow it at table. If you must spit, leave the room.'

But the wife was not expected to impose her views in a forceful manner since it was essential to her success that she should do good by stealth. The quality she needed, above all, was modesty:

It is not merely an adornment, but it is a passport to the hearts and confidence of both sexes. A bold, forward, presuming woman destroys her own influence. She may be upon an errand of mercy, and be actuated by the highest motives; but a masculine forwardness defeats the object of her mission. She never inspires confidence. Distrust rather springs up in her path. . . . [Modesty] is essential to the attainment of the highest controlling influence over society. No woman can be truly successful in performing the mission of life without it.[11]

Once they had secured their own social training women were expected to perpetuate the feminine ideal by persuading their daughters that 'the true secret of happiness is to learn to place delight in the performance of duty'. This included hints on the art of home administration such as the importance of buying in bulk to save money, the virtue of making regular payments to tradesmen and the need to absorb the wisdom of Mrs Beeton's *Household Management* or, on a less ambitious level, Mrs Moore's *Cheap Repository* ('the lesson there given and the examples exhibited, judiciously blend amusement with instruction').[12]

But the exponents of the feminine ideal were not insistent that the virtues of middle-class women should be reserved exclusively for the home. By the 1830s what Florence Nightingale described as 'poor peopling' was widely practised. Ladies were able to win approval by visiting the homes of the poorer citizens. An example of how this charitable activity could work out in practice was provided by Mrs Reaney, who wrote about the 'place and power' of English girls:

In one cottage she finds Mrs B in great trouble. Work has been slack of late, and the reduced wages brought home on Saturday have not lasted out the week. An empty cupboard, the children hungry, the good man expected home to dine as usual. Mrs B is overcome with the sadness of her lot, and hugs her babe in silence to her heart while forcing back the too redily flowing tears.

Now this is an occasion when tact and judgement are in great use. The English girl might be lavish in her sympathy; might open her purse and pour out its contents upon the cottage table . . . but the good thus accomplished would be doubtful. Mrs B's sorrow might be lessened for the moment, but her resources for self-help and self-reliance would be impoverished for the future, and that despondency which is the poor's greatest bane to happiness would be fostered and strengthened. The English girl is equal to the occasion. With a cheerful word and sunny smile she slips off her walking attire, turns up her sleeves, and forthwith proceeds to make a tasty dinner out of such supply as the cupboard affords in its extreme poverty. A little flour, a few small onions, a pinch of salt and pepper, and in five minutes an onion dumpling, costing from $1\frac{3}{4}$d to $2\frac{1}{2}$d is boiling steadily in the saucepan, and the poor wife is pouring out her gratitude. . . .[13]

A brief reading from the Bible and an offer to escort the older children to Sunday school rounds off the visit. The story is excruciatingly patronizing today but it is as unwise to dismiss out of hand the philosophy of self-help as it is to ridicule the Victorian idea of feminine perfection. Some credit is due for the effort to temper the harsher aspects of a rapidly expanding industrial society by emphasizing what were regarded as peculiarly female virtues – gentleness, loyalty, generosity and self-sacrifice.

'Human happiness,' said the Rev. Gisborne in poetic mood, 'is much less affected by great and infrequent events, whether of prosperity or of adversity, of benefit or of injury, than by small and perpetually recurring incidents of good and evil. Of the latter description are the effects which the influence of the female character produces. It is not like the periodical inundation of a river, which overspreads once in a year a desert with transient plenty. It is like the dew of heaven which descends at all seasons, returns after short intervals, and permanently nourishes every herb of the field.'[14]

The trouble, of course, was that too rarely was the ideal transformed into anything approaching reality. Men of wealth were totally sympathetic to the submissive role for women but often enough that is about as far as it went. However much they might have prattled on about the joys of Christian living and the need for charitable service most of them continued to regard their wives partly as household managers and child minders but chiefly as status symbols, whose value in social terms corresponded to the proportion of their time spent in leisure pursuits of varying degrees of banality. For most of the century girls' education was still dominated by 'the accomplishments'. When promoters of the feminine ideal attacked the 'pretensions to gentility', which consisted of 'idleness, dress and dissipation', they were answered with the claim that learned women did not make the best educators of children. It was feared that development of the intellect would lead them to neglect their innate virtues and to forget their responsibilities.

It was a short step from this argument to the conviction that, in fact, women were incapable of exerting their brains and imagination. 'If women's minds are as strong and powerful as men's,' asked the Rev. Morris, 'how is it that they have acquiesced for the last six thousand years in the contrary notion?' He went on to list a few of their intellectual failings which included a notable lack of geographical acumen. 'I have often been struck with the incapacity of women to find their way if lost in a strange part of the country; if they choose a road by the best guess they can make, it is almost certain to be a wrong one.'

What transpired, therefore, was that women were naturally more stupid than men but if, as seemed likely, there were exceptions to the rule it was unwise to give these brighter females too much encouragement in case they should lose their essential femininity. From all this it automatically followed that women should be excluded from political responsibilities, business interests and even from exercising legal rights. Thus a married woman lost all claims on property unless, by some happy chance, her parents were wealthy enough and sufficiently enlightened to make a settlement on her behalf. Even her body was not her own. Until 1884 she could be imprisoned for denying her husband his conjugal rights and if she tried to leave home he was entitled to keep her there by force. In a more passive and conservative period such disabilities would probably have remained unchallenged. But Victorian England experienced unprecedented economic and social change. The commercial boom that gave wealth and power to the manufacturers and traders, and leisure for their home partners, also stimulated a reaction among intelligent women against a system which kept them in a state of genteel slavery.

Florence Nightingale, who discovered a freedom of sorts by extending the idea of 'poor peopling' to full-time nursing, described in an unpublished manuscript the awful frustration of a bright girl brought up in a prosperous home. The morning was spent 'sitting round a table in the drawing-room, looking at prints, doing worsted work and reading little books. . . . Everybody reads aloud out of their own book or newspaper and every five minutes something is said. And what is it to be "read aloud to"? The most miserable exercise of the human intellect. It is like lying on one's back with one's hands tied and having liquid poured down one's throat'. The afternoon was devoted to a little drive in the country:

We can never pursue any object for a single two hours for we can never command any solitude; and in social and domestic life one is bound, under pain of being thought sulky, to make a remark every two minutes. . . . Come the night and women suffer – even physically . . . the accumulation of nervous energy, which has had nothing to do during the day, makes them feel every night, when they go to bed, as if they are going mad; they are obliged to lie long in bed in the morning to let it evaporate and keep it down. . . . Some are only deterred from suicide because it is in the most distinct manner to say to God 'I will not do as Thou would'st have me'.[15]

There were others who, like Florence Nightingale, found that they could achieve a measure of independence and creative fulfilment by really giving a serious interpretation to the feminine ideal of service and self-sacrifice and applying it in what, to most people, seemed to be the most unlikely circumstances. Elizabeth Fry spent her energy on helping women prisoners and in setting up a school in Newgate for their children; Mary Carpenter worked in Bristol slums where she tried to bring education to the wild gangs of juvenile criminals; Louisa Twining pioneered reform of the workhouses and organized some practical training for pauper girls; and Octavia Hill pursued schemes for rehousing some of London's poorest citizens. These women were loners in the sense that they were more in favour of individual initiative than a broad-based campaign for improving the social status of their sex.

But for those who were attracted to group activities there was founded, in the 1850s, a very special sort of women's club. The instigators acquired a house in central London close to what today is the site of Broadcasting House, and they opened a reading room, a luncheon room and an employment bureau exclusively for women. Also, they launched a new monthly magazine, *The English Woman's Journal*, which quickly became the main channel of communication between those seeking redress for the most blatant feminine grievances. The pioneers of the Ladies' Circle, or the Langham Place Circle as it was later called, were Adelaide Proctor, wealthy daughter of the poet Barry Cornwall, who was set to follow her father's career as a writer of the tear-jerking monologue verse much loved by the Victorians; Bessie Rayner Parkes, also remembered as the mother of Hilaire Belloc; and Barbara Leigh-Smith, a cousin of Florence Nightingale whose father was both rich and radical, and who believed in giving his daughter an allowance generous enough to enable her to lead an independent life.

The group came in for some savage ridicule which was inspired by the belief that they were dangerous revolutionaries. In fact, they were very mild reformers who, for the most part, approved of the Victorian concept of the feminine ideal and made a great issue of the potential benefits to the community if there was less restraint on the exercise of the 'gentler capacities of the gentler sex'. What they aimed to achieve was a social environment better suited to the functioning of female talents, a softening of male arrogance and a recognition that women were something more than 'a mere appendage to men'.[16]

The Langham Place Circle provided the training ground for several of the leaders of what was later to be called the women's rights movement and attracted the interest and support of women like George Eliot and Mrs Gaskell, who had already achieved eminence in a men's world. One of the Circle's earliest achievements was to educate public opinion for a change in the antiquated laws that applied to married women. In 1854 Barbara Leigh-Smith published *A Brief Summary in Plain Language of the Most Important Laws Concerning Women*. It was a straightforward and unemotional treatise but she revealed a situation that was so patently unfair that the book caused a sensation. Public interest was kept at a high point by the appearance of a longer and more passionate inquiry by Caroline Norton, whose heavily publicized marital disruption and consequent battle to gain access to her children had already led to an important change in the law of custody.

General opinion was sufficiently sympathetic for the Law Amendment Society to agree to sponsor a bill which extended property rights and the power to make wills to married women. Supporting meetings organized by the Ladies' Circle resulted in petitions backed by 24,000 signatures including those of Mrs Gaskell, Mrs Carlyle and Mrs Browning. The Married Women's Property Bill was given a kindly reception but it was blocked after the second reading, more because of a legislative technicality than the strength of the opposition. The consolation prize was the 1857 Marriage and Divorce Bill which made divorce possible other than by act of Parliament and incorporated some financial rights for deserted wives. At the same time the legislators emphasized that while any man might divorce his wife for adultery, a moral lapse on the part of the husband was not alone sufficient ground for a woman to obtain a divorce. It was not until 1870 that the principle of married women controlling their own possessions was accepted by Parliament and even then three more acts had to be passed before Barbara Leigh-Smith's proposals were fully implemented.

The Ladies' Circle also stimulated the demand for women's votes. Here again, the campaign was conducted with a sense of gentility befitting those who believed essentially in the basic tenets of Victorian society. There were none of the rough tactics associated with the later suffragettes and the main effort was concentrated on persuading men to allow the gentler sex wider opportunities to exercise their beneficial influences. Ironically, this aroused strong fears among those who believed that the feminine ideal was perfectly commendable as long as it applied only to women. Now, suddenly, they were struck with the terrible possibility that if women were enfranchised they would enforce their strict moral codes on men, a conviction that was reinforced by Josephine Butler's successful crusade against the Contagious Diseases Acts which were supposed to allow for some official regulation of prostitution and a check on the spread of venereal disease in garrison towns.

More sympathetic were those politicians who had discovered the practical advantages of recruiting women helpers in the constituencies. Manchester women collected more than 50,000 signatures for the Anti-Corn Law campaign and throughout the country middle-class wives organized social and money-raising functions on behalf of the League. In 1848 Richard Cobden supported a motion in the House of Commons to give the vote to all householders – men and women. Disraeli, who had not yet held office, was one of those who spoke in favour. J. S. Mill, whose reasoned appeal for electoral equality was contained in his much-discussed *The Subjection of Women* (published in the very year that women were allowed the vote in municipal elections), was an active Parliamentary petitioner whose attempts to extend the franchise led the way for a succession of debates on a question that was not to be finally settled for another forty years.

But the strongest interest of the early women's movement and the founder members of the Ladies' Circle in particular, and the area in which they achieved their greatest successes, was education. Barbara Leigh-Smith devoted part of her allowance to establishing the Portman Hall School for children of primary age from both sexes and any religion or class; Bessie Rayner Parkes published her *Remarks on the Education of Girls*, which included a plea for courses of physical as well as mental exercise; and Adelaide Proctor taught shop girls in evening classes.

Their concern for intellectual training was closely linked to their interpretation of the feminine ideal. 'It is the destiny of the masculine or evil principle in the universe to be finally reabsorbed into the feminine or good principle, and so annihilated,' wrote one of their supporters.[17] And how else was this to be achieved except by a rational system of education which could nourish and strengthen the female imagination? Even the *Saturday Review*, which was soon to accommodate the literary exercises of all the major opponents of the women's movement, volunteered the thought: 'There is no greater mistake than to assume that to be womanly and to be frivolous, are simply exchangeable ideas. A girl will be none the less feminine because she has some serious interests in life, none the less graceful because her tastes have a wider range than mere schoolroom accomplishments. . . .'[18]

But even if such lofty considerations of social philosophy were set aside there was still a strong argument for reform based on common-sense justice. Middle-class feminists were inclined to exaggerate the quality of education provided by Church and State for the children of the lower orders but it was nevertheless true that broadly speaking both sexes shared the same curriculum in the same schools. By contrast, the endowed public and grammar schools were dominated almost exclusively by boys. What made the whole situation even more ridiculous was the fact that teaching was one of the few acceptable occupations for women, yet so many were denied the opportunity of qualifying themselves for the job.

The typical victim of this paradox was the governess, who was compelled to provide for herself, yet because she was badly trained or had no training at all, lacked any real confidence in her task or any security in her employment. The 1851 Census revealed that the number of spinsters in this occupation approached 25,000 and it is a fair guess that an overwhelming proportion had no other source of income or any expectation of finding husbands to provide for them.

The few rather sad attempts to alleviate the slave labour conditions under which most of these creatures worked centred on the activities of the Governesses' Mutual Assurance Society founded in 1829. This organization which successively changed its name to the Governesses' Benevolent and Provident Association (1841) and then to the

Governesses' Benevolent Association (1843) before settling down to being known quite simply as the GBI, tried to give help to the unemployed and the incapacitated. Since the GBI income was derived from subscriptions the amount of assistance it could offer depended on the generosity of its sympathizers, who, more often than not, felt that other charitable institutions had a stronger claim on their funds. Thus in 1848 the GBI could provide only three annuities for which there were ninety-five applicants. Grants to cover short periods of unemployment were more plentiful but even in a good year there were unlikely to be many more than one hundred beneficiaries, and these represented only a small proportion of those who were unable to find a living. One of the best proposals for utilizing the income of the Association was implemented in 1846 with the purchase of a house in Harley Street, which became a temporary residence for governesses seeking work.

But there were more ways of helping the profession than by direct subsidy. By the mid-1840s the Rev. David Laing, the energetic secretary of the GBI, was thinking in terms of introducing qualifying examinations and certificates of proficiency, which he anticipated would raise the status of governesses and improve their bargaining powers. The government sympathized with the scheme, as did the National Society, but Laing needed hard cash which was to be acquired from a totally unexpected quarter.

The Honourable Amelia Murray, maid of honour to Queen Victoria, managed to reconcile her services to royalty with a frenzied enthusiasm for philanthropic causes. Among those who engaged her sympathy were slaves of the Southern States and the governesses of England, groups that had more in common than polite society dared imagine. While Laing was canvassing support, Amelia Murray was also pursuing the idea of instituting qualifying tests for governesses. Her hope was that the recently founded College of Preceptors would do the academic groundwork, which in many ways might have been the best solution since the College was already compiling a register for all teachers – not just governesses – and was prepared to recognize the claims of women. But events moved too slowly for the Queen's companion and in an effort to stimulate activity she transferred her interest and, more significantly, her money to the GBI.

Support of a different character came from a group of King's College academics led by F. D. Maurice, a theologian of some note and a social-political activist of considerable courage whose concern for the welfare of governesses was inspired by his experience as an only boy with seven sisters, most of whom were compelled to earn their living from teaching. Maurice, who was a member of the governing committee of the GBI, and several of his friends offered to give the lectures that would form the base of a course of instruction, while Amelia Murray gave the money to buy suitable accommodation for the students. A house was purchased in Harley Street next to the GBI and the Queen 'readily and graciously' gave the use of her title. In this way Queen's College was founded.

Queen's was more a school than a college. The minimum age of entry was set at twelve and most of the students were in their early teens. This produced the curious but apparently acceptable situation in which girls of meagre intellectual pretensions began their formal education by grappling with the thoughts of such as Professor O'Brien, whose Natural Philosophy course, described as a general approach to the subject, covered Astronomy, Optics, Acoustics, Heat, Electricity, Magnetism, and Mechanical Sciences. O'Brien's lectures were thought to be dull and uninteresting; but not so those of Charles Kingsley, a close friend and Christian Socialist partner of Maurice, who urged his listeners, in what some thought to be most immoderate terms, to think for themselves and to reject 'all hearsay and second-hand information'.[19]

The students at Queen's were predominantly middle- or upper-middle-class, the lower social order being excluded by the scale of fees, which ranged from £22 to £28 a year with an extra charge for special subjects. Of those who did attend, by no means all were intending to go in for teaching, let alone become governesses. Early on it was decided that lectures should be open to all – or at least to all those who could afford to come. Maurice defended this policy by pointing out that every woman is a teacher of her own if not of other people's children and 'those who had no dream of entering upon such a work [as teaching] this year, might be forced by some reverse of fortune to think of it next year'.[20]

Despite the academic formality of the staff and the almost mystical reverence in which they were held by their pupils (although at least one of these later recalled that the professors were quite as much afraid of the girls as the girls were of them), the atmosphere at Queen's was in no way subdued. Disputes about the style and content of the instruction were commonplace and usually centred on the complaints of the Lady Visitors, a formidable group of matrons whose chief claim to attention was their willingness to attend lectures in the capacity of chaperones. Early on their interest was kept alive by the chance that one of the male teachers would become so inflamed by the sight of acres of crinoline that he would attempt to rape half the class but when this possibility receded, the Lady Visitors found little to occupy their thoughts except gossip and intrigue.

One popular topic was the character of F. D. Maurice, whose thoughts were so far beyond the understanding of ordinary people that no one could decide whether he was very clever or very stupid. The general impression was that he held dangerous radical views, a suspicion confirmed by his support for Christian Socialism (surely the most heavily diluted form of socialism ever conceived by man) and his sympathy for the Chartists, which went so far as to produce a newspaper for the working classes designed to give 'short, pithy, weekly comments on the great questions of the day in a religious spirit'. His co-producer in this short-lived enterprise, as in so many other social projects, was Charles Kingsley, a teacher who projected ideas, both spoken and written, with passion and conviction. His lectures at Queen's were so popular that one Lady Visitor complained of gate-crashers. But for the conservative elders Kingsley's Christian Socialism was made more threatening by his facility for writing novels, a craft thought to be so pernicious in its influence that it attracted the strength of criticism that nowadays might be reserved for the practitioners of television violence.

Kingsley spent only a short time at Queen's – ill-health, not his enemies, forced him out – but Maurice was persuaded by his friends to remain as Chairman of the Education Committee, a post he held until 1852 when the combination of press criticism, theological squabbles at King's and his own reluctance to stay where he was not wanted, determined his resignation. Thereafter he was a frequent lecturer at Queen's but did not contribute to the administration of the College. Before his departure he negotiated a break with the GBI which was not difficult to arrange since Laing was conscious that he had lost control of events almost as soon as Maurice put in his appearance. He also helped set up a preparatory class for girls of nine and over, which was later to be known as Queen's College School.

Altogether the survival, let alone the expansion of Queen's (in 1849 there were 276 day and evening students), was a remarkable achievement in an age when parents were still deeply suspicious of the intentions of professional educators. The College can claim credit for inspiring the interest of several of the leaders of girls' education, notably Miss Beale and Miss Buss, and for establishing a model on which other schools, founded later in the century, were able to base their standards. But the most lasting influence was on the middle-class imagination which was gradually absorbing the philosophy, already well accepted among those involved in working-class education, that girls should be taught not to get above themselves or to supplant men as the natural governors of society, but to give a better account of themselves as promoters of gentleness and charity in their own families and in society at large; to act as civilizing agents in what was admitted to be a very wicked world.

The academic staff at Queen's liked to think that they were participating in an experiment in higher education even though entry standards were minimal. In retrospect it seems ludicrous that they should even have tried to graft on to Queen's the image of a university college. Yet their preoccupation with status at least initiated and helped keep alive the debate on the wisdom of introducing women to advanced learning. There was no real knowledge of how women stood up to university courses because they were excluded from nearly all the established institutions. University College, London, made a small concession when, in 1828, ladies were permitted to attend some lectures on Italian culture, and the London Mechanics' Institute (later Birkbeck College) admitted women, although here the authorities worried excessively about such matters of the moment as 'the propriety of admitting females . . . through the front entrance'.[21] But elsewhere attempts to give lectures to mixed audiences led to strict rules forbidding the attendance of women.

Whitelands, and the other women's training colleges, offered some form of advanced education but the courses were weighted heavily in favour of domestic economy, a subject which figured prominently in the girls' curriculum in the elementary schools. Aside from Queen's, the most hopeful development of this period was the creation of Bedford College. The inspiration for this enterprise came from Mrs Elizabeth Reid, a rich widow whose interest in education extended to arranging lectures for her friends in her own house.

These were so popular that she was encouraged to use her fortune to establish a college, which she accommodated in a house in Bedford Square. The first students were virtually indistinguishable from those who attended Queen's – the minimum entry age was twelve and the starting level of knowledge extremely low. But they joined an institution that was undenominational (Mrs Reid was a Unitarian), and one that, unlike Queen's, could boast a governing body that included women. Moreover, the ambition of the founder, and of those who administered the College after her death, was clearly directed towards achieving university status. This took nearly thirty years but in the end Bedford won the academic lead from Queen's, which eventually settled down to being a superior type of school.

After the foundation of Bedford College, the campaign for higher education for girls found a leader in Emily Davies, the daughter of a rural parson, who came to London after the death of her father and who quickly involved herself in the activities of the Ladies' Circle. She was exceptional not only for her intelligence and perseverance but for her conviction that women were in every way the equal of men. For Miss Davies there was no sense of inhibition that sprang from a loyalty to the feminine ideal. She was the first of the new breed of feminists who were convinced that, given the chance, women could prove that the social and economic distinctions between the sexes were totally artificial and overdue for demolition. Her reluctance to compromise placed her in a curiously ambiguous relationship with those who were ostensibly her allies, but the full implications of her particular philosophy did not become apparent to the wider public until the last years of the century. And by then it was too late for second thoughts.

One of her early plans was to persuade the governors of Queen's to work for affiliation to the University of Cambridge and to this end she even applied for the post of Assistant Secretary. She soon had to think of an alternative scheme because she failed to get the job, although later she may have derived some consolation from the appointment of her brother, Llewelyn Davies, to the principalship. Her next idea was to try to persuade the older universities to admit girls to their local examinations, which had been instituted a few years earlier to test the abilities of candidates from the boys' schools. It was a policy thought by some to be over-optimistic and others just plain foolish. Oxford and Cambridge were notoriously archaic institutions which had only recently given way to pressure to provide higher learning in subjects other than theology and the classics and to broaden the undergraduate intake. Among the ancient traditions much loved by the ruling professors was the aversion to women's influence which, in the case of Cambridge, was so strong that up till 1882 Fellows were compelled to accept the rule of celibacy.

Undeterred by the strength of the opposition Emily Davies formed an action committee which included Barbara Leigh-Smith (now Barbara Bodichon) and a few usefully-influential male sympathizers. One of these was H. R. Tomkinson, a Cambridge graduate and a successful businessman who also happened to be secretary of the London centre of the Cambridge local examinations. The first appeal was to Oxford, where the proposal for allowing girls to participate in the locals, though not exactly rejected, was answered by counter-suggestions that were totally unacceptable to Emily Davies. Girls and boys could not sit for the locals but some consideration might be given to instituting a special test that was framed to suit the idiosyncrasies of the female intellect. Realizing that there was some sympathy for the idea, even within her own ranks, she brought the negotiations to an abrupt conclusion.

At least she had learned something of the skill of academic in-fighting. Her next effort, which was a similar proposal to Cambridge, was framed with such deference to male sensitivities that it was scarcely a proposal at all. With Tomkinson's declared approval she asked merely for permission to set up an experiment whereby a group of young ladies might enter the locals to test the validity of the argument that studious girls were liable to suffer undue emotional strain if they were called upon to prove their talents. Her committee would make all the arrangements, said Miss Davies, including the invitation to examiners to assess the work. All that was needed was a spare set of papers. It was a suggestion that the university could scarcely refuse, although there was probably some amusement at the thought that Emily Davies had only six weeks to find her candidates. She recruited close on one hundred applicants of which eighty-three eventually sat for the examinations. The results were a disappointment, with only thirty-three successes. The most serious academic weakness was in mathematics but at least one of the examiners pointed out that the failure was a consequence not of low pupil ability but of inferior teaching. It was during this period, however, that two of the leading girls' schools were founded by two of the most famous pioneers of girls' education.

Dorothea Beale came from a prosperous and deeply religious family in which culture was held to be synonymous with the study of theology and the classics. She picked up her earliest formal learning at home from a governess, and at a small boarding school. Then, at sixteen, she went to a finishing school in Paris but was hurriedly brought home when, in 1848, the French reasserted their enthusiasm for revolutionary pursuits. Of her Continental education she said, 'I felt thought was killed. Still, I know now that the time was well spent. The mechanical order, the system of the French school was worth seeing, worth living, but not for long.' But perhaps she stayed too long for her own good, for while her enthusiasm for knowledge can be judged by her subsequent decision to attend lectures at Queen's College, and while she was undoubtedly well-read (she collected nine certificates at Queen's), her views were narrow and she frequently showed herself to be an insufferable prig.

She was also self-confident, determined and outspoken. On one occasion she cut across the instructions of her German tutor by indicating that 'she thought Faust objectionable reading for young girls'. The story as told by her biographer, Elizabeth Raikes, continues: 'Dr Bernays looked just a little annoyed, but listened quite kindly. He said it was a pity the books had been bought, but put it to the class what should be done. Such was Miss Beale's influence that all decided to submit to her judgement.'[22]

Miss Beale was a passionate believer in middle-class values. Her aim as a teacher, she told the National Association for the Promotion of Social Science, was to discover 'what seems to be the right means of training girls, so that they may best perform that subordinate part in the world to which I believe they have been called'.[23] She did not approve of Emily Davies's attempts to break down the front doors of the universities, but this did not mean that she was in any way satisfied with the standard of teaching in girls' schools. These, she thought, were mostly supported by unknowing and uncaring parents who were prepared to pay £100 or £200 a year merely to have someone else take the responsibility for supervising their daughters. As a teacher she had quite different notions of her proper functions. One of her pupils recalled: '... the first task which Miss Beale and her fellow pioneers set themselves was simply to do away with that corruption of the ideal by which girls were taught to use their fingers only, while their mental powers were left untrained, and their characters undeveloped, so that, being housekeepers rather than helpmates, they failed in the very work for which they were supposed to be prepared.'[24]

Dorothea did so well at Queen's that she was offered the post of mathematics tutor and shortly afterwards was appointed head of the College preparatory school. The job did not last long because she wanted – but was not given – more authority to arrest what she regarded as declining standards in the College. Her next employment, as head of the Clergy Daughters' School at Casterton, was equally unsatisfactory. When she demanded reforms in the style and content of the teaching the governors responded with a notice of dismissal. Perhaps they thought that at twenty-six her experience was not such as to warrant her high-handed criticisms, though if Emily Brontë's account of educational practice at Casterton is anything to go by, Miss Beale was almost certainly in the right. She departed in the last days of 1857 and went to Cheltenham Young Ladies' College which had opened three years previously and was now threatened with closure unless the new headmistress could attract enough business to balance the accounts. When Miss Beale arrived the reserve capital was down from £2,000 to £400. There were only sixty-nine pupils, of whom fifteen were about to leave, and there were complaints from parents that the curriculum was inappropriate for girls.

One parent commented after withdrawing his daughter, 'My dear lady, if the girls were going to be bankers it would be very well to teach them arithmetic as you do, but really there is no need.' The sequel to this incident, which Miss Beale was fond of relating to other parents, was that the man died and left his daughter a large fortune which she was mentally ill-equipped to manage.

Cheltenham was governed by a male-dominated council but Miss Beale pursued her reforms with such energy and success that she seldom had any problems in winning their approval. Her early efforts were concentrated on improving the amenities of the school. The accommodation was expanded, the curriculum reorganized, better teachers employed (though these were not easy to find) and, to allow for the changes, fees were raised. She emphatically denied any intention of making her girls career-minded but insisted that intelligence and knowledge were virtues that were important to marriage as much as to commerce and the professions. Academic rivalry was discouraged and Miss Beale intensely disliked the idea of competitive examinations though each of her pupils was required to perform a weekly written test in at least one subject.

Her support came from a narrow social group – chiefly clergymen, army officers and those described as 'private gentlemen' – who trusted her sober judgement and competence and who could afford the luxury of educating their daughters at what was now known simply as Cheltenham Ladies' College. Attendance increased to over 130 and annual income to £4,000 by the mid-1860s; new buildings were opened in 1873; the number of pupils went up to 300 and more; and a kindergarten was established.

To her pupils Miss Beale always seemed to be an aloof though kindly person. She was never good at small talk even with colleagues and parents and there are many anecdotes about her reserve. A visiting examiner who was invited to lunch broke a long silence with the happy observation 'I see your buildings are nearing completion', and was rewarded with the stern retort, 'Completion means death'. In her later years Miss Beale embraced religion with fanatical ardour and even considered founding a religious order, an idea which was apparently inspired by her belief that she was the reincarnation of St Hilda of Whitby. But she did not allow her excursions into theology to diminish her interest in education. She lectured to trainee teachers (there was a thriving training department attached to the College) and was listened to in respectful silence even when, as often happened, she rambled incoherently through a succession of un-related thoughts. Staff as well as students began to have problems in following her instructions when she took to the habit of writing notes in a form of shorthand. Thus 'Sum r 2 yg' was eventually translated as 'Some are too young', but the teacher who received the written advice 'Better not, DB' was never able to discover from what action she was supposed to refrain.[25] Miss Beale died in her seventy-fifth year, just two weeks after her final retirement from the classroom.

 If Cheltenham Ladies' College was the forerunner for the best of the girls' boarding schools, the pattern for middle-class day education was established by the North London Collegiate. Here the ruling lady was Miss Frances Mary Buss, who set herself up as a headmistress when she was a mere twenty-three. Apart from her early dedication to teaching she had in common with Miss Beale an obsession with the education needs of the social group she defined as 'the tax and rate payer, the voter and that middle class of the community in whose hands our lives, our prosperity, nay, even our liberty depends'.[26]

Miss Buss, however, was a more extrovert character. She took a strong interest in the broader issues of girls' education and was President of the Schoolmistresses Association for twenty years and helped launch the Association of Headmistresses. She believed that intelligent girls made the best wives and mothers, but realized that even if they never had the chance to be either, they still needed to be intellectually equipped for decent careers. She had no worries about the effect of examinations (although she disliked competition for its own sake) and was keen that girls should show that they could match the boys' academic prowess. Miss Buss was the daughter of an unsuccessful artist, one of the legion of brush scribblers who tried to make a living by immortalizing the faces of the Victorian *nouveau riche*. She had a little schooling from her mother, enough to give her an enthusiasm for learning, and at fourteen she was already earning a living as a teacher. Her studies continued with a course at the Home and Colonial School Society and evening classes at Queen's College in French, German and Historical Geography.

The North London Collegiate School opened in 1859 in the Buss family house in Camden Street. The position was thought to be ideal since 'its proximity to the City and the busy part of London on one hand and on the other to Regent's Park and the open parts about Hampstead, and Highgate and Holloway render it peculiarly convenient as a place of residence for that large and influential part of Society known as the middle class'.[27]

To begin with there were thirty-five pupils, whose fathers were 'retired gentlemen, surgeons, artists, clerks and the most respectable tradesmen in the neighbourhood'. There was no problem of recruiting staff since the children were taught chiefly by members of the Buss family. Instruction in science and art was given by Mr Buss; his two sons, both of whom were ordained, covered Latin and arithmetic; Mrs Buss looked after the youngest pupils and Miss Buss taught languages, geography and history. Scripture lessons were provided by the Rev. David Laing of Queen's College.

The local demand for education was as strong as Miss Buss could possibly have hoped. By the end of the first year there were 135 pupils and a growing waiting list. Adjoining buildings were taken over but the increase in numbers more than kept up with the expansion and after Miss Buss opened a boarding house the pressure on space became so great that in 1870 the school moved to more spacious premises at 202 Camden Road. Miss Buss, however, who was always averse to losing any opportunity for expansion, decided to keep the old property for another school, which would cater for the less affluent sector of the West London middle-class.

Thus the Camden School for Girls opened in 1871 with Miss Elford, an ex-pupil of Miss Buss, as the headmistress. Forty pupils turned up on the first day. They were the children of clerks, tailors, civil servants, two builders, two grocers, a clergyman, a pianoforte tuner, a bootmaker, a boarding-house keeper, an inspector of police and (curiously) an engineer at the British Museum. Miss Buss commented, 'The ignorance of the children is beyond belief.' The entrance examination results for 1872 showed that thirty-one girls had failed to give a correct answer in any subject.[28]

Nevertheless, the enterprise had an immediate appeal. By the end of the first year there were well over two hundred pupils, with many more children waiting for places. The teaching conditions were poor but this did not greatly worry the parents, who preferred the fees to be kept to the minimum. It is agreed even by her most fervent admirers that Miss Buss was not a brilliant woman, but she had great organizational talent and was a fantastic worker. That she put a great deal, possibly too much, into her vocation was clear to her friends, who saw that she looked old and tired when most women were still in their prime.

The work of Miss Buss and Miss Beale received early recognition from the wider public as a result of a Commission set up by the government to report on the schools 'attended by the children of such of the gentry, clergy, professional and commercial men as are of limited means, and of farmers and of tradesmen'. It might seem from this brief that there was little excuse to exclude any children blessed with middle-class parents, yet the indifference to girls' education was such that at first the Commissioners showed interest only in what was happening in the boys' sector. As Matthew Arnold pointed out in a letter to Emily Davies, 'I can hardly think that the new Commission, with all it will have on its hands, will be willing to undertake the enquiry into the girls schools as well as that into boys.'[29]

But despite Arnold's view, the Commissioners responded to

pressure from Miss Davies and her friends, while leaving themselves some hope of avoiding too much extra work, by pointing out that most girls were educated in private schools where headmistresses had the right to refuse inspection.

Many heads did take advantage of this right but the number and distribution of schools visited was quite sufficient for the Taunton Commission to arrive at a fair estimate of the state of girls' education: 'Want of thoroughness and foundation; want of system; slovenliness and showy superficiality; inattention to rudiments; and those not taught intelligently, or in any scientific manner; want of organization.'[30]

There were only four public girls' schools in London providing education for students up to the age of eighteen – Queen's, Bedford, the Clergy Orphan School and the Adult Orphan Institution. Of these the Commissioners listed Queen's and Bedford Colleges as the highest institutions for female education in England, comparing them with public schools for boys. But the report on the school attached to Queen's was a little less favourable. It was described as 'better than the majority of private schools for girls of this social grade, though not equal to some'. The inspector concluded, 'If more vigorously conducted it might be of very great use to the college.'[31]

Cheltenham Ladies' College and the North London Collegiate earned fulsome praise, but elsewhere:

We find, as a rule, a very small amount of professional skill, an inferior set of school books, a vast deal of dry, uninteresting task work, rules put into the memory with no explanation of their principles, no system of examination worthy of the name, a very false estimate of the relative value of the several kinds of acquirement, a reference to effect rather than to solid worth, a tendency to fill and adorn rather than to strengthen the mind.

In some places reading and spelling were not badly taught but there was rarely competent instruction in arithmetic while basic science was 'read from textbooks' and 'commonly unintelligible'. As for language tuition, a facility which the girls' schools claimed to be one of their special distinctions, one Assistant Commissioner wrote, 'Young ladies of 16 or 18, whose parents were paying from £100 to £150 a year for their education, were found ignorant of the inflections of the most common irregular verbs, and unable to turn a simple sentence into French without blunders.' Music was taught almost as badly, despite evidence showing that the average school allocated twenty-five per cent of the working week to this subject. 'It is no exaggeration to say,' claimed another Assistant Commissioner, 'that in the mass of girls' schools the intellectual aims are very low, and the attainments lower than the aims.' The pupils who suffered most were those from lower-middle-class families – the daughters of clerks or tradesmen earning about £200 a year, who hoped their children would achieve social advance by making good marriages:

She is nearly ten years old when she goes [to school], and has learnt at home little but reading and how to hold a needle, that being pretty nearly all her mother or elder sister can teach her. In the school, which is a small one, she is perfected in reading, learns spelling from a book, of which she repeats half a column daily; learns geography and English grammar – both by rote; does sums out of an arithmetical text-book twice or thrice a week, and reads in Goldsmith's *History of England*. After two or three years this course is extended to include chronology, geology, and mythology, with other branches of science and general information, which she learns by committing to memory the answers in Mangnall's *Questions*, or some one of the numerous catechisms already mentioned. An hour or two in the afternoon is also devoted to needlework, plain and ornamental, the latter being especially precious in the eyes of farmers' wives. And if her parents are rather more ambitious than their neighbours she is also taught French, and takes lessons on the pianoforte, spending, however, far less time in practising than is spent by pupils in the genteel schools. This course of study – interrupted, of course, by frequent absences from school when the day is wet, or she is wanted to mind the baby – continues till the girl is 14 or 15. . . .

Sometimes she was sent to a boarding school 'to finish' which meant that she had to go through the whole dismal routine for another year.

Then at 16 she goes home 'for good'. She displays the two or three pieces of ornamental needlework, each of which has occupied her three months, and some drawings, copies from the flat of figures and landscapes, whose high finish betrays the drawing master's hand.

A neighbour drops in, conversation turns upon Jane's return from school, and the mother bids her play one of the pieces she learnt there. For two or three weeks this exhibition of skill is repeated at intervals, and then it ceases, the piano is no more touched, the dates of inventions, the relationships of the heathen gods, the number of houses burnt in the fire of London, and other interesting facts contained in Mangnall are soon forgotten and the girl is as though she had never been to school at all.[32]

Teachers were often prepared to admit academic failings yet they did not appear to suffer any great sense of inferiority because they were so busy declaiming their vital contribution to smoothing the way of each generation of girls to marriage and maternity. Unfortunately, their competence even in this area was not so immediately apparent as they assumed:

I cannot find that any part of the training given in ladies schools educates them for domestic life, or prepares them for duties which are supposed to be especially womanly,

wrote Mr Fitch, a school inspector who was the Commission investigator for York and the West Riding:

I am repeatedly told that cooking, the government of servants, the superintendance of their work, the right management of the purse, and the power to economise all the resources of the household, are of more importance to a girl than learning. All this is confessedly true. But then these things are not taught in the schools. Nor are the laws of health, the elements of chemistry, the physiology which would be helpful in the case of children ... nor any of those studies which seem to stand in close relation to the work woman has to do in the world.

The Taunton Commission recognized that many of the complaints against the girls' schools applied with equal or greater force to boys' education. Both sexes were taught by rote rather than by thought so that learning was interpreted as practice of memory instead of practice of intellectual power. Nonetheless, the general conclusion was that girls were worse off than boys. The girls' schools were twice as expensive yet were too small to offer anything like a rounded education. Efficient teachers were in short supply (unlike their colleagues in the elementary schools they had no training facilities). There were no examinations or system of inspection so it was almost impossible to keep a running check on the quality of education offered by any particular establishment.

Given the political philosophy of the time, reform could not be imposed on the private sector and there was no logic in taxing the middle class in order to return their money in the form of a state-controlled structure of education. There was a strong feeling that the parents themselves were chiefly responsible for the situation which they could easily remedy. Unfortunately, as was pointed out by James Bryce who represented the Commission in Birkenhead and Lancashire, 'Although the world has existed several thousand years the notion that women have minds as cultivable and as well worth cultivating as men's minds, is still regarded by the ordinary British parent as an offensive, not to say a revolutionary, paradox.'

But there were two things the Commission could do very effectively: to make known the facts (which, incredibly enough, came as a great surprise to many teachers, let alone parents) and to encourage action by giving authoritative support to new ideas. After hearing evidence from the leading exponents of girls' education and bearing in mind the experience in America where women were regarded as in no way intellectually incapacitated, the Commission decided, 'There is mighty evidence to the effect that the essential capacity for learning is the same, or nearly the same, in the two sexes.'

The recommendations that followed were mild enough but nonetheless welcome. It was suggested that schools should submit themselves to regular inspection, and that boys and girls should be allowed to share examinations where 'the subjects dealt with are the great fundamental ones of general knowledge'. This was a direct encouragement to Emily Davies, who was still fighting for girls' entry to the university local examinations on a regular basis.

Using the Social Science Association as a platform for her campaign, she had collected the signatures of over one thousand educationists for a petition to the Cambridge Senate. In 1865 the university local examinations were officially opened to girls on condition that they should be relieved of some of the competitive tension by not having their names published in class lists – a proposal endorsed by the Taunton Commission. London followed in 1869 but with a special examination for women, which was accepted under protest by Emily Davies, but was welcomed by Miss Beale and those educationists who believed that some distinctions between the sexes were worth preserving.

The Taunton Commission proposed that girls' secondary schools, modelled on the North London Collegiate, should be established in every town of four thousand or more inhabitants but did not go into details as to the means whereby this ambitious scheme might be implemented. The only practical measure suggested was the re-distribution of endowments which had been unfairly concentrated in the boys' sector of education. It was calculated that while boys' schools received about £177,000 a year, less than £3,000 was given to girls' schools, most of which were attuned to the needs of lower-class children, concentrated in Lancashire, Cumberland and Westmorland. The remedy was provided by an Endowed Schools Commission set up by Parliament in 1869 to ensure, among other things, that 'provision shall be made ... for extending to girls the benefits of endowments'.

One of the curious features of the continuing debate on girls' education was the ease with which middle-class feminists persuaded themselves that working-class girls were adequately provided for by the Church and State system of elementary schools. One critic even suggested there was a danger of 'their becoming more intelligent than the class above them'.[33] The eagerness with which they grabbed what they regarded as their rightful share of the endowments is a good illustration of their social myopia, though in fairness it must be added that some of the best-known of the boys' public schools were subsidized from funds originally intended for children from poor families. The myth that working-class girls were blessed with all the educational advantages they deserved and needed was strengthened by the 1870 Education Act which committed the Education Department to provide school accommodation in districts where facilities were below certain minimum standards.

Yet ignoring any question of unfairness in the distinction between secondary schooling for middle-class children and elementary instruction for the lower orders, it could still be shown clearly that working-class girls suffered quite serious educational disabilities. Inspectors agreed that girls failed more frequently than boys in all subjects and in all standards. This was accounted for not by intellectual inferiority, but 'partly to previous neglect and partly to the comparative indifference with which even sensible parents still regard the education of their daughters'. In 1854, out of 80,000 women who married, more than 68,000 were unable to sign their names in the register.[34] However, middle-class feminists were still convinced that they alone were the objects of a particularly invidious form of education discrimination. The Taunton Commission gave them the incentive to fight back.

The most successful of the new educational enterprises was the Girls' Public Day School Company founded in 1872. Its origins, however, can be traced back twenty-two years earlier, to the publication of a book called *Thoughts on Self-Culture*, which related to contemporary attitudes towards women on whose behalf the authors proclaimed the right to intellectual equality. Woman's position, they complained, was one of 'entire subjection'. They wrote, 'Her opinions are passed over in silence in questions that most nearly concern herself, her claims are unheard in national councils, in everything she is subordinate and powerless.'[35] Among the remedies they proposed for this situation was the reform of girls' education. They wanted a broadening of the curriculum to take account of such unwomanly subjects as economics, science and mathematics, a change of attitude to teaching music and art so that they could become 'profitable to something better than mere drawing-room display', and a revolution in teaching techniques that would make love of knowledge the first priority.

The authors were Miss Emily Shirreff and Mrs Maria Grey, daughters of well-to-do if unconventional parents. Their father, Admiral Shirreff, a bluff and proud man, started his career in the service after running away from school at the age of ten. But he had no objection in principle to education, even for women of whom he said he did not care how blue their stockings were as long as their petticoats were long enough to hide them. When his children were very young he provided them with a Swiss governess and then sent them to a school in Paris. They were not there for long because Emily had a serious illness and the Admiral was posted to Gibraltar and wanted his daughters with him. Although they were still in their early teens their formal education ended, but they were sufficiently well-equipped with academic skills to pursue their interests in languages and writing. They produced a travel book and a novel before they developed their thoughts on girls' education. By this time they were back in England. During her marriage to a wine merchant Maria was concerned with domestic life but Emily persevered with her reflections on the upbringing of girls and published a stern moral tract called *Intellectual Education and its Influence on Women*, which stressed the need for hard work as an agency for moral welfare.

The Taunton Commission confirmed the sisters' criticisms of the middle-class schools but it was some years before they could be persuaded to take an active role in the reform movement. When, in 1871, the election for the first School Board of London was announced, it was suggested that either Emily or Maria should stand as a candidate for Chelsea. Emily refused immediately since her views on women's place in the world were not as advanced as to accommodate the crude squabbling of the hustings. Maria also refused but a few days later changed her mind. As a widow of independent means with no family responsibilities she wanted an outlet for her energies. She lost the election but made such an impression on her supporters that they urged her to continue her work for the education of girls.

Maria compiled a declaration of intent for promoting girls' education 'for all classes above those attending the public elementary schools'. Next she gave two lectures, the first to the Society of Arts in 1871, the second a few months later to the Social Science Congress at Leeds. She claimed that existing schools were dismissed as totally ineffectual even as training centres for housekeepers. The pupils 'are not educated to be wives, but to get husbands'. An alternative system needed to be based on three principles:

> The equal right of all women to the education recognised as the best for human beings; the equal right of girls to a share in the existing educational endowments of the country, and to be considered, no less than boys, in the creation of any new endowments; and the registration of teachers, with such other measures as may raise teaching to a profession as honourable and honoured for women as for men.[36]

Maria Grey, together with her sister and their sympathizers, among whom there were now quite a few notables with money to back up their ideas, went ahead with an action plan. 1872 was the birth year of the National Union for Improving the Education of Women of all Classes above the Elementary (the last three words of the title were later dropped but the social bias of the organization remained unchanged). The Union, in turn, created the Teachers' Training and Registration Society to administer a new college. It opened in premises in Bishopsgate in 1878, with four students, but the demand for more places forced a move to a larger house in Fitzroy Street. Within a decade the Maria Grey Training College was sending out qualified teachers to fill a wide variety of responsible posts. The 1890 prospectus noted that 'students of the College are to be found in most of the chief schools in the United Kingdom'. But heading the honours board were the 'empire builders', who included the Inspectress General of Girls' Schools in the Punjab, the Principal of the Government Training College in Jamaica and the headmistress of Queen's College, Barbados, not to mention the head of the Royal School for Officers' Daughters at Bath who, despite her home base, qualified for the top group by caring for the offspring of the imperial guardians.

But it was the offshoot of the National Union – the Girls' Public Day School Company – that made the biggest impact on girls' education. The idea was to sell education to the Victorian middle classes in terms they could best understand. A school, said Mrs Grey and Miss Shirreff, did not have to be a charity or a state-supported institution; it could just as easily be run as a business with a profit and loss account.

The scheme for setting up a limited liability company to create and administer girls' schools was launched at a public meeting at the Albert Hall in May 1872. Some of those who attended had reservations as to the potential customer appeal of such schools. Mrs Grey reported that she was asked time and time again whether she was mad enough to suppose that any gentleman would send his daughter to a public school, while the Bishop of Manchester, who was one of the leading speakers at the Albert Hall gathering, went out of his way to assure his audience that the schools were intended for the lower middle class only.[37]

There was no problem, however, in attracting financial support for the new company. Amongst the earliest shareholders were Miss Buss, Miss Beale, Kay-Shuttleworth, the Duke of Devonshire, the Worshipful Company of Clothmakers and two active campaigners who worked closely with the Shirreff sisters and who today are recognized as co-founders of the GPDSC, Mary Gurney and Lady Stanley of Alderley. The first school (later to become Kensington High School) opened in Chelsea in January 1873 with twenty pupils. Like most of the subsequent Company foundations it was modelled on the North London Collegiate. Nine months later Notting Hill High School was established in premises acquired by Miss Shirreff and leased to the Company on nominal terms. By 1874 the governing committee felt strong enough to venture into the suburbs to set up a school in Croydon. The total number of pupils in the care of the GPDSC was now 350 and the rush of appeals for assistance from local education bodies suggested that future expansion was guaranteed.

Some idea of the enthusiasm that was generated is shown in a letter from a group of parents in Wimbledon. They assured the Company that promises to take up three hundred shares had already been received and that another hundred would be sold as soon as it was known that an alliance with the GPDSC was under consideration. They justified their confidence with this evidence:

1. The population of Wimbledon is rapidly increasing and consists largely of professional and mercantile people who while they require and make sacrifices to obtain a good education for their daughters are obliged to consider the question of expense.

2. Lectures given by lecturers appointed by the Society for the extension of University teaching have been held here with success for the last three years. These have been attended chiefly by ladies. Two sets of lectures of a similar kind have just commenced. It appears by the reports of the examiners that the students profited much by the lectures.

3. Some of the people living in the neighbourhood have joined together to have at a private house classes for their girls conducted by first-rate masters from London.

4. Several families resident in the district have been in the habit of sending their girls to the high school at Croydon.

There is no endowed school in the neighbourhood. The access from several of the neighbouring suburbs of London to this place is easy. Tooting, Kingston, Surbiton, Hampton Court are within a short distance by rail.

The Wimbledon parents won their campaign. So did the parents of Norwich, Clapham, Nottingham, Bath, Oxford, Brighton, Gateshead, Newcastle, Maida Vale, Sheffield, Ipswich, Dulwich, Blackheath, Liverpool, Portsmouth, Tunbridge Wells, Sutton, Shrewsbury, Streatham Hill, Sydenham, Birkenhead and East Putney. In 1876 the GPDSC had over a thousand pupils in nine schools. By 1893 – the peak year – there were as many as thirty-six schools with over seven thousand pupils. Thereafter competition from the state system forced a number of schools to close. 'Ah, well,' murmured the Secretary when a depressing decision was taken, 'this is, after all, a business.' What had been the original and even the inspiring quality of the organization – that it was run like a profit-making commercial concern – was more a liability in an age when the local authorities were creating their own high schools with the resources of the taxpayer.

In 1898 the articles of association were amended to preclude the payment of dividends higher than four per cent so that the Company could be eligible for grants from public funds. Shortly afterwards the financial situation was given another shake-up when the Company was converted into a trust. Local authorities were given representation on the governing bodies and, in return for Board of Education grants, a number of free places were offered to girls from public elementary schools.

Among the supporters of the GPDSC were several eminent clerics, but if at times they were less than wholehearted in their enthusiasm it was because the Company was officially undenominational. Inevitably there was talk of setting up a similar organization with allegiance to the Established Church and in 1883, when it was evident that the GPDSC had hit on a successful formula, there was a move to create a Church Schools' Company. Except for religious policy the two concerns were united in their aspirations to rescue from ignorance the women of the middle classes. They even shared the same illusions about the quality of education provided for the rest of society. There was no mistaking the social tone of the manifesto for the Church

Schools' Company: '... while the children of those who live by manual labour are most liberally and amply supplied everywhere, both in town and country, with means and opportunity of good education, the children of those above the wage-earning classes are placed at much disadvantage in the preparation for the battle of life'.[38]

Applications from interested groups poured in. In the first year eight girls' schools were opened; also two for boys. One of the girls' schools was a relaunch of a run-down establishment previously controlled by the Drapers' Company at Tottenham. Miss Buss and Miss Beale were co-opted on to the governing committee and Miss Buss took an active part in the affairs of the Company, arbitrating in disputes between staff and trying to improve contacts between headmistresses so that they could share their problems and their experiences. In 1897 there were twenty-eight schools catering for about 2,500 pupils. Even more encouraging, all the mortgages had been paid. Shareholders were rewarded for their perseverance with a higher dividend. But the Church Schools' Company had the same long-term problem as the GPDSC – competition from the state and from a much enlivened private sector. Eventually most of the schools were either sold or closed or handed over to local Church management.

Another Church-controlled organization which made an impressive contribution to middle-class girls' education was the Woodard Corporation. There was a certain irony in this because the founder, Canon Woodard, had little regard for feminine qualities. As he told a colleague after sponsoring his first girls' school, 'So slippery are women that we must watch our own progress before we promise more.'[39] By 'our own progress' he meant the pursuit of the middle-class ideal in boys' education, a cause for which he devoted most of his energy and his very considerable talent for money-raising. Following the model of the early Victorian public school foundations – Marlborough, Rossall, Brighton, Radley – Woodard established Shoreham Grammar in 1847 and, two years later, Hurstpierpoint and St Nicolas' (known to later generations as Lancing). His patrons were chosen for their wealth and their willingness to part with it. In five years Woodard collected £40,000 for Hurstpierpoint and £30,000 for Lancing. He would invite a carefully selected group of potential philanthropists to an expensive lunch, the cost of which was more than justified by the value of the donations. A lunch attended by some two hundred of the leading citizens of Manchester produced a net gain of £20,000. But sometimes the individual approach paid off just as handsomely. The banker, Henry Tritton, was persuaded to give £10,000 a year to the Corporation.[40]

Was it possible that he could achieve for girls' education what he had succeeded in doing for the boys' schools? The answer was no. The Canon did not have the enthusiasm to chase after what he regarded as a totally separate issue. In any case, all the evidence suggested that even the wealthiest sympathizers were not prepared to give on behalf of their daughters until they were satisfied that there was adequate education provision for their sons. But Woodard's chief lieutenant, the Rev. Edward Lowe, was more optimistic about the prospects for girls' schools. Lowe, who was the first head of Hurstpierpoint and later Provost of Lancing, may have been influenced by his sisters, who ran a small boarding school for girls in Middlesex, but he took his main inspiration from the writer and teacher Mrs Elizabeth Sewell, whose school in the Isle of Wight was dedicated to religion and piety.

In 1865 he took responsibility for St Michael's, a girls' private boarding school at Bognor, which had been offered to Woodard on the retirement of the owner and headmistress, and accepted, under protest, as a result of Lowe's assurances that he could make a success of the enterprise. 'Public schools for girls are of very doubtful merit,' Woodard wrote. 'Religious homes, or convents, are more in harmony with my ideas.'[41] Lowe was less extreme in his religious views of women and it was fortunate that Woodard contributed little except advice to the development of the school. The experiment was a success, at least to the extent of encouraging Lowe to establish another girls' school, this time in Staffordshire, where the Woodard Corporation was already represented by Denstone College. A fund was launched for St Anne's, Abbots Bromley, which was opened in 1874. Mrs Lowe's sister was appointed Lady Warden, which involved responsibility for the moral and spiritual training of the girls.

Six years later a second school, St Mary's, was opened just across the street from St Anne's to cater for lower-middle-class children. 'Our aim,' said Lowe, 'is to combine, with sound general instruction, such training in practical, and perhaps, industrial matters, as will qualify girls leaving school for undertaking some of those remunerative occupations which are daily being opened more and more to women.'[42] The Woodard Corporation subsequently added several other girls' schools to its portfolio, including Queen Margaret's at Scarborough where the pupils earned a certain notoriety by experiencing an attack from a German warship in 1914.

References
1. William M. Thayer, *The True Woman* (Hodder and Stoughton, 1839), p. 35.
2. Rev. John Todd, *The Daughter at School* (Nelson, 1853), p. 219.
3. *Girls' Own Paper*, 16 April 1892.
4. *Girls' Own Paper*, 26 December 1885.
5. *Girls' Own Paper*, 28 April 1883.
6. Gisborne, op. cit., p. 230.
7. *Girls' Own Paper*, 7 May 1892.
8. *Girls' Own Paper*, 16 April 1892.
9. Ibid.
10. Mrs Ellis, *Wives of England* (1843), p. 146.
11. Thayer, op. cit., p. 81.
12. Mrs Taylor, *Practical Hints to Young Females* (Taylor and Hessey, 1818), p. 41.
13. Mrs G. S. Reaney, *English Girls, Their Place and Power* (Kegan Paul, 1879), pp. 44, 45.
14. Gisborne, op. cit., pp. 11, 12.
15. Cecil Woodham Smith, *Florence Nightingale* (Constable, 1950), pp. 94, 95.
16. Harriet Taylor, quoted by Margaret Maison, *The Listener*, 22 July 1971.
17. Henry Dalton, *The Education of Girls* (Watts and Co., 1877).
18. *Saturday Review*, 6 August 1864.
19. Elaine Kaye, *A History of Queen's College* (Chatto and Windus, 1972), pp. 47, 48.
20. Ibid., p. 39.
21. Ibid., p. 35.
22. Elizabeth Raikes, *Dorothea Beale of Cheltenham* (1908), p. 420.
23. *Address to the National Association for the Promotion of Social Science* (Sheffield, 1865).
24. F. Cecily Steadman, *In the Days of Miss Beale* (Burrow and Co. Ltd, 1931), p. 41.
25. Ibid., p. 171.

26. *The North London Collegiate School 1850–1950* (Oxford University Press, 1950), p. 29.
27. Ibid., p. 25.
28. Doris Burchell, *Miss Buss' Second School* (Frances Mary Buss Foundation, 1971), pp. 2, 12.
29. Barbara Stephen, *Emily Davies and Girton College* (1927), pp. 130–1.
30. *Reports of the Schools Enquiry Commission on Education of Girls*, reprinted with extracts from evidence and preface by D. Beale (1870).
31. *Report of the Schools Enquiry Commission*, Vol. IX, 1868, p. 581.
32. Ibid., pp. 826–9.
33. *Ancient Charities and Endowed Schools, Their Uses and Shortcomings* (1865).
34. *Report of the Committee of the Council on Education*, 1869–70, p. 28.
35. Quoted in Kathleen B. Littlewood, *Account of the History of the Girls' Public Day School Trust* (GPDST, 1960), p. 6.
36. Magnus, op. cit., pp. 9, 11.
37. Littlewood, op. cit., p. 11.
38. E. Moberly Bell, *A History of the Church Schools' Company, 1883–1958* (SPCK, 1958), p. 9.
39. K. E. Kirk, *The Story of the Woodard Schools* (Hodder and Stoughton, 1937), p. 144.
40. Ibid., p. 36.
41. Marcia Alice Rice, *The Story of St Mary's, Abbots Bromley* (1947), p. 21.
42. Ibid., p. 35.

Chapter five

Age of expansion

So, dear hearts, remember always,
All of us have work to do;
Every dawning brings fresh lessons,
Every year brings something new.
Learn them well, and say them rightly,
Day by day, and one by one;
Then, my darlings, school-time over,
God Himself will say 'Well done'.

Girls' Own Paper, 6 February 1892

There was scarcely a large urban area that did not have its local society for the improvement of girls' education. In Leeds there were actually two – the Ladies Educational Association and the Yorkshire Ladies Council of Education – which cooperated in giving practical shape to their ideas. The plans for Leeds Girls' High School were completed in 1876 when two of Miss Beale's teachers were appointed headmistress and second mistress in charge of forty-two pupils.[1]

There were, however, schools started without help from any established educational organization or even much in the way of local support. Redland High School in Bristol opened with four pupils, and two of these were the daughters of the founder, the Rev. T. G. Rose, who also taught most of the academic subjects. It is possible that Rose found some encouragement in the knowledge that his establishment could hardly achieve a worse record than its eighteenth-century predecessor, where some 'forty poor girls were taught to read, but not to write, by two mistresses, one of whom could not sign her own name'.[2]

St George's School began with an advertisement in *The Scotsman* inviting young ladies who wanted preparation for the Edinburgh Local Examination to join a class organized by a small local group of education enthusiasts. This modest enterprise led to a proposal for a course in teacher training which in turn inspired the idea of a girls' day school. After 1888, the college and school shared premises in Melville Street, Edinburgh, and during the next few years purchased adjoining houses.[3]

Minority religious groups were active. Edgehill College in Devon was founded by a small Methodist denomination whose members pursued the causes of temperance and education with equal fervour and who looked to a girls' school as an extension of their success in establishing Shebbear College for boys. The first headmistress was a daughter of a minister of the group and the wife of another. She inspired respect and even fear by reserving for her most unruly pupils the dreadful warning 'I am afraid I shall never see *you* in paradise.'[4]

The Wesleyan Methodists also had their pioneer, the Reverend F. Payne, a minister in North Wales, who established Penrhos College at Colwyn Bay long before the town was a popular resort. He persuaded two ladies who ran a small boarding school in Norfolk to take charge and they had sixty pupils by the end of the first year.[5]

There were also new schools that developed from old charitable foundations. Merchant Taylors' School for Girls at Crosby, Liverpool, can trace its history back to 1618, when £500 from the will of John Harrison went to providing education for local children. Until 1876 the investment was used exclusively for the benefit of boys, but when they migrated to new premises the girls were moved into the original building which was renovated and re-opened in 1888 to cater for about fifty pupils.[6]

The fashion for girls' education provided a welcome source of income for impoverished middle-class families. With the moral backing of a few clerical and commercial dignitaries it was not too difficult for a respectable, if otherwise undistinguished, single lady or married couple, to raise enough capital to start a small school. A few of these establishments survived the twentieth-century expansion of State education and still prosper today. An example is Moira House, originally situated in Croydon and founded in 1875 by Charles Barlow Ingham, his wife Annie, and his sisters-in-law, Mary and Leah Connah.

Ingham's daughter recalls that her father, who was trained as an engineer, was always an educationist at heart:

When therefore, in 1874, my grandmother Connah, a widow with a family of five daughters and three young sons, was suddenly faced with the fact that her fortune had been squandered by a relation in the USA my father decided that the only thing to do was to start a school which could be run by the two unmarried daughters, my mother and himself![7]

Unlike many of his contemporaries, who turned to education for want of something more remunerative, Ingham was a gifted and imaginative teacher. He bought a supply of equipment and instructional aids from New York because he considered the furniture in use in British schools 'was unwieldey and stiff in appearance'. There were no examinations or marks for study and conduct at Moira House, and the girls were allowed the freedom to work and play without continuous supervision.

Other schools were founded by wealthy and benevolent parents to create employment for their unmarried or unmarriageable daughters. Westbourne, the oldest of the girls' schools in Glasgow, was opened in 1877 as The Westbourne Gardens School for the Education of Young Ladies conducted by The Misses Lavack, of whom there were no less than six.[8] Two of these subsequently found husbands and retired to their drawing-rooms, but the others persevered with their attempts to inspire youth with a love of high thinking and plain living.

St James' School, West Malvern, originated with a parental suggestion that the Baird twins, Alice and Katrine, could make best use of their own expensive education by teaching others. Mr Baird, who was manager of Lord Home's sixty-thousand-acre estate in Lanarkshire, was well able to afford the investment in a school, which later provided work and income for five of his six daughters.[9]

Most of these new establishments started with not more than twenty pupils but this did not necessarily simplify the teaching programme. Notting Hill and Ealing High School opened with ten girls but they were of such disparate age and achievement that they had to be divided into three forms. This was a continuing problem in nearly all schools because there was no recognized starting or leaving age and parents were liable to pay for their teenage daughters to attend only for a few terms in the hope of supplementing a private education which varied in quality from one home to another.

Occasionally, the initial response was so disappointing that financial revenues were exhausted before schools had a chance to get established. A school at Guildford attracted only three pupils in its first month and was threatened with closure until the Church Schools' Company relaunched the school in January 1888 as Guildford High School. Even then there were only twenty-two pupils, but by Easter there were thirty-five.

Francis Holland Church of England School for Girls, which opened in 1881 in a house in Graham Street, London, recruited twenty-six pupils within six weeks, a respectable total by comparative standards, but one which failed to satisfy the sponsors. The headmistress was warned that unless demand increased closure was inevitable. 'It was even suggested that I should personally canvas the neighbourhood, but I really could not see myself calling at houses and asking for pupils.'[10] But within a year the demand for places had increased so much that additional space was urgently needed.

There was a similar problem at the Cheltenham Ladies' College, which in 1873 moved into new buildings designed for 220 pupils. At that time there were 70 vacancies, but within two years numbers were up to 300. Further construction was approved but was not sufficient to keep up with the rising level of admissions. By 1877, 470 pupils were crammed into the College.[11]

But this penalty of success was felt most severely by the North London Collegiate which, in the mid-1870s, had five hundred girls in the upper school and nearly four hundred in the lower. New and larger premises in the Camden Road were occupied in 1871 but the old building was immediately taken over by the Camden School for Girls, which started with forty pupils and ended the first year with over two hundred. In 1873 the headmistress could write: 'I know of a child and her mother, hearing that there were many new ones applying, were up at six o'clock in the morning to come by the first train from Acton in order to be in time, but there was no vacancy!'[12]

This type of 'second grade school' for children of clerks, trades people and craftsmen was later adopted by the Church Schools' Company, which opened an establishment in Brighton for girls 'whose parents were unwilling to send them to elementary schools but could not aspire to high schools'.[13] The process of class division was carried further by the Woodard Girls' Schools, where 'industrials' were taken in. These were girls who in return for doing housework and paying a small fee received an elementary education and were eventually sent out into domestic service.[14]

Overall, prices were kept at a surprisingly moderate level. At none of the ten foundations of the Church Schools' Company were the fees in excess of eighteen guineas a year, while the Girls' Public Day School Trust seldom charged more than twenty-five guineas.

Elsewhere, prices varied according to the number of subjects studied, the social pretensions of the school and the age of the children. Ambitious head teachers tried to produce a formula to suit all incomes. The junior section of Westbourne School offered seven study programmes ranging from the three Rs with Bible knowledge and needlework at two guineas a term, to the full curriculum including Latin and Elocution at five guineas. Special rates were offered to families who sent more than two girls to the school.[15]

Initially, boarding was charged on scales that were not noticeably different from those for day pupils, but charges increased rapidly as parents came to demand higher standards. When Penrhos College opened in 1880, the fees were from sixteen to eighteen guineas a term. But this increased to twenty-five guineas in the early 1890s and by the end of the century parents were paying forty guineas a term.

St Mary's, one of the two Woodard Schools at Abbots Bromley, offered a course for 'the daughters of tradesmen, farmers and others of moderate means' at seventeen or twenty-one guineas a year according to their age of entry, while for 'the daughters of gentlemen' a more elaborate curriculum was provided at sixty guineas a year.[16] This second group 'join the middle school at meals but have a separate governess and schoolroom and take their walks and amusements separately'. They were required to bring to school 'a silver fork and spoon, two pairs of sheets, eight towels and six dinner napkins'.[17] The other girls were not expected to bring anything except a plain, simple dress, and although the school provided them with basic necessities these did not include knives and forks – 'They eat their food with their fingers.'

Some of the best schools were also the cheapest. At the North London Collegiate the Lower School charged four to six guineas a term while in the Higher School fees went up to between nine and fifteen guineas.[18] But for education on an economy budget, the best bargain was offered by the Camden School at four guineas a year. Indeed, Miss Buss even had the idea of lowering the cost of education still further by instigating a plan for teaching on a half-time basis. She spoke approvingly of a school in Copenhagen where two thousand children were taught on a shift system. This was a time when the finishing schools, which offered little except a working knowledge of 'the accomplishments', demanded anything from £80 to £300 a year, while at the other end of the social scale even the elementary schools charged one or two pennies a week.[19]

Schools that prided themselves on asking parents only for moderate contributions were seldom able to rely on alternative sources of income such as gifts from wealthy sympathizers or public subscriptions. In 1871 an appeal to launch the Camden School for Girls realised just £42 2s 6d, while, at about the same time, a project to build a new boys' school in the City was supported to the tune of £60,000, which was raised without exceptional publicity. The Camden School plan was eventually saved by a few large donations including money from the Brewers' Company, but the risk of failure had been great and other schools that could not rely on the patronage of such a prestigious figure as Miss Buss quickly learned that survival depended on a strict economy. The first headmistress of St Mary's, Abbots Bromley, was told on her appointment that her chief responsibility was to run the school on the 'smallest possible budget'.[20]

Attempts to keep down the cost meant that school life was liable to reflect not so much the Victorian as the Spartan ideal. Buildings were inadequate and badly sited, grounds were restricted and basic equipment such as desks and seats were in short supply. The schools of the Girls' Public Day School Trust were distinguished by their insistence on a separate room for each class. The usual practice was for several classes to study together in one large room divided by curtains, which could be pulled back when several groups had to be supervised by a single teacher.

Francis Holland School was situated in a slum district. The view from the window of the head teacher's drawing-room was a public house. At midnight the inmates, including children from the neighbourhood, were pitched out into the street. For at least one teacher 'it was difficult to reconcile the contrast between the squalor and lack of opportunities for the children outside, with the rich opportunities for the children in our school'.[21] In the 1870s Loughborough High was forced to move out of its premises into temporary accommodation because of an outbreak of typhoid.[22] In spite of, or perhaps because of, health hazards, girls were constantly urged to acquire the skill of self-diagnosis. As the readers of *Girls' Own Paper* were solemnly warned: 'A bad cough, not properly treated because "it is so tiresome to stay indoors for ever", a lingering consumption, or short and sharp attack on the lungs, prepares the way for a flower-covered mound in the churchyard, and a vacant chair in the home.'[23]

Boarders were fed with a surfeit of bread and butter, weak tea or coffee and puddings of various complexions. Meat and fresh milk seldom appeared unless parents were prepared to pay extra. Sleeping accommodation was simple but each girl could expect at least a small chest of drawers to contain her possessions and, possibly, a looking-glass. Washing water was plentiful but it was usually cold, even in winter. Lighting was by oil lamps and candles – rarely by gas. When, at the Welsh Girls' School, the pipes were frozen, 'no means of cooking was possible but a fire in the yard'.[24]

The great majority of the Victorian middle-class girls' schools held their first lessons in what until recently had been private homes. This was inconvenient for teachers and pupils but was justified chiefly for reasons of economy. The overall cost of conversion was often greater than the investment needed for a new building, but improvements could be spread over several years, which made it easier to raise the necessary capital. Also, for parents who were still getting used to the idea of putting their girls into the custody of strangers, there was a certain feeling of security associated with a former private house. There could even be prestige for a school if its premises had historical associations. Clapham High achieved a notable coup by moving into the Georgian home of Captain Cook, while the girls of Oxford High had their first lessons in the Judges' Lodgings, an expedient which allowed them to enjoy extra holidays at the time of the Assizes.

Notting Hill and Ealing High took over a boys' school and in July 1873 '. . . the darkness outside was reflected by the blackness inside the large hall. It had been the boys' general school room, and was exactly as they had left it. Ink, ink, everywhere. Walls, floors, desks, benches were all black.'

Accommodation gradually improved as schools took on more pupils and increased their incomes. In 1885, five years after its foundation, Redland High School, now with over one hundred pupils, moved from two small houses in Bristol to a country mansion. Latin lessons were given in the stables and chemistry was taught in the hay loft.[25]

When Brighton High School wanted larger premises the governors bought a stately home which was known as The Temple because it was supposed to have been designed to the measurements of Solomon's palace. The most distinctive feature of this building was the huge centre dome but since charm could not be allowed to impede scholarship this eccentric piece of architecture was later removed to make room for larger science laboratories.

Even when schools were purpose-built, architects suffered an irresistible urge to design them like country mansions. Blackheath, erected in 1879, had a 'wide central vestibule with Headmistress's and Staff rooms on either side, leading into a loggia of five arches, through which there is a view into the Hall below, the main and characteristic feature of the building, lighted from above, with eight classrooms opening out of it. Two balustrade staircases lead down from the entrance, forming at their intersection, a little rostrum commanding the Hall. At the far end stands the figure of Venus de Milo; on the wall above, a cast of the Parthenon frieze; on the walls on either side, panels for the Honours lists and between them brackets for classical busts.'[26]

Charming rural settings could be less appealing after the Christmas holidays. The girls of St Anne's, Abbots Bromley, in the heart of rural Staffordshire, dreaded the journey from the station to their school:

There was no covering to the conveyance, [writes an ex-pupil], but an icy wind blowing; the Uttoxeter road half hidden in snowdrifts, the woods on either side weirdly white, and gloom in front and behind and around . . . girls wait while the men work to ease the wheels and to force a way through the snowdrifts. . . . The day seems an eternity, parents and home far away and unreal, only cold and loneliness and hunger are realities and grim ones.[27]

The reluctance of some schools to settle in one building, or even one area for more than a few years, was disconcerting for parents and students. Moira House, which was established in Croydon in 1875, moved to Bournemouth seven years later because the headmaster was in poor health and his parents lived there. While Bournemouth was thought to be ideal for invalids and the elderly, doctors advised parents not to send their children to the resort unless they suffered from some physical weakness. Thus, within two years Moira House resettled in Eastbourne, which turned out to be a more suitable neighbourhood for girls' education. But as numbers and income increased there was a final move to a new, purpose-designed building on the edge of the Downs.[28]

The Baird twins opened their school in a house at Southborne and by the end of the second term there were three pupils, who were delighted with the 'pleasant, homely atmosphere'. They enjoyed the excitement of the wind on the cliff and a rough sea, picnics on the beach and bathing at Boscombe. 'Overall was that wonderful sense of security and wellbeing . . . and if we did eat a peck of dirt in the form of flying sand it did us no harm.' To survive the school moved to Crowborough near the Ashdown Forest before settling at West Malvern.[29]

School uniforms were rare but plain, unexciting outfits were preferred, which meant that jewellery was automatically forbidden. Hair was tied back or plaited. Sailor suits were strongly favoured for the youngest girls while the more mature students wore long full skirts. Flat-heeled shoes were required for all indoor activities.

But teachers were less preoccupied with sartorial conformity than with achieving a standard of dress that permitted the healthy growth of young people. Miss Buss had a particular aversion to the fashionable stiff-boned corsets, which she assumed, quite rightly, had a deleterious effect on breathing. She was also concerned about her girls catching cold. 'I hope your daughter wears woollen combinations in winter,' she told one parent. 'That is of more importance to her than passing matriculation.' Her concern for the health of her pupils, which by modern standards might seem to be over-protective, was entirely justified by the school medical inspections which revealed frequent cases of 'rheumatic poor heart' and 'spinal curvature', quite apart from a whole range of less serious complaints.[30]

Almost every school had a great number of rules for the behaviour of pupils and teachers. Some were merely exhortations to economize on the use of pens, paper and other costly materials. Others were inspired by the idiosyncratic nature of particular head teachers, such as the law on ink spots imposed by Miss Buss at the Camden School. Teachers were liable to a fine of one penny whenever ink stains were found on their desks or ink was spilt by any of the children under their care.[31]

But most of the rules were aimed at securing the confidence of parents and public who needed to be convinced that girls were not risking any moral dangers by leaving the security of their families.

There was a particular fear of the harmful effect of popular novels, which were thought to implant dreadful temptations in the minds of impressionable teenagers. 'What shall I say of novels and romances?' wrote the Reverend John Todd. 'Where shall they come in and how large a place shall they occupy? I reply, as the physician did to his patient who importuned him to know if a little brandy would hurt him much: "No, a little won't hurt you much, but none at all won't hurt you any." '[32] Girls were generally forbidden to bring any novel to school without permission – and permission was granted only when the book in question was beyond all possible criticism from the guardian of purity. As late as 1896, the approved list of books for school libraries issued by the Girls' Public Day School Trust emphasized the virtue of established classics and works of reference but failed to recommend a single contemporary novel.[33]

Every conceivable effort was made to control and supervise the movements of pupils. At Bromley High School, which was fairly typical in this respect, 'The girls, when they come (not earlier than 8.40), must go straight to the Cloakroom, straight up to the Form Room, and stay in their own Form Room unless they have special permission from their Form Mistress. At dismissal they must go straight to the Cloakroom.'

The daily routine of Wimbledon High School was controlled by a series of bell chimes to which teachers and pupils responded like Pavlovian dogs:

At 11.30 play the mistress first on the list stays in, rings the small bell, and times the girls. The other mistresses go out, and when the bell rings the second on the list goes to the Studio landing, the third to the Office landing, and the fourth to the Hall or gallery. . . . When the second bell rings girls should get into line according to height, and line up in Hall in that order. . . . If a girl speaks after she enters the Hall she must be sent back to her classroom and receive a Disorder mark.

Chaperoning was a particular problem in urban schools where accommodation was spread over several buildings. When the girls of Francis Holland School needed to change rooms they joined a crocodile procession and embarked on a 'weary plod round and round the same streets, backwards and forwards, to drop one member and pick up another according to the extra classes and lessons'.[34]

Any form of communication between pupils that was not related to their studies was automatically associated with subversive activities and notes written, received or delivered without permission were immediately suspect, several establishments trying to ban them

But the most onerous and unpopular restriction was the infamous silence rule, first instituted by Miss Buss and Miss Beale, and subsequently adopted by nearly all the schools that were modelled on the North London Collegiate and Cheltenham Ladies' College.

The law at Cheltenham was so uncompromising as to be almost impossible to obey:

Leave must be asked from the class teacher before speaking to another pupil. Leave must be obtained from both class teachers before speaking to a pupil in another class. Conversation must be finished in the place where permission is given, and may not be carried on in dressing-rooms, corridors or staircases.[35]

Miss Beale went so far as to encourage parents to cooperate by preventing all 'indiscriminate conversation'.[36]

The pupils at Kensington High were quite simply 'forbidden to hold any communication with each other during school hours' and an old girl of Belvedere School, Liverpool, recalls that the silence rule was 'nearly as strict as in a Trappist monastery'. There were even attempts to dampen the exuberance of girls at play; Miss Moberly, headmistress of Tunbridge Wells High, was thought to be most enlightened when she advised those in her charge, 'you may shout, but not *scream*'.[37]

In fairness to the teachers, it must be said that the silence rule was much favoured by parents, who were often worried by the thought of their children chattering to strangers about home affairs. Gossiping was believed to be essentially a female vice and middle-class wives had more time and opportunity than the men to indulge in this pastime. But it was unjust to attempt to restrain their daughters in what, for many of them, was subsequently to be their chief intellectual exercise.

Regulations were frequently extended to activities beyond the boundaries of the school. At Wimbledon High 'girls below Form Upper VI may not have lunch or tea at shops in the town without an escort from home'. When an older girl at Oxford High was reproved for walking unchaperoned with a boy she found it was no defence to point out that her companion was also her brother. 'Remember,' said the head teacher, '*everyone* does not know it was your brother.'[38] Many schools decreed that pupils were not even allowed to come to school with friends of their own sex without permission.

If teachers had been asked to justify their complex systems of rules from an educational point of view they might reasonably have replied that in some measure they compensated for the almost total absence of the traditional disciplinary technique. The prefect system was not popular. There was hardly every any question of using corporal punishment, though occasionally a teacher might be technically guilty of physical assault when she took some precipitative action such as hurling a book at an offender in the back row of the class. Rule breakers at St Mary's Hall, Brighton, were sent to bed during the day or sentenced to take their meals alone.[39] At other places the order 'stand in the corner' could mean hours of lonely reflection on the harshness of life.

More usually, however, an ordered, smooth-running organization was maintained by promoting the laws of school behaviour to an almost mystical significance. A pupil at Tunbridge Wells in the mid-1880s recalled: 'I do remember that soon after I arrived I was told to write my name in a dreadful thing called the Black Book, because I had forgotten to take a book home with me and could not do my preparation. There was another book called the Red Book for good people, but I never got into that.'[40]

The reading out of conduct and work marks, usually once a week, was always a great ceremony. Lazy pupils and wrong-doers were made to feel the full shame of their inadequacies by having them revealed to the entire school. Miss Buss was quite pleased with her success in persuading her pupils to report on themselves if they were guilty of serious faults.

At Norwich High it was the rule for girls to file into prayers carrying their books in their right hands and holding their left hands behind their backs. It took a little while for new pupils to realize that this haloed tradition effectively prevented them from pulling the hair of the girls in front.[41]

Then there were well-meaning attempts to counteract the boredom that was inevitably involved in rote learning. An old girl of Westbourne, Glasgow, recalls:

> We had our lessons chiefly in the library and dining-room and in both rooms we sat round a long table with a heap of counters in the middle, helping ourselves to one each time we answered correctly . . . the library counters were dull – mere haricot beans. But the dining-room ones were bright coloured tiddlywinks, a source of joy and also distraction, the great game among us being to build up some elegant colour scheme as we accumulated our marks.[42]

Prize-giving was a widely accepted technique for stimulating the interest and excitement of pupils, though some schools did away with special awards when they realised that girls were putting too much emphasis on winning first place. A popular compromise, which boys' schools might have done well to copy, was to give form prizes to any girl who achieved a certain percentage of marks in her exams.

The ceremony of handing out the prizes was an occasion for impressive exercises in public relations. In 1876 over eight hundred girls from the Camden School and the North London Collegiate turned out in their best summer dresses for a joint prize day. The newspapers commented favourably on the display and confessed admiringly that nothing like it had been seen before in England. Subsequently, the Girls' Public Day School Trust regularly organized mass prize-givings for the girls of all of their schools. These events, which were held in the Albert Hall or the Crystal Palace, were usually attended by a member of the Royal Family.

The final arbiter of disciplinary and intellectual standards was the headmistress. In most schools she was a shadowy figure keeping herself aloof from the students and staff, like the ruler of a small state who fears that familiarity with the populace might breed rebellion. To be called before the headmistress meant that a pupil was destined either for the highest praise or the most terrible rebuke.

An old girl of Westbourne School remembers the 'awesome interview' that could be expected by a pupil who committed what was regarded as a grave misdemeanour:

> The culprit was ushered from the school half of the building to the private half, to which we never otherwise had access, and the interview took place in the drawing-room. The lady-like well-dressed figure of the headmistress received the quaking schoolgirl in an atmosphere of polite formality. This was no heart-to-heart talk with an acknowledgement of human frailty. It was a cold rebuke spoken in a firm quiet tone and all the more impressive for the lack of mobility in the face and voice delivering it.[43]

But to be successful a headmistress required a two-sided personality. In her dealings with parents she was open, welcoming and extremely tactful. After all, these were business clients whose custom she was hoping to attract.

One of her major tasks was to ensure that term reports were carefully composed. Any suggestion that a girl was not making good use of her opportunities was liable to reflect badly on the school, which stood to lose income if the parents decided that their child might do better elsewhere. Thus staff who made unhelpful comments – such as the language teacher at Francis Holland School, who described a girl's 'progress' as 'steadily going backwards' – were severely reprimanded and their opinions struck from the record.[44]

The image of a Victorian headmistress as a stern but motherly creature implies that she was also a mature personality enjoying the wisdom of her middle years. In fact, school administration was a young woman's profession. The average age of appointment was under thirty (Miss Buss was only twenty-three when she founded the North London Collegiate) and it was not uncommon for a teacher to apply for senior posts after only two or three years' experience in the classroom.

These jobs were open to the young because there was no one else to fill them. The supply of competent staff was well short of demand and most of those who were in any way qualified had graduated from such recently established institutions as Queen's College and Bedford College or from the training establishments linked to the new middle-class schools. Their rivals were a sad collection of social casualties who made the task of sifting applications for educational employment a depressing experience. Emily Shirreff reported that when the principal of a ladies' college advertised for a superintendent to take charge of scholastic work she received replies from nine hundred teachers. Of these, ninety-five per cent 'showed every variety of incapacity and ignorance, and furnished examples of every kind of sin against common sense and the English language'.[45]

Salaries for head teachers varied enormously but were usually related to the profitability of their schools, often by a system of bonus payments. The head of Merchant Taylors' School, Crosby, was contracted for a basic £120 a year with an additional £2 to £4 for every pupil. Her colleague at the St Martin's Endowed School for Girls was paid a minimum of £180 with £1 for each pupil in residence. At Francis Holland School the head received £250 plus one guinea for every pupil recruited in excess of 150.

These rates were not wildly different from those paid to headmasters of boys' schools. In at least one case, Woolwich Girls', the head, who earned £200 a year, was paid the same as the head of Woolwich Boys'.[46] At the other extreme, the headmistress of St Anne's, Abbots Bromley – or Lady in Residence to use her proper title – refused to accept a salary and instead offered her services 'for love of God'.[47] But it was more common for heads to feel that their rewards were not commensurate with their duties. An experienced teacher, who was offered the headship of South Kensington High School, rejected the post because 'I did not think the right kind of person would come forward for a fixed salary of £200. I said the offer ought to be either £250 or £200 plus a capitation fee for every pupil over a hundred.'[48]

For assistant mistresses salaries could be as low as £30 a year with residence. Miss Beale was thought to be uncommonly generous when she offered teachers £60, which was about £10 above the average. By contrast, the earnings for a teacher in a boys' school were closer to £100, a salary which their female colleagues were able to acquire only at the very end of the century. But then the distance between the sexes was as wide as ever, since men's earnings had increased proportionately.

School hours were short. The usual timetable, and one adopted at all the schools controlled by the GPDST, was from 9 a.m. to 1 p.m. five days a week. This was in deference to the popular view that girls would suffer ill-health and neurosis if their faculties were over-stretched. The urge to protect the very young from intellectual exertion was particularly strong. One respected medical adviser held the view that the brain was too soft for anything like mental labour before seven years of age. There was also a need to consider the social demands on girls who were expected to be 'at home' with their mothers in the afternoons ready to help with the reception of visitors. Optional lessons such as cookery, drawing, music and dancing were invariably offered for those who wanted to put in extra hours and pupils were given homework. But there were strict rules about the amount of time to be devoted to preparing for lessons and head-mistresses insisted on being informed if any child showed signs of unusual intellectual exertion.

This exaggerated concern for the welfare of pupils did not extend to staff who were expected to put in a full day's work. In the poorer schools this could even involve domestic chores. The headmistress who informed the Church Schools' Company that it was impossible to ask any member of staff to work afternoons because the only one who had done so had broken down, was regarded as most eccentric.[49] But why it should have been thought that a work load that was intoler-able for girls should be suitable for young women, is difficult to understand.

Of course, there were establishments where girls experienced tougher-minded régimes. Daily routine for the boarders at St Anne's, Abbots Bromley, began at 6 a.m. with three-quarters of an hour allowed for dressing before the girls attended their first lesson. But early rising did not imply a greater emphasis on scholastic studies. Needlework and music were judged to be more suitable for the early hours than mathematics or history.[50]

In the early days physical exercise consisted of drill lessons which were invariably supervised by a visiting NCO from the local regiment. Schools advertised top-class drill instructors in their prospectuses with all the flourish usually reserved for distinguished academics. The Central Newcastle High School enthusiastically informed parents that it had secured the services of Mr Leblique, late chief instructor of the military gymnasium of Aldershot and Curragh

Camp, and Redland High referred admiringly to the talents of Sergeant-Major O'Reilly who, each week, marched the girls for an hour or two.

During Lent the girls of St Anne's had an extra quarter hour of drill before breakfast, and thoughout winter 'there were walks, long walks and, on Saturdays, very long walks',[51] while at Francis Holland School, Corporal Major McPherson of the Blues, who 'could curtsy better than any dancing mistress', introduced the foursome reel and 'made less noise on the wooden floor than any of his gym shoe clad pupils, though he was a big man and wore boots'.[52]

As a supplement to these exercises pupils were courteously reminded to sit back and upright in their seats. In many schools there were back-boards on which girls with round shoulders or weak backs were compelled to lie – sometimes for a whole hour or two. The pupils of Tunbridge Wells High School had to march with round, flat pads filled with sand perched on their heads, a routine that was supposed to prevent stooping. 'There was also an exercise called "Satellites run" in which at the command one girl of each couple had to run round her companion in a given number of steps, and if the companion was large it was a most breathless performance.'[53]

The most irksome feature of drill instruction was the heavy costume that girls were compelled to wear. For instance, the drill-dress at Belvedere School consisted of 'a coat-like garment in scratchy blue serge, buttoning up to the neck and reaching decently below the knees, with a velvet collar and a long row of gilt buttons; voluminous knickers to match and long black woollen stockings'.[54]

Early attempts to supplement drill with more beneficial forms of exercise brought hardly any support from parents and teachers who believed that a girl was doing all that could be expected of her if she learned to keep her head up, her stomach in and her back straight. Anyway, was it not thoroughly undignified for the daughters of gentlemen to fling themselves into various ungainly postures to conform with some dubious theory of muscle development? Even dancing was suspect unless it could be 'divorced from the surroundings of fashionable dissipation and restored to arcadian simplicity',[55] which meant that girls were allowed merely to indulge in the nymphlike prancing known as calisthenic exercises.

Opinion was eventually liberalized by the example of the London School Board which led the campaign for proper physical education in the State schools. The Swedish system of gymnastics which emphasized the 'harmonious development of the whole body'[56] was much favoured by the London administrators, who realized that the children in their care needed some antidote to the noxious environment in which most of them were raised. In 1878, the LSB created the post of Lady Superintendent of Physical Exercises and appointed a graduate of the Central Gymnastics Institute in Stockholm. But there was opposition from teachers and ratepayers and after less than a year she departed to find more congenial employment. Her successor, Martina Bergman-Österberg, who was a product of the Stockholm Institute, had a much stronger will and a fanatical desire to popularize the strenuous exercises that have since become part of the folklore of education. 'poSITION! hips – FIRM! poSITION! repeat – ONE, TWO! rePOSE. poSITION! feet – CLOSE! feet – OPEN! repeat – ONE, TWO! rePOSE! – and so on.

Martina Bergman-Österberg had the sense to realize that she could make the greatest impact by working through the training colleges. She even set up one of her own – the Hampstead Physical Training College in Broadhurst Gardens. Gradually the message spread to the middle-class schools where she earned respect as an intelligent and cultured woman who had dedicated herself to public service. The sergeant-majors of the drill halls, who were unable to compete with such formidable opposition, were soon demoted to light duties and eventually retired from the active list of teachers.

A more controversial debate was the question of outdoor games which many parents and teachers considered undesirably boyish compared with graceful calisthenics or even Swedish gymnastics. Educationists who favoured competitive sports for girls supported their case by arguing that the release of physical energy would do much to help discipline, relieve mental strain and even stimulate a greater interest in book work.

Teachers of the GPDST were told:

It is found that after a certain time at lessons children begin to get restless. If the lessons are continued they get more and more troublesome, until it is absolutely impossible to keep them quiet any longer. . . . The remedy is a good game, which is not only exercise but true recreation, or re-creation of brain, by employing an entirely fresh and unused set of nerve cells.[57]

The argument made sense in schools where playing grounds were spacious and decently secluded and teachers were blessed with a little daring.

'We are looking for great results from these outdoor sports,' wrote the headmistress of Redland High in her 1885 report to parents. 'We anticipate that the daily increasing energy which we see developing in physical exercise will aid the girls in attaining a higher standard of energy and courage in mental work.'[58]

Skipping, rowing, running, jumping, rounders, fives and tennis were thought to be particularly suitable for girls and though cycling was initially condemned as an ungainly activity it was also much favoured before the end of the century. The great advantage of cycling was that schools could use the public highway as a sports track, an expedient which was attractively economical even if it hurt the pride of some headmistresses to find that their pupils were providing apparently limitless entertainment for incredulous pedestrians. After 1892, when the Lady Cyclists' Association got under way, clubs were quickly set up all over the country and various schemes were introduced to allow girls to hire or buy cycles at reasonable cost. For instance, the members of Mowbray House Cycling Association, who paid an annual subscription of four guineas, were, at the end of each year, allowed the option of buying their machines at a concessional rate.

Swimming was popular where there were baths, although at schools situated in the coastal resorts only a form of bathing was possible since 'the long gowns hired from the van-men were of heavy serge with half sleeves and dragged the wearer down'.[59]

Netball was another much-loved sport, although in the early days, when equipment was unobtainable through commercial suppliers, the participants had to improvise. The girls at the North London Collegiate constructed goals by fixing waste paper baskets to the top of jumping poles.[60]

Hockey and cricket took longer to get established because they involved a greater risk of injury. When Miss Beale saw her first hockey match she reacted with the comment: 'The children will hurt themselves if they all run about after one ball; get some more balls at once.' As it turned out she had the right idea, since the obvious way of removing the fear of physical danger was to amend the rules. For instance, the national summer sport was played with a miniature bat and stump and a string ball by specialists in underarm bowling. This certainly put some pace into the game but there were still complaints of what one school report described as 'conversational fielding'. Hockey was also made safer by the use of a soft ball and large, square-handled sticks. In the early days girls often played with walking sticks but it was soon realized that these were more hazardous than proper sticks. When a new games mistress arrived at Alice Ottley School in Worcester she found that girls were using 'ash sticks of varying degrees of curve' which 'sent the ball up in a highly dangerous manner'. When she had solved that problem she attempted to persuade her pupils to give some attention to the spirit of the game. 'The forwards keep the ball to themselves,' she complained, 'chasing each other madly, and never giving the backs a chance' so that 'the whole of both sides seem always in a seething mass, clawing at each other's feet.'[61]

Efforts to remove the physical risk from field sports was scorned by a small, select group of schools that modelled themselves closely on boys' public education.

St Andrews, opened in 1877, Roedean, which started in a modest way at Brighton in 1885, and Wycombe Abbey, founded in 1896, favoured the traditional rules and regulation equipment. Eventually the others, not wanting to be looked upon as second raters, followed their example.

All sorts of attempts were made to discover convincing precedents for the female invasion of the playing fields. A manuscript dated 1344 was extracted from the Bodleian Library showing a figure, apparently female, in the act of bowling to the straight bat of a man surrounded by a mixed group of fielders. Cynics argued that this claim to antecedence was false; what casual observers had assumed was a group of women was in fact a party of monks. What was indisputable, though of less impact, was a note made by Robert Southey in his commonplace book of a cricket match played in 1797 between eleven married women of the parish of Bury and eleven maidens. The former won, and it was said that the Bury women were so famous for their sporting prowess that they could beat any team in any village in their county. The first reference to cricket in a girls' school appeared in the *Shepton Mallet Journal* in 1868, when it was reported that 'In a ladies' school near Frome the pupils are allowed to play cricket, and the best cricketers are said to be the best scholars.'

At Clifton High the prestige of cricket was considerably enhanced when W. G. Grace sent his two daughters to the school. Brighton High School even went so far as to start a football club. But parents complained that their daughters wore out their shoes on the gravel and after a window was broken and the headmistress made a rule that the ball was never to be kicked unless on the ground, enthusiasm for the game waned and the club disbanded.

By 1900 there were some great annual events in the girls' sporting calendar, such as the cricket match between Wycombe and Roedean and the Rounders' Tournament of the Liverpool schools, when the girls turned out in straw hats decorated with their school hat-band, ate picnic lunches and shouted themselves hoarse.

For many schools, however, organized games remained a mixed blessing. Playing fields were not always within easy distance and London teachers dreaded the experience of umpiring hockey matches on grounds in Fulham, Richmond and Epping or tennis in Battersea Park, where male audiences gathered in strength.

The problem of designing costumes for physical exercise, which allowed some freedom of movement without offending public morality, became more difficult as schools introduced competitive sports. At Tunbridge Wells High School, where tight-fitting bodices, high collars and flowing skirts were the regulation dress, teenage girls on the hockey field looked like sober matrons experiencing an attack of hysterics. Players quickly became skilled in the art of hiding the ball in the folds of their dresses, a practice, warned an instructor, 'which always arouses the wrath of the sterner sex'. In the end the Scarlet Runners or first eleven wore scarlet tam o' shanters, scarlet ribbon bows at the neck, white blouses and blue skirts, and the Blue Beans (second eleven) a similar costume, but blue. Ties were suggested as another item of apparel but were not considered lady-like.[62] Most schools adopted a broadly similar outfit and the berets known as tam o' shanters were popular everywhere.

Some of these sartorial traditions died hard. As late as 1962 the girls of St George's were expected to race in divided skirts and though permitted to high jump in blue knickers they were told to replace their skirts as soon as the jumping was over.[63]

References

1. K. E. Proctor, *A Short History of Leeds Girls' High School*, Part 1, *1876–1906*.
2. M. G. Shaw, *Redland High School* (1932), p. 8.
3. *The Story of St George's School*, pp. 1, 2.
4. Richard Pyke, *Edgehill College 1884–1957* (Epworth Press, 1957).
5. Rosa Harvey, *Penrhos 1880–1930* (1931).
6. E. Fordham, *John Harrison and His School* (1929).
7. D. J. Foxton, *History of Moira House*, pp. 1, 5.
8. *Scottish Field*, June 1964.
9. Alice Baird (Ed.), *I Was There* (Littlebury and Co., 1956).
10. Beatrice Dunning (Ed.), *Graham Street Memories* (Hazell Watson and Viney Ltd, 1931), p. 4.
11. Steadman, op. cit.
12. Doris Burchell, op. cit., pp. 11, 12.
13. Moberly Bell, op. cit., p. 22.
14. Kirk, op. cit., p. 146.
15. *Scottish Field*, June 1964.
16. Rice, op. cit.
17. Edward C. Lowe, *St Nicolas College and its Schools, A Record of Thirty Years Work* (Parker and Co., 1878), p. 61.
18. Mary Gurney, *Are We to Have Education for Our Middle Class Girls* (National Union for Improving the Education of Women of All Classes, 1872).
19. Ibid.
20. Rice, op. cit., p. 77.
21. Dunning, op. cit., p. 78.
22. *The Loughborough High School Magazine*, Jubilee Reunion Number, June 1930.
23. *Girls' Own Paper*, 9 May 1891.
24. Leighton, op. cit., p. 116.
25. Shaw, op. cit., p. 24.
26. Magnus, op. cit., p. 119.
27. Violet Mary MacPherson, *The Story of St Anne's, Abbots Bromley* (1924), p. 20.
28. Foxton, op. cit., p. 3.
29. Baird, op. cit., pp. 71, 72.

30. *North London Collegiate School, 1850–1950* (Oxford University Press, 1950), pp. 63, 123.
31. Burchell, op. cit.
32. Todd, op. cit., p. 130.
33. *Girls' Own Paper*, 9 April 1892.
34. Dunning, op. cit., p. 64.
35. Steadman, op. cit., p. 113.
36. Josephine Kamm, *How Different From Us* (Bodley Head, 1958), p. 61.
37. *Tunbridge Wells High School Jubilee Record, 1883–1933*, p. 8.
38. V. E. Stack, *Oxford High School, 1875–1960* (1963), p. 59.
39. Meades, op. cit., p. 12.
40. *Tunbridge Wells Jubilee Record*, p. 9.
41. *Norwich High School, 1875–1950*, pp. 82, 83.
42. *Scottish Field*, June 1964.
43. Ibid.
44. Dunning, op. cit., pp. 27, 28.
45. Emily Sherriff, *The Work of the National Union* (1873), p. 25.
46. Moberly Bell, op. cit., p. 25.
47. Rice, op. cit., p. 45.
48. Magnus, op. cit., p. 42.
49. Moberly Bell, op. cit., p. 30.
50. MacPherson, op. cit., p. 20.
51. Ibid., p. 39.
52. Dunning, op. cit., pp. 157, 183.
53. *Tunbridge Wells Jubilee Record*, p. 7.
54. 'An Old Girl Looks Back', *Belvedere School Chronicle*, 1950.
55. Alfred Schofield, *Lecture on the Physical Education of Girls* (Girls' Public Day School Trust, June 1889).
56. Jonathan May, *Madame Bergman-Österberg* (Harrap, 1969), p. 8.
57. Schofield, op. cit.
58. Shaw, op. cit., p. 24.
59. Harvey, op. cit., p. 17.
60. *The North London Collegiate School*, p. 65.
61. Valentine Noalse, *History of the Alice Ottley School* (1952), p. 183.
62. *Tunbridge Wells Jubilee Record*, p. 15.
63. *The Story of St George's School*, p. 2.

Chapter six

Hockey sticks and typewriters

> Make the most of life, girls!
>   As you go along,
> Do not dream, at labour pouting,
> Life is just a summer outing,
>   Filled with fun and song.
> Life is duty, urgent, needing
>   All that heart can give;
> Those who pass its claims unheeding
>   Have not learned to live.
> Do not idle through the present,
> Choosing only what is pleasant,
>   Making self your aim;
> In the workers' noble army
>   Strive to win a name!

Girls' Own Paper, 20 June 1891

The new schools achieved wide publicity but not everyone was clear about their proper functions. The headmistress of Notting Hill and Ealing High had to deal with a request for admission by a lady who wanted to improve her sight; after all, it was an Eye School. And a postcard was sent to Francis Holland School asking for details of admission and enquiring 'Do you finish girls off?'. The best schools were very good indeed. At Manchester High:

Girls in the sixth form studied English Grammar and Literature, French, Geography, History, Latin, Mathematics, and
German (from which a few girls were exempted), and Drawing
and Harmony were taken by most girls. Singing, Pianoforte

playing, and Political Economy were each taken by a few pupils. Greek was as a rule only studied by those who were going to Oxford or Cambridge, and a custom early grew up in Girls' High Schools of making German alternative to Latin.[1]

Elsewhere, syllabuses were seldom so comprehensive, especially in the early days when really good staff were hard to find. Only a minority of teachers managed to combine intelligence, learning and an imaginative approach to their work. This is not really surprising since, even by the end of the century, training and higher education facilities were sadly restricted. In any case, only a small proportion of those recruited to the profession regarded it as a vocation. For the majority, teaching offered a respectable, if ill-paid, career in conditions that came as near as possible to a domestic environment, without actually involving marriage. One of the members of the Taunton Commission described teaching as 'the noblest of professions, but the sorriest of trades'.

But if women teachers were not always of the highest calibre, male staff were no better. The burden that almost every school had to bear was the clergyman who believed that his calling entitled him to give interminable lectures. At Penrhos College 'the mathematics master was very dark and rather terrifying, and most girls failed to make any progress. A curtain divided the large classroom from a smaller one in which a kind mistress sat so that she might supplement his teaching with the necessary explanations. . . . The Harmony master was a rather fiery person and had a habit of taking snuff . . . the Drawing master was an extremely shy individual who never looked at anyone and spoke in the lowest tones.'[2]

It is true that in a multitude of memoirs and reminiscences the old girls pay tribute to their mentors, recalling, often with heavily sentimentalized affection, the happiest days of their lives. But occasionally it is possible to check the character and effectiveness of a teacher against evidence that is more revealing than pupils' testimonials, and the results are not always encouraging. Consider, for instance, the reputation of J. A. Cramb, Professor of Modern History at Queen's College at the turn of the century, who, according to numerous dedications, was a teacher of rare talent and personality. Yet judging by his lectures, which he was reckless enough to publish, he projected a philosophy that derived from a maniacal preoccupation with military adventure and the thrill of violence. A student of German politics, he employed Hegelian logic to justify his faith in the eventual ascendancy of the British Empire over all other imperialist states. The South African War excited him greatly as a sign that Britain was at last meeting the challenge of her destiny and while the conflict continued he subjected his students at Queen's – all those nice middle-class girls – to melodramatic recitations of Empire patriotism in action:

> The soldier after Spion Kop, his jaw torn off, death threatening him, signs for a paper and pencil to write, not a farewell message to wife or kin, but Wolfe's question on the Plains of Abraham – 'Have we won?'. Another, his side raked by a hideous wound, dying, breathes out the undying resolution of his heart, 'Roll me aside, men, and go on!'[3]

Even those male ogres, the university examiners, on whose judge-ment the schools depended for their academic reputation, were some-times frighteningly incompetent. A Cambridge examiner who visited Francis Holland School and made a great show of assessing the knowledge the girls had acquired, later returned all the test papers – unmarked. The head teacher records, '. . . he regretted that he did not feel equal to completing the work he had undertaken – he was not feeling very well. He was also suffering from pecuniary embarrass-ment and would I kindly lend him £50'. She adds '. . . at that point our brief acquaintance ended'.[4]

Many lessons were still simple memory exercises totally unrelated to each other or to any broader concept of academic understanding. Geography at Westbourne

> . . . was largely a matter of memorising the rivers, mountains, chief towns, and products of Europe (never, never, the overseas dominions or other outlandish places). We were often set to draw maps, filling in the mountains into feathery lines like hairy caterpillars or the backbone of a sardine; and this occupation took place in the midst of the lesson when our teacher vanished into the private half of the house and returned brushing crumbs from her satin bosom.[5]

Headmistresses boasted in their annual reports of the number of pupils who were able to recite the most famous passages from

Chaucer, Spenser and Shakespeare. History teachers 'practically dictate notes to the girls; others give half the lesson by means of questions and answers, and the other half by lecture'.[6] This criticism came from an examiner who wanted girls to develop their imagination and intellectual powers by actually practising history.

Croydon High School was exceptional in that regular expeditions were arranged to places of historical interest, and the pupils organized a research project based on the history of Old Croydon. When visits were impossible, lantern lectures were substituted. The headmistress had only one complaint: the limited scope of the examinations imposed an irritating restriction on her experimental work. 'It is to be regretted,' she said, 'that the style of papers is still sometimes of an antiquated character – showing that the Examiners are not in touch with modern methods in the Schools.'[7]

Certainly, examinations were rarely very imaginative. A selection from the papers of Bedford College at a time when it was still basically a school gives some idea of the general standard.

English Language:	State what you know of any poem of either Gray or Wordsworth.
	Define adverb. How do you distinguish adverbs from adjectives and prepositions?
English Literature:	Sketch a short history of English metres.
Geography:	Enumerate in order the principal islands on the coast of Great Britain.
History:	Give a life of St Thomas à Becket, with dates.
Arithmetic, junior:	A man walks 80 miles in 5 days; he begins by walking 4 hours a day, at the rate of 5 miles an hour; and each day, increasing the number of hours by one, he diminishes the pace by one mile per hour; how many hours does he walk?
Arithmetic, senior:	A carpenter makes 2 chairs in 3 days, and 3 chairs and 1 table in 8 days; in what time would he make 6 chairs and 3 tables?

There was little time in the curriculum allocated to science. It was thought not to be of much practical use to girls and, in any case, the schools could seldom afford the expense of laboratories and equipment. When the Government set up a Science and Art Department of the Board of Trade to stimulate greater interest in science and technology, special grants were allocated to education but none to girls' schools. The science room at Belvedere School was tucked away in a corner of the building where two or three Bunsen burners and a few test tubes were stored. Tunbridge High had a cupboard at the top of the house which was known as the laboratory. Botany was quite popular in many schools because it was considered suitable for girls and had the advantage of not requiring costly equipment. Gateshead High School went in for botany excursions but 'other schools never dreamt of such things. They learnt all their botany in neat little rows of desks'.[8] Still, some pupils at least managed to combine ignorance with charm, like the girl who, when asked to explain how ivy climbs a vertical surface, wrote on her test paper 'Ivy clings 1, with little hands 2, with little feet'.[9]

Even in schools where science was taught, it was unusual for a pupil to acquire an adequate grounding for advanced study. 'She has learnt some scientific facts,' said a lecturer at Newnham, 'probably too many – but has not in the least gained the scientific frame of mind. She cannot, in correct terse English, describe an experiment she has herself performed or that she has seen performed. . . . When she comes to College the best thing that can happen to her . . . is that she should rapidly forget all she has learnt at school.'[10]

The middle-class schools counted as their first objective the training of good mothers and home-makers yet they were curiously negligent in providing instruction. The GPDST believed that cookery was an unsuitable subject for a high-school course. One reason was that 'the girls who attend the schools are all drawn from the class that habitually employs servants. It is unnecessary and undesirable, therefore, for young girls to work in the kitchen at home: hence, their cookery at school would have no practical bearing, and if taught some time before they leave school would be forgotten by the time they might fittingly practise the art at home.' Anyway, there was not enough time to accommodate an additional subject and 'it is better not to teach a subject at all than to teach it inadequately', and 'a good scientific basis for later instruction in cookery is laid in our science course'.

Hygiene was also thought to be an undesirable subject for girls between the ages of twelve and sixteen because certain aspects of the study might have an unfortunate effect on feminine sensibilities. On the other hand, 'the parts of hygiene to which no exception can be taken are included in every well-thought-out scheme of elementary science'. That left only needlework, which the Council of the GPDST was happy to accept as an important element in the curriculum for younger girls.[11]

Some schools offered domestic courses for students who had completed their academic training. At Brighton and Hove High School the syllabus included cookery, needlework, dressmaking, millinery, household management, hygiene, home nursing and first aid. Students had to be at least seventeen and were charged six guineas a term. A similar scheme at Bromley High School was open to outsiders but they had to pay extra – eight guineas a term. Other schools provided voluntary classes in cooking on Saturday mornings or between three and four in the afternoon. Clapham was one of the few high schools to develop a really successful domestic science department. From the beginning of the century to the First World War about five hundred Housewives' Certificates were awarded and over one hundred domestic science teachers were trained. But when money was short the department was automatically sacrificed.

If pupils' intellectual standards were generally modest, however, this was not altogether the fault of the schools. Parents had little idea of what serious study really involved and were inclined to believe that a few months spent in the company of teachers was sufficient for a reasonable education. The average school life of a girl at Cheltenham Ladies' College was less than two years and elsewhere it was almost certainly much shorter. Furthermore, they came knowing little or nothing about the standard subjects.

A major problem was the continuing shortage of good textbooks. A pupil of Cheltenham Ladies' College retained to old age memories of a history text 'published in three grades, in which progress was chiefly marked by increasing detail concerning horrors connected with murders, executions and deaths by horrible disease'.[12] A popular Latin course required students to translate such elevating observations as 'Elephants have large legs and small heads' or, on a following page, 'Elephants have small heads and large legs'.

The serious defects of the system did not go unrecognized. In seminars and conferences educationists protested against the policy of cramming the memory with a catalogue of facts and called for a training that was more likely to strengthen and develop understanding and logical thought. A vocal minority enthused over the Froebel philosophy, believing that the schools were too much preoccupied with containing the enthusiasm and curiosity of children so that they became passive creatures, incapable of using their imagination independently of their elders.

'Constant jumping up and down from the seats, talking at wrong times, undue and disturbing interest taken in other children's work and concerns are not mere troublesomeness which we have to suppress as far as we can,' said Elinor Welldon, headmistress of the Kindergarten Training Department at Cheltenham Ladies' College, when she spoke at a teachers conference in London, '. . . they are signs which ought to rejoice every teacher's heart, speaking of the bubbling over of energy, of the healthy flow of life on all sides; our work is to direct this energy aright, by giving each child something to do, as well as something to learn.'[13]

There was a growing realization of the possibilities of restructuring the standard curriculum to make it more appealing. Criticism was directed at the system of keeping subjects rigidly separated 'as if the pupil-recipient offers herself in the form of a collection of receptacles, each one of which is labelled with the name of some special branch of information or learning'.[14] This and a great quantity of other advice was taken seriously by the teachers. Wimbledon High School, for example, introduced a correlated scheme for English Literature, History and Geography which required pupils to combine, say, the study of Roman history to the first century AD and the reading of Macaulay's *Horatius* and Shakespeare's *Coriolanus* and *Julius Caesar*, with relevant instruction in the geography of the British Isles. The scheme was soon adopted in several other schools.

With reforms in higher education and the training of teachers, standards of school instruction improved immensely. There was a cumulative process created whereby the schools turned out better-qualified students, a large proportion of whom became teachers with knowledge, ideas and techniques that were quite beyond the scope of their predecessors. Ironically, this worried some observers of the education scene who thought that the race towards academic distinction was being pursued at the expense of that other major objective, the moral training of future wives and mothers. When, in 1896, the Bishop of Hereford was invited to speak at Redland High, he took the opportunity to warn young women 'especially of the upper and middle classes' against aping men's fashions and manners. 'I sometimes see,' complained the bishop, 'very smart young ladies in waistcoats and so on, which suggest imitation of men and I always feel it a mistake.' He offered the slogan 'sympathy before comic sections'. The following week *Punch* commented that the attack came with a very bad grace from a middle-aged gentleman who habitually attired himself in lawn sleeves and an apron.[15]

But the bishop was not entirely misguided. It was true to say that the high schools were introducing modifications into the feminine ideal and in some schools there appeared to be a complete restructuring process in operation. The change was most obvious in those establishments that modelled themselves on the boys' public schools. The 'jolly hockey sticks' philosophy adopted by St Leonard's and Wycombe Abbey, among others, and popularized by writers like Angela Brazil, produced an image of the muscle girl who was all set to beat men at their own games, on and off the playing fields:

Ellinor Cooper, whose arm was the strongest in the school, wielded her hockey stick with all her force and hit Winona across the shin.

Instantly there was a commotion. Winona, white with the agony of the blow, leaned hard against Bessie Kirk, and clenched her fists to avoid crying out . . . 'I'll manage, thanks! Yes, really! Please don't worry yourselves about me!'

The game recommenced, and Winona, with a supreme effort, continued to play. The pain was still acute, but she realised that on her presence or absence depended victory or defeat. Without her, the courage of the team would collapse. How she lived through the time she never knew.

Inspired by the heroic example of their captain, the girls were playing for all they were worth. The score, which had been against them was now even. Time was almost up. Winona set her teeth. The ball went spinning. Next minute she was leaning against the goal post, trembling with the violence of her effort, while the High School hoorayed itself hoarse in the joy of the hard won victory.

'I say, old girl, were you really hurt?' asked Bessie anxiously. 'You're looking the colour of chalk!'

'Never mind, it's over now! Yes, I am hurt. Give me your arm, and I'll go back to the hostel.'

'You're an absolute Joan of Arc today,' purred Bessie. . . .

That extract from Angela Brazil's novel *The Luckiest Girl in the School* reads like a parody, but glancing through actual schoolgirl reminiscences of the time it is easy to see where Miss Brazil found her ideas. For instance, this is how Penelope Elphinstone Dalrymple, a pupil at St James', Malvern, recorded the climax to a vital lacrosse match: 'Rhoda, our leader, thundering down the muddy field, utterly ignoring a badly dislocated knee, shoots the final goal and brings us to victory. "Oh! Well played, Rhoda! Does it hurt? Oh, jolly well played!" With true British phlegm Rhoda refuses to discuss her injury. Thinking only of her team, she limps at the head of her men.'[16]

The interesting thing here is that in almost every other respect St James' was a school that was totally dedicated to the original version of the Victorian feminine ideal. In fact, there was a strong link with an even earlier tradition, since a large share of the curriculum was devoted to the 'accomplishments' and preparation for the social round of hunt balls, Ascot frocks, Henley punts, the Court curtsey, and the ices and strawberries of tennis parties and garden fêtes. One ex-pupil, remembering the school at the turn of the century, wrote

... my favourite recollection is that of Miss Price, the little dancing mistress in a gown the colour of ripe bananas, with her hair curled all over her head, sitting sideways at the piano with one hand on the keys, putting us through the drill which she called Deportment. 'You are alone in your mother's drawing-room,' she would say crisply to some gawky pupil. 'The door opens and the maid announces a caller. What will you do? Not, I hope,' with infinite scorn, 'blush and run away, muttering something about fetching your mother. The maid will do that. No, you must rise gracefully, resting your weight on your back foot as you do so; you must come forward, put out your hand with an agreeable smile and say . . .' but I forget now what it was we were to say, something very elegant and appropriate, I feel sure.[17]

St James' was able to attract the daughters of top families who could, if they wished, take advantage of some good-quality academic tuition. But there were many other establishments of lesser status where 'Both for the young women and their mothers, the potential occurrence that loomed largest upon the horizon was marriage, and in spite of the undaunted persistence with which the Principals upheld their own progressive ideals of public service, almost every girl left school with only two ambitions – to return at the first possible moment to impress her school-fellows with the glory of the grown-up toilette, and to get engaged before anybody else.'[18]

Some of these schools, which prospered well into the twentieth century, made no pretence at all at sympathizing with any sort of 'progressive ideals', a fact discovered by a contributor to the *London Mercury* as late as 1920:

The daughter of a rich friend of mine came to see us yesterday. Her age is sixteen, and she is at a French 'finishing-school' in Mayfair. The school, which moved over here from Paris during the war and will shortly move back again, counts among the most fashionable of the kind, and is, I suppose, an example of the best and costliest that the rich have managed to get organised for the education of their daughters in the mediaeval year 1920. It has 28 pupils. Miranda told us that there were no rules. I discovered, however, that there was at any rate one. Namely, that pupils, out alone, may not acknowledge salutes from male acquaintances in the street. I asked Miranda whether if I met her she would cut me. She replied that she would not. Mistresses and pupils rise at about 8.30 a.m., but Miranda rises an hour earlier in order to practise the piano, of which she is very fond. She 'learns' nothing but music and French. Nothing. She shares a bedroom with three other girls. All the pupils are English, but only French may be spoken in the presence of mistresses, who nevertheless are beloved. I should say that such a school would 'finish' any girl unless she happened to have a very powerful and unfinishable personality. The Renaissance seems nearly due.[19]

But in the best of the high schools the Renaissance was already in evidence. Not only were academic standards improving but there were other encouraging signs that girls' education was creating its own ethos that was clearly distinguishable from the tradition of the boys' schools. There was less emphasis on the virtue of competition; most schools did not even go in for the hearty games-playing so beloved of the fiction writers. There was not the pressure to be the top person either in academic or social activity. The house and prefect system seldom took a powerful hold on the imagination of the pupils. Discipline was not dependent on the threat of physical reprisal and though the rule structure was often complicated and unduly restrictive, as time went on schools adopted a more relaxed attitude towards the pupils. Of course, there were (and still are for that matter) girls' schools that did not begin to fit in to this pattern but it is unfair to treat them as in any way typical.

The leading high schools remained loyal to the essence of the feminine ideal but brought in modifications to suit a new generation of women who were less inclined to assume the passive role – to do good by stealth. The feminine ideal was pursued with a stronger spirit and a much broader interpretation was given to the concept of service to the community. This was most vividly reflected in some of the remarkable careers forged by high-school graduates. Lillian Hamilton left Cheltenham Ladies' College in 1877. She spent three years in Germany, returned for a short period of teaching at her old school, trained as a nurse and then qualified as a doctor at the universities of Glasgow, Edinburgh and Brussels. It was at this point that her life really began because she departed for India and after working in Calcutta for a time took up a post as medical adviser to the Emir of Afghanistan. '. . . before long there was hardly a family in Cabul which she had not helped.'[20]

The schools were also a fruitful recruiting ground for the suffragettes. Sophie Bryant, Miss Buss's successor at the North London Collegiate, was an active campaigner and one of the first to sign the 1906 petition for women's votes. And it was an ex-pupil of St James', who, when presented to George V, shocked the entire Court and put her mother into a faint by saying to the King, 'Your Majesty, for God's sake, stop forcible feeding.'

Such indications of female independence, not to mention insubordination, created a furore of opposition from the conservatives. What had happened, they asked, to the 'tender, loving, retiring or domestic' girls of earlier years? Now they were beginning to adopt all sorts of unconventional social postures which earned them such derisive epithets as the New Girls, the Bachelor Girls, the Professional Girls, the Political Girls, and the Revolting Daughters. 'The question has advanced beyond the reach of banter,' said a writer in the *Quarterly Review*. 'England is not prepared for either female suffrage or a female Parliament, for women as Poor Law guardians, attendants at vestries, public lecturers, public speakers, doctors, lawyers, clergy, or even, to any much greater extent than at present, as authors.'[21]

The feminine ideal hit its lowest point of credibility in the time of the militant suffragettes. The antics of the Pankhursts and their followers, though scarcely as violent or as socially disruptive as the tactics frequently employed by political movements dominated by men, were nonetheless so far departed from the popular image of womanly behaviour that they jolted the male establishment into realizing that for too long too much had been taken for granted.

But while the Pankhursts belied the gentle and submissive nature of their sex by leading demonstrations, encouraging vandalism against public property, and disrupting the routine of His Majesty's prisons, there were many other campaigners seeking the same objectives who preferred the techniques of peaceful persuasion. This group was represented by Millicent Fawcett, who led the National Union of Women's Suffrage Societies, a rival though not an enemy of the Pankhurst-controlled Women's Social and Political Union. Millicent Fawcett was a democrat and a constitutionalist; Mrs Pankhurst and her daughters were dictatorial and intolerant. Even their closest allies, such as the Pethick-Lawrences, who gave all their energy and most of their fortune to the cause, were ruthlessly discarded when they showed signs of favouring a less militant policy. It was certainly no coincidence that during the First World War it was Mrs Pankhurst who devoted much of her time to recruitment speeches and toured America to win support for the British war effort, while the Pethick-Lawrences helped conscientious objectors and supported the peace movement.

But the influence of girls' education cannot be judged in the adventures of the empire builders or the triumph of the suffragettes. Of far greater long-term significance were the beginnings of a school-inspired mass movement into new areas of employment where women were eventually to mark out for themselves positions of influence and power.

In 1841 there were about two million women workers, nearly twenty-three per cent of the total female population, most of whom were employed in domestic service, textiles and agriculture. Ten years later the overall figure was up to three million and the proportion of women employed was twenty-nine per cent. Most of the increase was taken up by industry – for instance, there was a steep rise in the number employed in the metal trades. By 1861 nearly thirty per cent of all women were in employment. The proportion dropped slightly over the next two decades but the number of women workers was now over four million. Agriculture was claiming a decreasing share of the female labour market but domestic service and textiles were still way in front, with a work force of nearly three million. Then as now the great majority were in unskilled work because the education and training opportunities open to them did not prepare them for anything better. In fact, it was arguable that their education did not even give them much of a preface to domestic life, though it was often pointed out that a domestic servant made a much better wife after 'a dozen years' training in a well-managed family'.[22]

Acceptable occupations for middle-class women were those closely linked to the concept of the feminine ideal – teaching, nursing, and mission work. Since there were more spinsters and widows who needed to provide for themselves than there were job openings in these professions, salaries were low. Josephine Butler calculated that in the 1860s there were scarcely a thousand women in the country earning much more than £100.[23]

The Ladies' Circle took a strong interest in broadening employment opportunities for women. Barbara Bodichon (Leigh-Smith) wrote *Women and Work* as a plea to men to take a more tolerant view of the prospect of feminine infiltration of the professions. Adelaide Anne Proctor founded the Society for Promoting the Employment of Women, which provided useful information on training and career prospects. In the 1860s and 1870s there was little encouragement from employers. When the Society asked London hairdressers to train some women they were told that men would never tolerate an influx of such obviously inferior quality labour.[24]

'I cannot state too strongly my conviction of the necessity of more systematic and methodical training for girls,' wrote Miss King, Secretary of the Society for Promoting the Employment of Women.

'By far the greater number of those who apply to me for work are over 25 years of age. Many have never held any responsible position at home or elsewhere, nor have had any training for anything at all. The saddest cases we have to deal with are those of widows or deserted wives who are left with children dependent on them utterly unprovided for.'[25]

But the educationists formed a powerful pressure group in favour of reform and with the growing authority of the girls' schools, opinion started moving in favour of a better deal for the labour force of middle-class women. There was a gradual recognition that while 'marriage is the best profession for women . . . all women cannot enter its strait and narrow gate'.[26] Those who claimed that a stronger emphasis on work would distract women from their duties were out-manoeuvred by the argument (largely justified by subsequent experience) that for most girls employment would not be readily accepted as a substitute for marriage. 'However accessible professions may be,' said a government inspector, 'they will never be more attractive than the sacred and beautiful ambition of superintending a happy home.'[27]

If more women were allowed to take up positions of responsibility, some argued, they would be better able to exercise their civilizing influence over men. 'Every virtue which we regard as distinctively feminine,' said Josephine Butler, 'will, under conditions of greater freedom, develop more freely like plants brought out into the light from a cellar.'[28] The feeling that working women were not quite respectable was still very strong and some otherwise intelligent people supported their prejudice with fatuous theories on the economics of labour. One popular assertion was that the size of the national work force had reached the limit of its expansion and that the entry of more women into the market could only lead to a loss of employment for men. But undeterred by such dismal predictions – even if they believed them – the girls took to job-hunting with uncommon enthusiasm, and employment opportunities for middle-class girls broadened dramatically in the last two decades of the nineteenth century.

Employment agencies, such as that operated by the Young Women's Christian Association and the Lady-Guide Office in the Strand, offered a good range of occupations at average starting salaries of around £1 a week. The best chances of finding jobs were in areas where men had not already established a strong claim. Thus the expansion of commercial administration inspired the invention of the typewriter, and the telephone, the development of shorthand skills and the demand for a new breed of clerical workers who were mostly recruited from the reserve of female, middle-class labour.

City dwellers had no great difficulty in attending courses in shorthand and typing. The London girls were eligible for a bewildering selection of training institutions ranging from the College for Work-Women to the School of Business Training. Basic instruction, which was likely to include an introduction to book-keeping, could last anything from three to six months and the total cost was in the region of five to ten guineas. Then there was the option, attractive to those who lived out of town, of signing on for one of the many correspondence courses. It is difficult now to assess the quality of the businesses that offered to teach shorthand and typing as well as most academic subjects by post. Looking through the newspapers and journals of the time it is easy enough to spot establishments that were less than honest in their claims but few of them seemed to last very long and none offered serious competition to the recognized masters like Mr Isaac Pitman, self-styled Professor of Shorthand, who set up a highly successful correspondence college in Bath.

A welcome boost for women's employment was provided by the government when female clerical workers were admitted to the civil service. In 1872 the Post Office Savings Bank offered eleven vacancies to women and received over two thousand applications. Then the Post Office itself started employing female sorting clerks and telegraphists. Candidates had to be from fourteen to eighteen years of age (fourteen to twenty-five in the provinces) and at least five feet high. Their abilities were tested by a competitive examination which included dictation and the first four rules of arithmetic, but it was a help to know the local postmaster since it was he who made the final selection.[29]

In the late 1880s and 1890s competition became so intense that entry requirements were raised. Not only was the examination made harder but the medical tests were more demanding and the minimum age of entry was raised to twenty. More worrying was a corresponding fall in rates of starting pay. In 1880 a Post Office clerk engaged on routine work could expect to earn a minimum annual salary of £65. By 1890 this had dropped to £55. It was argued that the decrease was balanced by a new incremental scale of £2 10s a year up to £70 and then £5 a year up to £100. But relatively few women stayed long enough to earn the top rates since it was a strict rule that their employment ceased the day they married.

Salaries in other parts of the civil service were generally better. A Treasury clerk, for example, started at £60 but could progress to a maximum of £180. But very few were favoured with employment on this elevated level. More common was the plight of girls who failed the examination and who ended up working for organizations that were less demanding of intellectual skills and less generous in their terms of employment. Kelly's used exclusively female labour to compile Post Office directories. They worked from 9.30 a.m. to 5.30 p.m. except on Saturdays when they stopped at 3 p.m., and were paid on a scale that started at eight shillings a week and went up by two shillings a week each year. The United Telephone Company also employed a large staff of women. There was no entry examination but applicants had to be daughters of professional men or of gentlemen 'not engaged in business'. They were paid 10s a week.

Among other new areas of employment were the rapidly expanding occupations of printing and journalism. Emily Faithfull's Victoria Printing Press, which opened in 1858, was staffed almost exclusively by women and so many others followed her example that by the 1880s they thought it worthwhile to found a Women's Printing Society. The 1881 Census estimated a total of over 2,200 women printers. The apprenticeship for compositors was from three to four years and during this time they could earn from 15s to £1 3s a week. A good basic education, including a knowledge of foreign languages, was demanded for this work. W. T. Stead caused a sensation in 1882 by employing women journalists and paying them the same rate as men. But the first newspaperwomen took a long time to get established in what was traditionally regarded as a male preserve.

A woman magazine writer warned potential applicants, '. . . the girl reporter has to assume a bold mien when, with her notebook, she takes her place at a table among perhaps a dozen men, on whose province she is encroaching. It is not an occupation which tends to the development of feminine graces, and this will be as fully realised by the girl herself as by those with whom she comes in contact.'[30]

One suggestion for beginners was to invest in some photographic equipment, 'There is now so large a demand for illustrated articles,' said an adviser, 'that the girl photographer who can write passable English can generally place an article if accompanied by pictures.'[31] Photography was also recommended for upper-class girls who were able to countenance only the most genteel employment. They were assured that '. . . the taking of country seats, and even less pretentious dwellings, yields a fair profit'.[32] That this was reasonable advice was indicated by the 1881 Census, which found 3,500 women painters and photographers.

After teaching, undoubtedly the most popular career for middle-class girls was nursing. The 1881 Census calculated that there were over 35,000 (compared with nearly 124,000 teachers). One of the attractions of nursing was that the skills involved were of the greatest value even if they were not used to earn a living. As the writer of an instruction manual pointed out, 'The fact that almost every woman has at some time to act as a sick-nurse is generally acknowledged'.

Against this, competition for places was severe, the training hard and the financial rewards minimal. A probationer at one of the big hospitals could expect a salary of between £12 and £20 a year for her first three years and if later she wanted to apply for a senior appointment she was compelled to finance her own training. Board, lodging and uniform were provided free but these concessions failed to disassociate nursing from a depressing atmosphere of genteel poverty. And the work was very hard indeed:

Our day begins at seven o'clock a.m. at which time we rise. We breakfast at half-past seven; prayers at ten minutes to eight, read by our lady superintendent. We enter our wards at eight o'clock. . . . We proceed to scrub the tables, brighten the brass work, finishing up by putting on the day quilts, and dusting the lockers which stand by each bed, containing each patient's little necessaries. At half-past nine the ward must be ready for the visit of the house surgeon, the nurses in attendance. At ten the medicines are given and the dressings changed. At twelve the patients' dinners are served; the nurses dine at one. At two the medicines are again given, beds straightened, and preparations made for the visit of the physician or surgeon. At four the patients' teas are given round; an hour later the nurses take tea. At six p.m. medicines and dressings are again given and renewed, and all vessels emptied. At eight the patients have supper, the day quilts are changed for the night, the night pills and draughts given, prayers are read, and at nine p.m. the day nurse goes off duty and the night nurse goes on.[33]

An extension of nursing was the art of massage, which was thought to be an easier and more congenial occupation than tramping the hospital wards. But students were warned to preserve their 'vital energy' which could be too easily absorbed by an over-keen recipient of their energies:

> A really good constitution is essential in an operator, and the age, we should say, between twenty-five and forty. A masseuse should have had some training as a nurse, but not for so long a period as to have told in any degree on her health and strength. She should at least have had the benefit of rest and change of air to recuperate after the fatigue and strain on the mind and nervous system resulting from a course of hospital nursing.[34]

Pharmacy was another spin-off from nursing. The Pharmaceutical Society was opened to women in 1872 and since most of the pioneers became in some way involved in the training process, the possibilities for increasing the inflow of students were particularly good. Most hospital dispensers and several lady chemists supplemented their incomes by taking in pupils for a one-year or eighteen-months' apprenticeship and proudly advertised the success of those of their protégées who eventually set up in business on their own account. There were also courses run by the Pharmaceutical Society and the London School of Pharmacy, but fees were high – £150 to £200 for the full three years' training. Salaries were generally higher in commercial dispensing than in the hospitals but, ironically, competition was strongest for the lower-paid jobs because many middle-class girls did not want to give the impression that they were merely high-grade shop assistants.

But if serving behind the counter was thought to be a lowly form of employment (and certainly the pay and working conditions were generally dreadful) shop and business management was regarded as an acceptable occupation for the daughters of the middle class. The way in was to gain basic experience with, say, a high-class dressmaker or milliner whose approval and support, given after about three years' training, could lead to an appointment to a supervisory post. The fees for apprenticeship – an average of about £20 a year – were a good investment, yielding an income as high as £250 or £300 after ten years' work. But there were risks involved. Said one commentator, 'Many houses in the West End are absolutely unfit for any good or nice-minded girl to enter.'[35] Parents were even more wary of the hairdressing salons and perfumery businesses which were said to present 'Temptations that do not attack in other occupations'. Whatever the truth of this many girls who were attracted to the fashion trade were deterred from joining established firms and instead encouraged to occupy their talents at home – making dresses or fancy goods, for instance, to be sold privately or offered to shops on a commission basis.

Management skills of a different order were required for laundry work, which, somewhat surprisingly, seems to have been much favoured by middle-class girls. A possible attraction was the short period of training. At the Liverpool Technical College for Women it was calculated that a competent lecturer who based her lessons on Miss Calder's bestselling text, *A Teacher's Manual of Elementary Laundry Work*, could cover the entire subject in ten two-hour sessions. Technically, even a manageress needed only three months' practical training and if this was insufficient to secure well-paid employment (over £100 a year) there was always the option of setting up an independent business.

The first woman factory inspector was appointed in 1893. Training for this profession was offered by the National Health Society which set out to find students who were not too proud to delve into the practicalities of public hygiene. 'A woman who wishes to become an inspector must not be content to be able to give good written answers to questions only; she must try to obtain a thorough understanding of the principles of drainage, water supply etc. and avail herself of every chance of studying how pipes are laid.' Bedford College organized sanitary science courses for students who were prepared to 'visit various public works, and to have details of builders' and plumbers' work explained to them objectively'.[36] Successful applicants, who generally had some experience of nursing, often went on to be lecturers on hygiene, serving the poorer urban areas on behalf of such organizations as the National Health Society, the Ladies' Sanitary Association of Liverpool, and the Ladies' Health Society of Manchester.

Women of all classes had long been associated with farming, though they were seldom given credit either for their management abilities or their capacity for strenuous work. But in the late Victorian period there appeared a new participant in rural life – the 'lady agriculturalist'. She could be trained at Swanley Agricultural College in Kent to earn an independent living from vegetable growing, dairying or stock keeping. If she favoured market gardening she was urged to join a cooperative enterprise with five or six other women each of whom would contribute about £100 to the working capital. Another useful piece of advice was not to employ men until one was sufficiently experienced to forestall their attempts to filch the profits. The competent agriculturalist was capable of supplementing her income by lecturing to farmers who lacked the technical knowledge to apply modern techniques. Opportunities were particularly good in the West Country where Cheese and Butter Schools were a regular feature of rural education. Teachers were in such short supply that they were imported from America and Denmark.

Another area of adult education where women instructors were in strong demand was domestic economy. This was a factor over-looked by the secondary schools when they downgraded cookery to the tail of the syllabus. Middle-class girls who wanted to go into this area of work usually went to an establishment like the National Training School of Cookery in the Buckingham Palace Road where a general fourteen-week course cost eight guineas and a cooking instructor's course of twenty weeks was offered for twenty guineas. This establishment was one of the largest in the country but there were colleges in most of the large cities. Among those with the highest reputations were the Liverpool Technical College for Women, the Liverpool Training School of Cookery, the Sparhill Institute in Birmingham, the Yorkshire Training School in Leeds and the Sheffield School of Cookery. By the end of the century the supply of capable instructors had caught up with the demand and middle-class girls who were proficient in cookery were urged to take their skills into business or restaurants or even private homes. Those who were reluctant to take such a bold step were reminded that an imaginative cook had no trouble in earning two or three times as much as a governess.

The extent of a girl's freedom of choice of occupation depended on where she lived. In London and Birmingham girls were employed in the drawing departments of engineering firms. (One company arranged a work schedule so that the ladies could arrive and depart without actually encountering the male employees.) Library assistants were in demand but even the largest institutions, like the Manchester Free Libraries, paid very poor salaries. London and the university towns gave opportunities to indexers and in Westminster there was even a firm that took in apprentices. In the smarter districts of London young ladies could find employment chaperoning children to and from school or on holiday walks, making up wedding bouquets and funeral wreaths, tending house plants when families were away (there was a Woman's Gardening Association to administer this type of work), and playing or singing at rich people's parties. This last category could also make a living by giving private tuition. The 1881 Census calculated that there were over 11,000 music teachers in private employment.

For those with a social conscience (and the tradition of poor peopling retained a strong hold over the imagination of Victorian middle-class girls) there was an inexhaustible supply of poorly paid work in the slum settlements. Not that the supply of recruits was declining. Mission work at home and abroad ranked with teaching and nursing as the most popular occupations for those who graduated from the high schools. If they had difficulty in finding work in Britain many girls preferred to emigrate rather than take up some other occupation. The colonies were soon complaining that they had all the nurses, teachers and missionaries they could usefully absorb and would it not be a good idea to send across women who were prepared to put their backs into farming or such domestic tasks as 'nursing the baby, brightening the copper kettle, feeding the poultry, cooking the dinner and lending a hand at the ironing board'.

The Female Middle-Class Emigration Society was established in 1862 to organize what was fast becoming a major business. Information was given on climatic conditions and essential clothes and possessions, the availability of assisted passages (usually reserved for domestic servants), and the prospects of finding work when the travellers arrived at their destination. In the mid-1880s, for instance, the Society was warning against settling in New South Wales. 'The labour market is glutted, rents are high and living dear . . . In the bush, however, things are better.'

The Society did not work alone. There was the Church Emigration

Society, the Columbia Mission, the United British Women's Emigration Society, the Employment Department of the Girls' Friendly Society, the YWCA and the Ladies' Association for the Promotion of Female Education in India, all of which provided useful advice and services such as the provision of accommodation for ladies passing through London on the way to embarkation. The Colonial Office also ran an Emigrants' Information Department, which often directed applicants to the Government-sponsored Emigrants' Training Home in Salop, where women could learn domestic skills in preparation for employment or marriage.

The First World War did not create many new areas of women's employment unless such essentially short-term occupations as munition production are taken into account, but the emergency did produce a situation in which industry and commerce became accustomed to the more intensive use of skilled female labour. Many more nurses were needed than ever before, there was a big expansion in the office work associated with military administration, girls who had previously helped out on their parents' farms now became land girls and took on an increasing range of skilled occupations. A popular careers' guide published just after the War admitted enthusiastically that 'every year in greater numbers women compete with men in nearly every conceivable sphere of activity'. As an indication of the abrupt change in public attitudes the author went on to suggest to parents that they avoid blind-alley occupations for their daughters:

> It may be easy; it may be pleasant, involving perhaps the wearing and handling of pretty things in artistic surroundings or the cheerful bustle of office life; but if it is likely to bring the girl to a dead-end as regards salary and promotion in the mid-twenties it is to be avoided. When she has ceased to be a girl she may not wish to be married; and no thoughtful parent would wish her to be forced into marriage as a means of escape from a poorly paid and prospectless occupation.[37]

Parents could recognize the implication that with the awful expenditure of manpower on the Western Front more young girls would be compelled to make their own way in the world. Before the War there were about a million more women than men in Britain.

After 1918 the disproportion was more like one and three-quarter millions.

While inevitably this was a bleak prospect for some, the feminist leadership found great encouragement in the increasing demand for skilled female labour. The famous campaign cry of Olive Schreiner, who published *Woman and Labour* in 1911, was beginning to sound more realistic and practicable with every year that passed:

> From the judge's seat to the legislator's chair; from the states-man's closet to the merchant's office; from the chemist's labora-tory to the astronomer's tower, there is no post or form of toil for which it is not our intention to attempt to fit ourselves; and there is no closed door we do not intend to force open; and there is no fruit in the garden of knowledge it is not our determination to eat.

References

1. *Report of the Consultative Committee on the Differentiation of the Curriculum for Boys and Girls*, 1923, p. 33.
2. Harvey, op. cit., pp. 18, 19.
3. J. A. Cramb, *Origins and Destiny of Imperial Britain* (Murray, 1915), pp. 90, 91.
4. Dunning, op. cit., p. 6.
5. *Scottish Field*, June 1964.
6. Conference on Teaching of History (GPDST), December 1895.
7. Croydon High School Head's Annual Report to GPDST Council, 1900.
8. Olive Carter, *History of Gateshead High School, 1876–1907* (GPDST, 1957).
9. Dunning, op. cit., pp. 51, 52.
10. Paper by Miss Freund, Newnham College, to Conference on Teaching of Science (GPDST), June 1896.
11. Report from the Council of the GPDST, April 1907.
12. Steadman, op. cit., p. 44.
13. Elinor A. Welldon, *The Teacher of Young Children* (GPDST, 1896).
14. Foxton, op. cit., pp. 1, 5.
15. Shaw, op. cit., p. 41.
16. Baird, op. cit., p. 368.

17. Ibid., pp. 140, 141.
18. Vera Brittain, *Testament of Youth* (Gollancz, 1933), pp. 33, 34.
19. *London Mercury*, September 1920.
20. Steadman, op. cit., p. 20.
21. *Quarterly Review*, April 1869.
22. *Girls' Own Paper*, 19 July 1884.
23. Josephine Butler, *The Education and Employment of Women*, 1868.
24. Emily Faithfull, *Women's Work with Special Reference to Industrial Employment*, Society of Arts, 1871.
25. Mrs William Grey, *University Education of Women*, Paper to Society of Arts, May 1871, William Ridgeway, 1871, p. 23.
26. *Nineteenth Century*, January 1894.
27. J. G. Fitch, *Address to Students of Birkbeck Institution*, October 1872.
28. Josephine Butler, *The Education and Employment of Woman* (1868).
29. *Englishwoman's Year Book 1891* and *Guide to Female Employment in Government Offices* (Cassell, 1891).
30. *Girls' Own Paper*, 21 March 1891.
31. Ibid., 8 November 1902.
32. Ibid., 10 October 1891.
33. Ibid., 28 October 1882.
34. Ibid., 11 April 1891.
35. Ibid., 2 January 1892.
36. Ibid., 19 September 1903.
37. Sir Charles Cheers Wakefield, *On Leaving School and the Choice of a Career* (Hodder and Stoughton, 1920), pp. 213, 216.

Chapter seven

Higher and secondary

> Ah, were I something great! I wish I were
> Some mighty poetess, I would shame you then,
> That love to keep us children! O I wish
> That I were some great princess, I would build
> Far off from men a college like a man's,
> And I would teach them all that men are taught. . . .

Tennyson, The Princess, *1847*

By the 1870s committees working for higher education for girls were in evidence in most of the larger towns and cities. One of the earliest groups to be founded was the North of England Council for Promoting Higher Education of Women, with its offshoot, the Ladies' Council of the Yorkshire Council of Education. The main function of these organizations, apart from planning a long-term strategy for the admission of women into the universities, was to arrange lectures and classes in such popular subjects as history and English literature. Some of these enterprises were so successful that the curricula were broadened into the equivalent of complete college courses which were eventually merged with the established system of university education. Thus the Clifton classes were taken over by Bristol and the London Ladies' Association was transferred to University College. But long before this happened there were other important battles fought and won.

Emily Davies, who had already achieved some success in entering girls for university local examinations, now began to think in terms of setting up a women's college. She decided that Cambridge was to be the base for her venture since it was there that sympathy for her cause was strongest. Contributions came in slowly but when, at last, £2,000 were collected it was decided to go ahead with the next stage of the plan. In 1869 a small house was rented at Hitchin to accommodate the first five students. The project was 'designed to hold in relation to girls' schools and home teaching a position analogous to that occupied by the universities towards the public schools for boys'.[1]

The first prospectus promised a strict routine of study beginning at 8 a.m. and finishing at 6 p.m. The fees for board, lodging and instruction were £35 a term. Hitchin was twenty-six miles away from Cambridge which made it difficult to organize the regular attendance of university dons. Lectures, said one ex-student, were governed by the times of trains.[2] But at least parents had the comfort of knowing that their daughters were not exposed to the moral dangers of living in close proximity to male students.

At about the same time an alternative scheme was a topic of discussion for the North of England Council where Josephine Butler, who was president, and Anne Clough, founder and secretary, were preoccupied with their ideas for introducing women to a test of higher intellectual calibre than that of the university locals. They had the support of several eminent Cambridge scholars including the philosopher Henry Sidgwick, John Stuart Mill and Henry Fawcett, who did much to organize lectures for women. Inevitably there was the problem of accommodation and Miss Clough moved to Cambridge to take charge of a residence for female students. In 1875 they moved to another property which was to become Newnham College. A year earlier Emily Davies's establishment was transferred to roomier premises at Girton.

An American student recalled that each of the Girton girls was provided with a bedroom and a study. Discipline was not unduly onerous, at least by school standards. Students were required to enter their names on an attendance register three times daily and were expected to attend all lectures unless specifically excused. They had to be in College by 6 p.m. in winter and by dusk in summer unless they had an evening invitation (not more than one a week permitted) in which case they could remain out until 11 p.m. Men were not allowed in any of the private rooms. The morning was given over to individual study in preparation for lectures in the afternoon. After dinner the students entertained themselves with college songs or country dancing. Tea, coffee or cocoa was brought to their rooms by the servants before 9 p.m. but there was no rule against talking long into the night.[3]

Why was it necessary for Girton and Newnham to retain their separate identities? The reason was that Emily Davies and Anne Clough represented distinctly contrasting philosophies of girls' education. The division, already apparent in the schools, between the new feminists and those who adhered to the traditional feminine ideal, was much more clearly defined in the area of higher education. Miss Davies wanted complete equality. She dismissed the scare tactics of some of her critics, who liked to think that women who aimed at the academic heights would collapse with brain disease before they were even within striking distance. But her argument was less secure when she insisted that her girls should work for the examinations of the ordinary degree. Most academics of any note thought that the qualification was not worth the parchment on which it was commemorated. Henry Sidgwick, among others, believed that a new women's college should set an example of intellectual excellence which the men's colleges would be bound to follow. The challenge was resisted by Miss Davies, who asserted that 'a fancy test invented for women only, even if really higher, would never possess more than a fancy value'.[4]

That danger certainly existed, and taking into account Emily Davies's lack of sympathy with the feminine ideal, it is difficult to blame her for her uncompromising attitude. Now, however, with hindsight adding another dimension to the argument, how tempting it is to wish that she had taken the broader view. What could have been achieved in higher education if the feminists had stuck to their own line rather than accept what amounted to male leadership can be illustrated by the experiences of Anne Clough and the North of England Council. Miss Clough and her friends were prepared to go along with the idea that there should be a special women's examination; indeed they were very keen on the project partly because they believed in distinguishing between the sexes but chiefly because they calculated that they would have a greater influence on society and education if they retained their independence. Hence they petitioned Cambridge to create a new examination, for the particular purpose of assessing female abilities. The University granted the request and in 1869 the higher local examination was introduced, offering a choice of subjects including literature, history, arithmetic and political economy.

What chiefly distinguished it from the conventional courses was the refusal to allow it to be burdened by the dead weight of the Classics.

Emily Davies was firmly opposed to the scheme, although she was prepared to give grudging approval to a similar experiment launched by London University. She believed that this exam was 'not on the whole less difficult than the existing matriculation examination'.[5] But a professor who was involved in the administration of the scheme claimed that the standard expected of girls was incredibly high and he admitted, 'Would that all our young men had as much when they begin their university course'.[6] The Cambridge higher local attracted first-class lecturers and good quality students whose obvious need for a permanent study base was eventually satisfied by the creation of Newnham College. So successful was the examination that five years later it was opened to men, many of whom found the studies more suited to their interests than the traditional courses. There is a hint in this development that if the feminists had presented a united front they might have led the reform of the entire structure and content of higher education.

Men might have also have benefited if they had had access to a college run on the principles of Newnham, where the intellectual atmosphere was relaxed without encouraging apathy or indolence. Instead, the pattern for the future was set rather by Girton where the Emily Davies régime was dedicated to the frenzied pursuit of academic status and paper qualifications. She hoped by this means to create broader responsibilities for women outside as well as inside the home. '. . . all women are not made to be philanthropists,' she wrote. 'It would be considered unreasonable to expect that all men should take Holy Orders, or enrol themselves as town missionaries. . . .'[7] But this did not mean that she regarded education simply as a passport to a career. She told the Social Science Association:

> So long as education is treated only as a means of getting on in the world, nothing is easier to show that the women for whom the getting on has been done by other people do not want it. . . . The object of the new College is not to enable women to make money, though that may probably be among the results indirectly attained. . . . It will not be directed towards changing the occupations of women, but rather towards securing that whatever they do shall be done well.[8]

Perhaps Agnata Frances Ramsey had this in mind when, after being placed alone in the first division of the first class of the classical tripos for 1887, she promptly married the Master of Trinity. 'It is her goodness, not her Greek and Latin, that have stolen my heart,' said the bridegroom.[9]

At Oxford, local examinations were extended to girls in 1870. Lectures were organized by a group of academics who were sympathetic to the idea of women participating in higher education and these events were so popular that inevitably there was a move to introduce special courses and exams covering 'such kinds of learning as are particularly part of women's education as well as those which may from time to time be recognised in the Schools of the University'.[10] Modern languages were substituted for Latin and Greek and though great emphasis was put on the arts subjects, particularly history, the ladies were permitted to study Physics and Biology. Oxford also established two women's colleges – Lady Margaret Hall and Somerville. The difference between the founding groups was not so much social and educational as religious (Somerville was undenominational) but before long there was a split in educational aims as Somerville followed the Girton path towards sex equality while Lady Margaret Hall remained loyal to the feminine ideal. 'We want,' said the Principal, 'to turn out girls so that they will be capable of making homes happy.'[11]

The difference in aims was a continuing issue but with the formidable Emily Davies leading the campaign for the recognition of female academics there was a clearly detectable progression towards equality. Ironically, it was a victory that was founded on a defeat – or rather, an unconditional surrender to the male-dominated concept of higher education. A final and fruitless attempt to reverse the trend was made by Miss Beale when, on a slender budget, she founded St Hilda's so that her girls 'might do better service for the glory of the Creator and the relief of man's estate'. In 1875 Parliament legislated to enable universities to admit women if they wished. Shortly afterwards London revised its charter to allow for the award of degrees to women and their admission to all classes, lectures and examinations. This was a concession far in excess of anything offered by Oxford or Cambridge, where examination successes did not carry the right for female students to put B.A. after their names. It was not until 1920 that Oxford awarded degrees to women, while at Cambridge the die-hards held out until 1948.

Sir J. J. Thompson, who was Master of Trinity in the 1930s, recalls that:

> The proposal met with the most determined opposition. . . . On the day of the voting there was a great influx of non-residents and the proposal was thrown out by the crushing majority of 1707 to 661. I believe the number of voters has never been equalled. . . . The behaviour of some of the undergraduates after the poll was declared in the Senate House as exceptionally deplorable and disgraceful. A large band of them left the Senate House, proceeded to Newnham and damaged the bronze gates which had been put up as a memorial to Miss Clough.[12]

The liberals at London University urged Bedford College to abandon its remaining links with secondary schooling and encouraged the foundation of two more women's colleges. Westfield, which opened in Maresfield Gardens in 1882, was financed by a donation of £10,000 from Miss Dudin Brown, who wanted to 'establish a college for the higher education of women on Christian principles'. In 1891 the College moved to its present site in Kidderpore Avenue. Examinations were taken at University College but there was no pressure on students to round off their studies with a degree. Royal Holloway, founded by a pill manufacturer in memory of his mother, was opened in 1886. A few years later the 'ladies department' of King's College was merged with the formal university structure.

Elsewhere there were increasing opportunities for women to acquire degree status. By the mid-1890s all the Scottish, Irish and Welsh universities had abandoned discrimination, and women students were welcomed at Liverpool, Leeds and Manchester. Durham, the last of the English universities to open its courses to women, conceded in 1895.

But there was no question of higher education for any but the daughters of middle- and upper-class families. Fees were high and the few scholarships that were available usually went to the more illustrious of the high schools. In the mid-1890s Girton was at the top of the fee scale with minimum charges of £105 a year. Newnham fees varied from 75 to 96 guineas (fires in students' rooms and dinner wines were counted as extras), Lady Margaret Hall charged 75 guineas, St Hugh's £60, and Somerville £60. Costs were similar in London – at Royal Holloway, for example, the fee was £90 a year – but further afield parents could find economy courses for their daughters. Alexandra College, Dublin, offered higher education at prices from between £14 and £21 a year but this did not include accommodation. It may have been the cost that deterred some parents and certainly not all places were taken up. In 1870 the report of Bedford College Council regretted 'that the number of students is not larger, as the College could receive more students without any great increase of expense'.

In specialized vocational qualifications, as might be expected, conservatism was strongest where academic work was associated with the narrow mentality of the professions. In 1859 the British Medical Register contained the name of one woman doctor. Elizabeth Blackwell studied medicine in New York and when she came to London found that her American degree entitled her to professional recognition. It is unlikely that this contingency had ever entered the collective imagination of the Medical Council, where the prevailing opinion (shared by the medical schools) was that women, if they had to be employed, were best occupied in a supporting role. Anyway, they acted with more than customary haste to frustrate the ambitions of other precocious ladies by revising the Charter so that in future holders of foreign degrees could be excluded.

Elizabeth Blackwell later returned to America but before departing she gave lectures and classes to encourage others to take up the cause. One of those who was inspired by her example was Elizabeth Garrett, a friend of Emily Davies, who shared the same strength of will and infinite capacity for political warfare. She started as a nurse at the Middlesex Hospital but with the help of private coaching very quickly made her entrance to lectures and demonstrations. A succession of examination successes followed which stimulated jealousy and opposition from her male colleagues so that she was unable to complete the course.

The Society of Apothecaries held an examination which entitled successful candidates to be put on the Medical Register. There was no rule that excluded women simply because it was never anticipated that they would offer themselves for assessment. The Society tried to find excuses for refusing Elizabeth Garrett's application but gave way when legal action was threatened. In this way Miss Garrett became the second woman to appear on the Register and the medical establishment imposed another restrictive measure which ensured that in future the Society of Apothecaries only accepted candidates from the medical schools.

But the fight was only just beginning. A group of assailants led by Sophia Jex-Blake invaded the medical faculty of Edinburgh University. They asked only that they should be allowed to attend special lectures and classes which they were prepared to finance, but inevitably this was followed by a request to sit the examinations. Their obvious abilities and skilful public relations succeeded in winning limited concessions but as soon as they started to make real progress, the male students showed their disapproval. The women had only to put in an appearance at the school to be greeted like politicians on the hustings. Boos and catcalls were supplemented by such hearty demonstrations as pushing a live sheep into a crowded examination room. 'Leave it,' said the invigilator, 'it has more sense than those who sent it.'

There was triumph for the conservatives when Sophia Jex-Blake failed her examinations. The amount of effort she was putting into extra-curricular activities must have contributed to her failure, but even if she had succeeded, the university would have refused to give her a degree for she was unable to persuade the Senate to recognize women's claims to equality of opportunity. Undeterred, she founded the London School of Medicine for Women, which inspired support from public figures who had been appalled by the ill behaviour of the Edinburgh students. Four-year courses were offered to women who were prepared to pay from between £60 and £70 a term for board and lodging in addition to an £80 surgery fee and £45 for hospital instruction. Among the sympathisers were several eminent Parliamentarians who made their contribution by persuading their colleagues to approve an Enabling Bill. This permitted the medical schools to examine women even if they were technically forbidden to do so by the terms of their charters. This was the breakthrough, followed by a decision of Queen's University and the King's College of Physicians in Ireland to admit women to the Medical Register. Sophia Jex-Blake was one of the first to take advantage of this concession.

In 1876 the London University Senate supported the admission of women to medical degrees but Convocation insisted that approval should be postponed until the question of awarding all degrees had been considered. Subsequent debates went in favour of a policy of liberalization and in 1878 an amended Charter was accepted by Convocation by an absolute majority. One by one the other medical schools fell into line. By the turn of the century all the Scottish and Irish universities, the University of Durham, Victoria University (Leeds, Liverpool and Manchester), the Society of Apothecaries and the University of Birmingham admitted women to medical degrees. Fees averaged £130 a year plus £40 for the privilege of sitting the exams. But even after this quite considerable expenditure, women doctors could not be sure of obtaining the sort of employment they wanted. There were openings in missions, girls' schools and colleges, workhouses and asylums but it was virtually impossible to set up in private practice. In sheer frustration some of those who succeeded in obtaining good qualifications went abroad to work. In 1890 when there were 110 females on the Medical Register, 32 of them were practising in India.

Women art students found that training was available for them far more easily, partly because the profession was considered a much more ladylike pursuit and partly because several members of the Ladies' Circle were influential in art circles. The Society of Female Artists was formed in 1856 and five years later the Royal Academy schools were opened to women. By the turn of the century there were a considerable number of institutions offering courses for both sexes ranging from Metropolitan Art Schools run by the Board of Education and the Central School of Arts and Crafts in Regent Street (two shillings and sixpence a month for all classes) to Caldcron's School of Animal Painting (twenty-five guineas a year). For parents who worried about their daughters mixing with men, there was the Royal Female School of Art and the Wimbledon Art College for Ladies. Among those who qualified and tried to earn a living, the lucky ones found regular jobs in fashion houses or in publishing; the less fortunate designed greeting cards in their back parlours.

Music was another ladylike study. The Royal Academy of Music encouraged female applicants by offering forty scholarships. Unsubsidized students paid eleven guineas a term, about the same as the fee charged by the Royal College of Music and the Guildhall School of Music. There was also the option of preparing for the Bachelor of Music degree at London, Durham, Edinburgh or the universities of Wales and Ireland. Oxford and Cambridge allowed women to study music but, of course, did not permit them to take degrees.

An ever-growing sector of higher education for women was teacher training, which had the great advantage of combining academic studies with the promise of a steady career. Training for secondary school teaching was nonexistent until a demand for skilled staff was created by the girls' high schools. A teacher training department was founded at Cheltenham by Miss Beale, an example that was followed by several other schools. The Girls' Public Day School Trust took an early lead in providing training facilities and the National Union for Promoting the Education of Women was persuaded by Maria Grey to set up a college for secondary teachers. Miss Buss was active on the Council of the College of Preceptors, an organization set up to promote educational interests, which included the award of teaching diplomas.

An increasing proportion of middle-class girls found a vocation in elementary teaching. In 1873 Bishop Otter Memorial College at Chichester, which had previously trained schoolmasters, was reopened 'for the purpose of training ladies as elementary teachers in the principles of the Church of England'.[13] But there were numerous classless colleges which accepted both girls from the high schools and pupil-teachers from the elementary system. The first group were advised to sit for one of the university local exams and gain some practical experience before applying for admission. They paid their own fees, which varied from £20 to £40 a year. In rare cases loans could be arranged through such organizations as the Society for Promoting the Employment of Women or the Yorkshire Ladies' Council of Education. The second group were invariably holders of the Queen's Scholarship, which was awarded to those who survived a strenuous introduction to practical teaching. Kathleen Lee, who was a pupil-teacher with the East Ham authority in the early 1900s, has described how her career began:

The path was well-trodden; a year as Probationer, doing all the odd jobs, breaking up clay (no plasticene), winding hanks of new knitting cotton, sharpening pencils, cutting squares of flannel and calico straight to a thread for needlework specimens, cleaning and filling inkwells for the lowest classes, taking dunces for reading in a corner of the hall, playing the piano for drill lessons. Then I became a Candidate, with a rise to £8 per annum and a new Probationer under me. Half the day was spent at school and half at the centre, involving a great rush in the dinner hour. Homework occupied most of the evening.

In my sixteenth year I took the Government Exam on the result of which depended my formal apprenticeship to the local authority for three years. Having passed, I became a First Year pupil teacher at £20 per annum, rising in subsequent years to £26 and £32. The money was supposed to be put aside for training college fees. In my case it had to help with the home.

Kathleen Lee did not win a scholarship and though she was offered a place in a training college she could not afford the fees. Instead she went on to take the Government Certificate, an external exam for which she prepared by attending evening classes.[14]

Most cities had facilities for evening study. In London female students were welcomed at the Birkbeck Institute, which boasted a free library of nearly 10,000 volumes, the Regent Street Polytechnic, the College for Working Women in Fitzroy Street, the South-West London College and the People's Palace in the Mile End Road. Special classes were put on at such centres as the Wimbledon Lecture Hall and St Mark's School in St John's Wood.

The schools and the colleges together achieved a remarkable change of public attitude to girls' education. 'No girl,' wrote a contributor to a popular journal, 'should go into society until she has attained her eighteenth year. She ought to give her whole attentions to her education, reserving only due leisure for exercise, games of play, and meals.'[15] And a contributor to *Nineteenth Century* wrote: 'We have of late years elected to educate everybody, our daughters included . . . diplomas of proficiency are more plentiful than were blackberries last year.'[16]

This was something short of the truth, since the high schools were almost exclusively preoccupied with families who could afford to pay fees. There was a large group comprising the lower middle class and a section of the working class who could not spare much money for their daughters' education yet wanted to achieve more than could be offered by the elementary schools. The success of the high schools stimulated their envy and the Taunton Commission, reporting in secondary education, recommended the creation of a system ~onding 'roughly, but by no means exactly, to the gradations ~iety', but the proposal was ignored. Twenty years later the Cro~~ Commission, which examined elementary education, noted that some school boards were already setting up higher-grade schools which, in effect, were doing secondary level work. A minority report welcomed this development and suggested that the government should encourage further projects. Nothing was done – at least not on a systematic basis. But the more progressive school boards went ahead with their schemes helped by grants from industrial and public funds that were intended to stimulate technical education.

In some areas girls' education benefited from these developments. London's Technical Education Board, which was established as a department of the LCC in 1893, provided 600 junior county scholarships, of which just under half were awarded to girls from elementary schools. The holders were entitled to free secondary education for two years and an annual grant of £12. There were also intermediate and senior county scholarships which in 1895 enabled about fifty girls to attend high schools. Facilities varied from one area to another. Cheshire gave thirty scholarships a year to girls, Liverpool offered two. Surrey founded two secondary schools for girls – Wallington and South Wimbledon; Derbyshire took over a girls' high school in Chesterfield when it was threatened with closure and administered several co-educational grammar schools. Manchester awarded thirty scholarships, tenable at a technical school, a school of art, a grammar school or Owen's College. Hull's municipal technical school opened a women's section and Durham founded a School of Cookery and Household Economy.

The breakthrough for a State system of secondary education came with the 1902 Education Act, which enabled local authorities to maintain and assist secondary schools for both sexes. Now the nineteenth-century high schools were taken as a model (there was no other alternative available) for the creation of a much enlarged sector of girls' education. Thus, ironically, it was in the years of the militant suffragettes that education achieved its biggest ever recruitment for the gospel of the feminine ideal. Between 1897 and 1902 the number of girls educated in recognized schools increased from 20,000 to 185,000. By the beginning of the First World War the total exceeded half a million. But complete equality remained an elusive ideal. In 1936 the secondary schools catered for 150 boys every 10,000 of the male population and only 124 girls per 10,--- the female population.

In at least one respect the feminine ideal was given stronger recognition in the elementary schools, where the Board of Education did its best to compensate for a deficient social environment by putting a special emphasis on the need for instruction in home management. The 1876 Code identified domestic economy as the most important study for girls. A Grant of four shillings per pupil was paid to most schools after 1882 when there were about sixty thousand girls taking the subject. By the end of the century this figure had jumped to 122,000. But standards of instruction varied extensively from one school to another:

> At one extreme the inquirer would find a slovenly classroom, as often as not unswept, filled with the fumes of uncovered gas rings. Disposed about the various desks he would discover groups of girls, from four to six in number, under their ordinary class teachers, interfering with each other's efforts to make beef tea, rock cakes, and pancakes, or to recook cold meat cooked by the previous class. At the other extreme he would encounter large classes of girls drafted to cookery centres filled with elaborate stoves and appliances of a type they could never hope to see in their own humble homes, and by sheer weight of numbers compelling their harassed teachers to set them to endless rubbing of flour through sieves and the picking of every single stalk from every single currant. That there cannot have been very many centres of the latter type may, however, be inferred from the opinion expressed by one Inspector that £12 to £15 should be an ample allowance to provide the whole equipment required for cookery classes.[17]

Needlework was another subject supported by special grants, although here the chief difficulty was finding members of the all-male inspectorate who were qualified to judge the quality of the work. As Matthew Arnold complained, 'The new grant for needlework requires female help for the proper award of it. No one will seriously maintain that a set of men are fit judges, either of plans on which to teach needlework or of results in an examination in it.' In some schools it was the custom to bring out the same garments year after year in the hope that the inspector would not realize that he had seen and judged them on earlier occasions. After 1890 there were grants to encourage instruction in laundrywork and by 1902 the list of practical subjects embraced dairywork, household management, cottage gardening and – as a first hint of future equality – cookery for boys, but only for those who lived in seaside towns.

Then the larger authorities started experimenting with the use of domestic centres, the chief purpose of which was to break down the totally artificial barriers between the practical subjects. Eventually the best schools were equipped with modern housewifery flats where girls could relate their studies to realistic domestic situations. The aim was to persuade them to 'realise the value of the home as a social and national asset, to provide a model which will stimulate the desire for improved conditions in their own homes; to help them appreciate the importance of domestic and personal hygiene, well balanced economical meals and labour-saving methods in home organisation'.[18]

With developments of this sort there were hints in the 1920s that the philosophy of girls' education might begin to have a wider impact on the boys' schools. After all, the gradual move towards sex equality justified introducing both sexes to the principles of domestic well-being. And then there was the dawning awareness that the qualities of the good life as interpreted by the women educationists – gentleness, sensitivity, consideration for others – might usefully be given some stronger promotion by their male colleagues. It was surely no coincidence, as the psychologists pointed out, that anti-social and delinquent behaviour was invariably associated with the traditional characteristics of masculinity.

But the cross-fertilization between boys' and girls' education did not work out in quite the way that the optimists expected. For one thing, after the suffrage victory the enthusiasm went out of the feminist movement. Advances of the inter-war years, such as the Law Reform Act of 1935 which freed husbands from responsibility for their wives' torts or civil wrongs and included married women among the general body of adult people who could own property, were part of a legislative tidying-up process that raised little excitement. The classic exception was A. P. Herbert's Matrimonial Causes Act which introduced grounds for divorce other than adultery, but it is noteworthy that this reform was promoted and carried through by a man.

Women's employment did not achieve the advances predicted in the earlier years of the century. Two decades of economic depression saw to that. There was a slight uplift of interest in technology produced by the pioneering achievements of such as Amy Johnson (an economics graduate from Sheffield University) and Margaret Partridge, who established and administered a prosperous heating and lighting firm. Soon after the First World War a Women's Engineering Society was founded by Lady Parsons, the wife of the inventor of the turbine, who was an engineer in her own right. Advertising created a new area of women's work and the larger firms in the retail trade took to recruiting women for posts in senior management. But most female graduates veered towards teaching, while throughout the inter-war period only about ten per cent of university-trained women went into industry.[19]

The preference for teaching was not entirely based on convention. There was a better chance of achieving senior jobs in the schools and salaries were competitive with those in industry. In the 1920s a woman could start in an elementary school at £180 a year, rising to £261 after ten years. The maximum for a headmistress in a London elementary school was £486. In the secondary sector a woman graduate started at £264 a year and received £372 at the end of ten years. Corresponding salaries in the provinces were about £50 less. A secondary headship could be worth over £900 a year, a salary that compared favourably with the rewards of teaching in the private sector. The GPDST paid between £600 and £800 to heads of schools with 350 pupils or over, and £500 to £700 to heads with less than 350 pupils. Probably the most significant development over the whole field of women's employment was the decline in the proportion of females employed as domestic servants, a figure which dropped from forty per cent to about thirty per cent between the 1890s and the 1930s. The reduction was caused chiefly by the fall in the number of people who could afford two or more maids.

The high schools, now securely established institutions, reclined into conservatism. The headmistress of Loughborough reflected the view of most of her colleagues when, in the school magazine for 1930, she wrote:

In the present age there is a general lowering of standards; people work less hard, think and act less honestly, behave more selfishly and live more slackly than they did fifty years ago. In School you are taught that there are absolute standards, that is to say, unchanging standards of honesty, truth, decency, kindness: to those standards . . . you must try to cling, however much the standards of your generation may change.

Whatever one thinks of the quality of such sentiments their importance is that they are clearly distinguished from earlier statements of high school policy by the defensive manner in which they are expressed. Gone is the crusading zeal which enthused the women educationists of the nineteenth century into believing that they could change the world. Instead there is merely the hope that a lucky minority might 'cling' to certain basic values. The attitude persists today, as a glance at a few speech day addresses or school prospectuses will immediately confirm. In 1970 the headmistress of The Mount School told the parents, 'In an age when public opinion as well as the law allows ever wider freedoms in matters of smoking, drinking, sexual matters, waking and sleeping hours, we are likely for reasons of health, mental and moral welfare, and religious principle too, to find ourselves increasingly apart from the world around us. . . .'

The tragedy of the girls' schools in this century is that they have become isolated from the mainstream of educational progress. It is almost as if they have deliberately abrogated the responsibility of trying to change and improve the social ethic. Developments might have been very different if early on they had enthusiastically embraced the principles of coeducation. 'If boys and girls, young men and young women, may dance and sing and generally play and amuse themselves together with advantage,' commented an educational writer in the 1870s, 'is any special danger to be apprehended if they should also study together?' Without waiting for an answer he went on to point out the considerable benefits of such an arrangement. 'Might not the refining influence of the one sex upon the other be expected to continue, so that the boys aiming at a higher standard of conduct would be less prone to selfishness, bullying and rowdyism of whatever kind, while the girls were less given to frivolity, sentimentalism, and gossip.'[20]

The logic of his argument was hard to beat. Where the experiment had been tried abroad it was regarded as a success. For instance, the Americans quickly accustomed themselves to coeducation in the days when the colonists could not afford separate schools. Boston, New York and Philadelphia administered single-sex schools but most of the other northern cities preferred coeducation. The popular view was that mixed schools made boys less rough and girls less sentimental and generally raised the standard of discipline.[21]

But in Britain the traditionalists were not to be persuaded. The question was discussed on several occasions by the North of England Council for Promoting the Higher Education of Women. The consensus of opinion was in favour of coeducation but 'the social feeling and habits of the English people would be against such an education system'.[22]

When the Taunton Commission was carrying out its investigations, they discovered a small coeducation endowed school at Upholland in Lancashire. The Commissioners said that the arrangement was most unusual. But if they had looked a little more carefully they would have found at least a few other examples. The Quakers adopted a mild version of coeducation at Ackworth, founded in 1779 'for the education of children whose parents are not in affluence'. Boys and girls were taught in the same building but were invariably separated for particular classes and were not encouraged to mix socially.

Genuinely coeducational establishments made their debut in the 1850s. Barbara Leigh-Smith opened the Portman Hall School; W. A. Case founded a boarding and day school for boys and girls at Hampstead and in 1869 the Misses Lushington started a coeducational boarding school near Kingsley in Hampshire. Thirty boys and thirty-five girls were taught together in everything except needlework. Said the headmaster, 'No restrictions are placed upon the ordinary open intercourse of the two sexes, but with the elder children we have to guard against clandestine communications.'[23]

Later in the century authorities with scattered populations discovered that coeducation had great economic advantages. Derbyshire, for example, ran a mixed school at Heanor which supplied a training 'of a commercial and general character'. There was another coeducational Higher Grade School at Clay Cross and when, in 1896, the ancient grammar school foundation at Bakewell was revived, boys and girls were admitted. The success of these schemes led to a decision to accept girls at three rural grammar schools which were situated in 'such sparsely populated districts, that with boys alone they can never flourish'. Bedales, probably the most famous of the coeducational boarding schools, was opened in 1893, though girls were not admitted until 1898. J. H. Badley, the founder and first headmaster, found himself administering a mixed school when, '... the offer was made by a mother of one of our boys to open a house for girls and bring with her her own daughter and three other girls. ...'[24]

It was in the elementary sector that coeducation took a really strong hold. By 1900 about half these schools were mixed and the proportion was very much higher in the north and in Scotland. But the motive for this development was related to economics, not to ideology. Indeed, there was considerable worry that boys and girls might see too much of each other and special precautions were taken to make sure this did not happen – separate entrances to the building, for example, and divided playgrounds. But in middle-class schools even this mild form of coeducation remained something of a rarity. By 1919, out of 1,080 secondary schools recognized as efficient, only 224 were mixed. The reason why the middle-class insisted on a social and educational barrier between boys and girls was because they feared that sexual misbehaviour was an inevitable consequence of coeducation. Thus some of the best features of girls' schools were relegated to a backwater of education.

There was a little relaxation of public attitudes after the First World War, when the lessons of the Freudians gained popular currency and when the practicalities of contraception came within the area of general discussion. In 1918 Marie Stopes published *Wise Parenthood*, a practical handbook on birth control, the royalties from which helped her to establish Britain's first birth control clinic. But this was not so much a revolution as the beginning of a very long trek towards standards of liberal and tolerant behaviour which are not much in evidence even today. Certainly, in the 1920s, Victorian prudery remained dominant. Commenting on the quality of advice in marriage manuals of the 1920s, Alex Comfort describes them as projecting 'a Stopesian squareness which is enough to make one abandon the project before the banns are up'.[25] If this is a fair reflection of adult reticence, it is not really surprising that there was no change in educational philosophy.

'. . . in the man have been developed powers of acquisition, con bativeness and self-assertion; in the woman, of creation, endurance tenderness and foresight; or, dealing with intellectual differences, that the movement of man's mind is discursive; of woman's pene-trative. His task has been to subdue the world; hers, to maintain the home.'[26] And that apparently was how it was to remain.

In 1923 the Consultative Committee of the Board of Education published a report on the Differentiation of the Curriculum for Boys and Girls respectively in Secondary Schools. It contained a curious mixture of recommendations that were aimed at reconciling recent moves towards sexual equality with contemporary ideas from popular psychology. It was suggested that boys and girls should be given identical doses of mathematics and that girls should learn elementary physics and devote more time to 'the analysis and un-derstanding of the logical content of works of literature'. Girls might profitably learn woodwork and boys domestic science. But the report was stuck with the notion that between the sexes 'there are important differences in temperament and emotion'. Although it was recognized that these differences are chiefly the product of 'training and tradi-tion', the Committee seems to have worked on the assumption that the education system could not be used to change the status quo. Girls were assumed to suffer more readily from physical fatigue and overstrain so it was proposed that they should take School and Higher Certificates a year later than the boys and that research should be undertaken to discover the most appropriate sports and games for girls' schools.

In 1926 the Hadow Report recommended that 'wherever possible separate new post-primary schools should be provided for boys and girls respectively'. It was thought that single-sex schools were par-ticularly desirable for the younger adolescents. Twenty years later a discussion document published by the Ministry of Education sug-gested that while mixed classes were in order for youngsters at the primary and further stages of education, in the secondary sector '. . . boys and girls must be separated for physical education and major games, and there are other respects, too, in which their needs and interests will run rather apart. Where, therefore, numbers permit, the balance of advantage may be held to lie on the side of single-sex schools.'[27]

But this was nearly the last shot of the old guard. The arguments against coeducation were losing force because there was no longer any real conviction that single-sex schools were a guarantee against promiscuity. Ironically, modern research has not only confirmed this view but shown that single-sex schools can actually encourage the very social tendencies they were supposed to prevent:

> ... it is in the schools where the boys are deprived of the company of the opposite sex that their attitude is less desirable. It is the deprivation of such company that makes them desire it all the more and at the same time tends to create – in their own words – unhealthy attitudes and an outlook towards girls which falls considerably below the 'normal friendship' which is the predominant phrase in the replies about co-educational schools.[28]

Pupils in girls' schools are also inclined to suffer social disabilities in so far as they are more likely to be 'boy crazy' or 'obsessed with sex' or even 'terrified' of boys.

Referring to mixed comprehensive schools, Benn and Simon comment:

> Although we came across schools where there were gangs and occasionally violence, where there were discussions about the length of the girls' skirts or the boys' haircuts, where vandalism was a real problem and truanting endemic, we can truly say that in all the schools we visited and have personal knowledge of – and with all the comprehensive pupils, staff, heads and parents with whom we have talked – there was one subject conspicuous by its absence: problems of promiscuity.[29]

Today there are very few single-sex establishments in the primary, further and higher sectors of education. Coeducation still has a long way to go in the secondary area, particularly in urban authorities where the great majority of the single-sex schools are to be found, but even here the trend is favourable. In the maintained secondary sector of England and Wales in 1967, 58 per cent of the schools were mixed; by 1968 the proportion was 60 per cent and by 1970, 63·5 per cent. The spread of comprehensive education with the emphasis on large schools has stimulated progress towards coeducation. The Benn and

Simon survey of comprehensive schools found that 81 per mixed. In Scotland the figure jumps to 99 per cent. Whe authorities have retained one or two single-sex schools, the ...... has been to cater for parental choice or to make a concession to the staff of amalgamated grammar schools.[30] But the trend towards co-education is far less obvious in the independent sector. For instance, less than half a dozen public schools are coeducational.

The overwhelming proportion of teachers in coeducational schools strongly favour the system and most of those who have taught in both types of school prefer coeducation. Where there is significant opposition, in the girls' schools for instance, it is based not so much on objections to mixing the sexes as on the fear that women would have little chance of securing the top jobs in their profession if they were constantly up against the competition of men.[31]

The evidence suggests that most boys or girls are unlikely to suffer academically from the coeducational situation. On the contrary, it seems that the majority do much better in their studies, though a qualifying note is introduced by the Medical Research Council investigation which found that middle-class grammar and secondary modern boys achieve marginally superior results in single-sex schools.[32]

Girls have a better chance of studying the traditionally male-dominated subjects like physics and chemistry if they attend mixed schools, though there is still generally a noticeable dividing line between girls' and boys' subjects even in areas where coeducation is long established. Benn and Simon found that fifty per cent of all mixed comprehensive schools have some subjects limited to boys only (for example, technical drawing, gardening, engineering or car maintenance) while forty-nine per cent admitted to providing certain subjects exclusively for girls.

But what of the areas where boys' and girls' education merges? Here there is a strong suspicion that most of the concessions to unity have come from the girls' side; that coeducation, as currently practised, gives too much credit to the tradition of the boys' schools. To the extent that this trend is consciously planned, the justification must be that this is a man's world and if girls want a bigger share of the glory they must learn to behave more like men. But what can men learn from the tradition of girls' education? First, that contemporary society could be made less selfish and greedy by a strong injection of feminine virtue. Secondly that not enough time and attention is given to the assessment of the unique contribution that women make to the general economy, not so much in financial terms but in work style. As a recent PEP study has shown, women in senior administration tend to be more informal than men in their relationship with their juniors and to be 'less interested in empire building and office politics'. This is the sort of characteristic that even the most male-orientated teacher might think is worth encouraging.[33]

Meanwhile, we can be thankful for what coeducation is already achieving. According to Dale, ex-pupils talk of

> a natural 'family atmosphere' and friendly pupil–teacher relationships, more 'vivacity', 'variety' and 'Joie de vivre', less 'pettiness and bitchiness' among the girls, less 'rowdiness and bullying' among the boys. The male teachers use physical force 'on the boys appreciably less, with fewer extremes of harshness', while the women teachers are not enforcing a multiplicity of – to the girls – 'unnecessary rules' or, in extreme cases, ensuring the lengthy observance of 'silence bells'. As a result there is less gap between teacher and pupil than the pupils report in some girls' schools.[34]

Dale concludes:

> The evidence that the presence of girls improves the appearance, conduct and discipline of the boys is very strong. . . . Though the evidence that the presence of boys effects a corresponding improvement in the girls is less strong, its existence cannot be denied; the tidiness of the girls and their dress are noticeably better and, according to those women who have attended both a girls' and a co-educational school, they become less catty and vindictive and less inclined to group in cliques.[35]

It seems also that mutual understanding and toleration extend from the coeducational school into the adult life of the pupils. A survey of education and happiness in marriage found that seventy per cent of those who had been to coeducational schools felt that their learning environment had helped their everyday relations with the opposite sex while roughly one in three of married adults who had been to single-sex schools thought that their education had hindered them in this respect. Moreover, about forty-five per cent of the first group said that coeducation had positively improved their chances of making a happy marriage.[36]

References

1. Emily Davies, *Question Relating to Women, 1860–1908* (Bowes and Bowes, 1910), p. 167.
2. M. C. Bradbrook, *That Infidel Place, A Short History of Girton College* (Chatto and Windus, 1969), p. 96.
3. *An Interior View of Girton College* (London Association of Schoolmistresses, 1876).
4. Maria Grey, *The Women's Education Movement* (GPDST, 1883), p. 43.
5. Davies, op. cit., p. 167.
6. Professor Masson, *University Teaching for Women* (Edinburgh Ladies' Educational Association, 1868).
7. Davies, op. cit., p. 5.
8. Bradbrook, op. cit., p. 102.
9. Ibid., p. 96.
10. Annie M. A. H. Rogers, *Degrees by Degrees* (1938), p. 7.
11. Vera Brittain, *Women at Oxford*, p. 36.
12. Quoted in Virginia Woolf, *Three Guineas* (Hogarth Press, 1938; Penguin edn), pp. 53, 54.
13. Josephine Kamm, *Hope Deferred* (Methuen, 1965), p. 277.
14. *The Teacher*, 14 January 1972.
15. *Girls' Own Paper*, 8 March 1884.
16. *Nineteenth Century*, January 1884.
17. G. A. N. Lowndes, *The Silent Social Revolution* (Oxford University Press, 1937, 2nd edn, 1969), pp. 25, 26.
18. Miss C. A. Bright, Inspector of Domestic Subjects for London, quoted in Lowndes, op. cit., p. 135.
19. Michael Sanderson, *The Universities and British Industry, 1850–1970* (Routledge and Kegan Paul, 1972), p. 337.
20. Dudley Campbell, *Mixed Education for Boys and Girls in America* (1874).
21. Mary E. Beedly, *The Joint Education of Young Men and Women in the American Schools and Colleges* (Sunday Lecture Society, 1873).

22. Report of the North of England Council for Promoting the Higher Education of Women, June 1869.
23. Alfred W. Bennet, *Is it Desirable that Boys and Girls Should be Taught Together?* (Office of Women's Suffrage Society, 1875).
24. *The Times*, 2 April 1965.
25. Dr Alex Comfort, *Sex in Society* (1963), p. 155.
26. *The Relations of the Sexes*, Report to Conference on Christian Politics, Economics and Citizenship (Longmans, 1924), p. 28.
27. *The Nation's Schools, Their Plan and Purpose* (HMSO, 1945).
28. R. R. Dale, *Mixed or Single-Sex Schools* (Routledge and Kegan Paul, 1971), Vol. II, p. 188.
29. Caroline Benn and Brian Simon, *Half Way There* (McGraw Hill, 1970; Penguin, 1972), p. 415.
30. Ibid., p. 409.
31. Dale, op. cit., Vol. I, pp. 227, 228.
32. J. W. B. Douglas, J. M. Ross and H. R. Simpson, *All Our Future* (Peter Davies, 1968; Panther, 1971), Chapter 10.
33. *Women in Top Jobs* (Allen and Unwin, 1971), p. 15.
34. Dale, op. cit., Vol. I, p. 236.
35. Ibid., Vol. II, p. 215.
36. B. F. Atherton, 'Co-educational and single-sex schooling and happiness of marriage', *Educational Research*, Vol. 15, No. 3, June 1973.

another are unable to take jobs and has led to vocal protests from those who enter careers only to find that they are expected to fall into second place behind their male contemporaries. Women are overwhelmingly concentrated in the less skilled and less responsible areas of employment. About seventy-five per cent of them are in jobs which take less than six months to learn. In 1971 nearly thirty-six per cent of female school-leavers entered clerical employment; other favoured occupations for girls include clothing, footwear and hairdressing. They command about seventeen per cent of managerial positions and, as the 1966 Census revealed, their share of supervisory jobs is limited to eighteen per cent, a figure which is inflated by the high proportion who are in charge of typing pools.

Few occupations have a formal rule excluding women – at the moment that distinction is reserved for the priesthood of the Roman Catholic Church and the Church of England. But there are a whole range of jobs – such as printing, mining, bus-driving, train-driving and flying – for which girls are effectively barred by the knowledge that male opinion is convinced of their inability to perform the work. Even in areas of employment where they have gained a foothold – and this includes most of the professions – there is little in the way of active campaigning to attract more recruits and limited encouragement for those already installed to stretch their abilities.

Surveys in this country and elsewhere in Europe have shown that employers make a determined effort to perpetuate that part of the Victorian feminine ideal which identifies women as home-based creatures. The mere expectation of marriage and pregnancy are supposed to prove that a female employee is a poor long-term risk, although, of course, the days when a man was accustomed to stay half a lifetime in the same job are long past. There is a strongly-held and frequently-expressed view that women lack leadership qualities and should therefore be allocated to duties – preferably light and undemanding – where they can be accountable to male supervision.

In a recent Parliamentary debate Baroness Seear recalled some of the surprising reactions from male employers to her study of women in positions of responsibility:

We asked ... what jobs, in the view of those managers, women could not do because they were women; and in no single case of a job mentioned were we unable to find an example in one of the other companies of a woman who was performing that job. The reasons given by the managers why women could not be employed included: 'Women are emotional and cannot cope with crises': 'men never lose their tempers, never throw things about'. One seemingly rather fortunate man said, 'Women cannot speak forcibly and openly.' Some said, 'Women are not respected abroad.' One even said, 'Women cannot stay alone in hotels.'[1]

In many organizations there seems to be an unconscious effort to reproduce the housewife image in the factory or the office. Thus, one employer commenting on the virtues of secretarial work pointed out: 'It is more natural for women to work in such an occupation because it involves hostess-type functions.'[2] For women, work on the shop floor is frequently reminiscent of the mechanical routine associated with cleaning the house and feeding the family. In neither case are they required to exercise initiative or imagination or even expected to be gifted with these qualities.

A recurring theme is that even when there is a demand for women to take on responsible and well-paid jobs, it is rare to find candidates with the requisite training and interest. But it is here that we spin off into one of those circular arguments which seem to characterize the sex role debate. By the mere act of believing that men are better able to perform most of the more interesting jobs, employers discourage women from training and competing for such jobs. While women are not openly discouraged from aspiring to the professions, their entry into these often highly exclusive clubs and their success in winning promotion depends very much on their skill in circumventing male jealousy and prejudice. In the fifty years since the 1919 Sex Disqualification (Removal) Act provided that no person should be 'disqualified by sex or marriage from the exercise of a public function, or from being appointed to or holding any civil or Judicial office or post, or from entering or assuming or carrying on any civil profession or vocation', the leading professions have scarcely taken the first steps towards evening the balance of the sexes. And yet, as Alva Myrdal and Viola Klein point out in their classic discussion of *Women's Two Roles*: '. . . if women do not conquer the professions . . . they will not develop enough leaders of their own, and will not sufficiently influence policy; they will not give encouraging examples, or stimulate a change in public opinion – in short they will not achieve complete equality.'[3]

Engineering is almost exclusively male-orientated. Among 8,300 chemical engineers there are 70 women; of the 28,000 civil engineers only 18 are women; the 56,000 electrical engineers include 116 women and somewhere in the area of mechanical engineering there are 45 women out of a total force of 65,000. Also, there are 6,500 municipal engineers but not one of them is a woman.[4] Of the other professions, the law is predictably one of the most conservative. Eight per cent of barristers and two per cent of solicitors are women. Moreover, sixty-six per cent of the law chambers in England and Wales are closed to women barristers. Four per cent of architects and one per cent of chartered accountants are women. Journalism is a little more representative with about 4,500 women among the 20,000 members of the NUJ, which puts the profession roughly on a par with dentistry, with 5,000 women on a register of 16,000.

About twenty per cent of medical practitioners are women, a proportion which, despite the entry restrictions of the medical schools might seem to qualify the profession for a relatively high grading in this particular scale of values. But points are lost because the consultants, who have the highest pay and status, are nearly all men, while at the lower end of the pecking order, nursing is female-dominated. Bearing in mind the contribution women have made to the development of social work it is perhaps surprising that the local authorities employ only fourteen women directors of social services.

In the United States, where women take forty per cent of all university degrees, the careers situation is just as bad as it is here. Only one per cent of the nation's engineers are women, three per cent of its lawyers and seven per cent of its doctors. Nearly twenty per cent of women BAs are clerks, factory workers or cooks. In Britain teaching is the only profession where women outnumber men (190,000 out of a total of 326,000 in the maintained secondary and primary sectors) but even here they hold few of the senior posts. In fact, with the single exception of girls' secondary schools, men dominate the top jobs in every area of education (see following table).

	Men	Women
University Vice-Chancellors	44	0
Principals of Colleges of Further Education	616	22
Principals of Colleges of Agriculture	44	0
Principals of Medical Schools	23	1
Principals of Polytechnics	28	0
Principals of Colleges of Education	85	72
Headteachers of boys' secondary schools	879	0
Headteachers of girls' secondary schools	1	882
Headteachers of mixed secondary schools	941	53

Source – *Hansard*, 20 July 1972.

In the great majority of occupations in every country, except perhaps in Russia and Finland, it is rare for a woman to earn the same for her labour as her male colleague. In Britain her rate of pay can be anything from five to thirty-five per cent lower. In 1968, a report of the Government Social Survey won unexpected notoriety by announcing that over fifty per cent of women employees earned less than twenty-five pence an hour. The obvious injustice was tolerable only as long as women were regarded as part-time and half-effort workers – a criticism that was seriously believed even if it was logically indefensible. But now that women are once more on the social offensive, the arguments for reforming the structure of employment opportunities and rewards has attracted enough public sympathy and political support to put an Equal Pay Bill on the statute book. The promise of equal pay 'for the same or broadly similar work' by 1975 may not be achieved in every occupation, but at least a principle has been put on record which no future government can sidestep; a principle, incidentally, which the TUC first accepted in 1883. A common fear is that employers will frustrate the intentions of the Equal Pay Bill by speeding up the process of automation in areas where traditionally the work has been performed by cheap female labour. Already the Applied Economics Research Department at Cambridge has forecast a contraction in clerical and manual jobs where women are overwhelmingly employed. It is possible therefore that the achievement of equal pay will be accompanied by a sharp cut back in the employment prospects for women. But if the need for a growth economy is accepted, it is unlikely that a large-scale shortage of employment will be a lasting problem. What is far more urgent is to make certain that the decline in demand for unskilled labour is more than compensated by an increase in the proportion of skilled jobs available to women.

It follows that as a matter of justice and common sense, the remaining social barriers, which prevent women from making best use of their talents, should be broken once and for all. One possibility for the future is legislation outlawing discrimination against women in all areas of employment. With this aim in mind a Private Members' Bill was introduced in the House of Commons early in 1972 but was talked out. The promoters had better luck in 1973 when they achieved a favourable vote on the second reading. Meanwhile, a similar Bill was given a friendly reception in the House of Lords and after a successful second reading was referred to a Select Committee, a procedure subsequently adopted by the Commons for their measure. In response to all this activity the Conservative Government announced that it too was preparing legislation to broaden employment opportunities for women. The General Election and the advent of the minority Labour administration in early 1974 inevitably disrupted the Parliamentary timetable but, at the time of writing, a Bill to make illegal 'the refusal of employment on grounds of sex alone, the refusal or neglect to offer conditions of work or opportunities for training to all persons irrespective of sex, and dismissal on grounds of sex alone' is confidently anticipated.[5] To implement the law a body like the Race Relations Board will be set up, although complaints of discrimination in industry will be dealt with in the first instance at local level. A similar procedure already works successfully in the United States and Canada where the Civil Rights Commissions investigate discrimination on grounds of sex as well as race and religion.

Even if a strong watchdog committee can remove the major grievances of women workers, however, it is not at all certain that legislation can touch the sorts of discrimination which are embedded deeply in the tradition of social and academic education. Take first the evidence of unequal opportunity for boys and girls at school. Although girls do at least as well as boys up to the compulsory school leaving age and GCE O Level (about eight per cent of both sexes obtain at least eight passes and thirty-nine per cent of both sexes gain one or more passes) more boys stay on to attempt higher qualifications.

In 1969, of the sixteen-year-olds, thirty-three per cent of the girls were in school compared with thirty-five per cent of the boys. At eighteen, there were five per cent of the girls in schools and seven per cent of the boys. With A Level passes and university entrance the gap widens. For every ten boys with three or more A Levels entering university in 1969, there were five girls; for every ten boys with two A Levels going to university, only four girls. Men at university still outnumber women by two to one despite strong indications that in the sixth forms the girls are more enthusiastic about their academic work than the boys.[6] A recent memorandum from the Committee of Vice-Chancellors and Principals claimed that the university selection process seeks the best applicants irrespective of their sex but evidence to the Robbins Committee showed that, as a general rule, women need to be better qualified than men to obtain a university place. According to a survey in *Where* magazine brilliant girls are accepted straight-forwardly enough, but when it comes to a choice between an average boy and an average girl, the boy has it.[7]

In some areas of higher education a deliberate attempt is made to restrict the number of women students. The Royal Commission on Medical Education found several medical schools where the proportion of women entrants fell below the fifteen per cent minimum recommended by the University Grants Committee, and it is frequently claimed that most of the leading schools try to keep the intake of women down to about ten per cent. Ironically, this is in a profession where women have made far greater than average progress. Despite the fact that women account for twenty per cent of those employed in agriculture, one of the two women's colleges was closed recently because, it was said, girls would have wider opportunities in mixed colleges.[8] Yet hardly any attempt has been made to provide genuinely coeducational alternatives (the rugger-playing, pipe-smoking image prevails) and some of the major colleges, notably Cirencester, remain closed to women.

Oxford and Cambridge, the only two universities where the segregation of the sexes is still the rule, reserve a relatively small number of places for women. At Oxford in 1971, 1,872 men were accepted out of 3,851 applicants but only 510 women were successful out of 1,775 applicants. The latest figures for Cambridge tell a similar story: 2,410 men accepted out of 4,810 applicants – in contrast to 497 women out of 2,033 applicants. Indeed, the proportion of women at Cambridge has actually fallen from eighteen per cent in the 1920s to the present level of sixteen per cent. But the overall position may gradually improve now that some of the men's colleges at both universities have decided to allocate a small quota of places to women.

Other universities are more liberally-disposed to women, although few can match the enthusiasm of Reading where a widely-publicized appeal has been made for more women applicants for the mathematics and science faculties. On full-time and sandwich advanced courses in further education, including those at the polytechnics, the ratio of men to women is ten to three. In some disciplines the contrast is so great it takes more than the customary act of faith to believe the statistics. Advanced courses in engineering are catering for fifty thousand men but less than one hundred women. Building courses are provided for nearly twelve thousand students of whom thirty are women.

Only about ten per cent of girls aged fifteen to seventeen in employment are getting day- or block-release compared with almost forty per cent of the boys. Even more pronounced is the disparity between the numbers of male and female apprentices. Only 7·5 per cent of girls enter apprenticeships and of these 4·5 take up hairdressing. The skilled craft occupations can boast 110 female apprentices out of a total force of over 12,000. Systematic training for related semi-skilled work accounts for another 400 girls, but in this context training can amount 'to little more than sitting next to Nellie'.[9] The contrast is particularly depressing for those who put their faith in the 1964 Industrial Training Act. It was hoped that one of the important responsibilities of the Industrial Training Boards established under the Act would be 'to expand and improve the quality of training provided for women and girls'.[10] Instead, as a report to the 1972 TUC Women's Conference reveals, 'although the levy has been paid by companies on the number of their women workers as well as on the number of men, the overwhelming majority of training programmes are designed for men'.[11]

The report also notes that the industries which have the lowest proportion of young women receiving day-release are those which employ the largest proportion of women. Five major industries share the booby prize for having less than five per cent of their young women on day-release – clothing and footwear; distributive trades; insurance, banking, finance and business services; textiles; and paper, publishing and printing. But industry as a whole must share the blame for failing to provide any sort of apprenticeship for clerical workers, two-thirds of whom are women. 'The majority of undertakings,' says the TUC Report, 'still expect the woman to have learned the basis of her shorthand and typing skills before recruitment and to perfect them outside working hours.' Ironically, the Commercial and Clerical Training Committee of the Central Training Council which produced several enlightened reports on training and employment opportunities for girls, was closed in 1969, while the ITB, dealing with hairdressing, that other major area of female employment, was abolished almost immediately following its constitution.

But for all that the other boards have achieved in the way of broadening the scope of women's employment, they too might as well put up the shutters. A survey carried out by the Association of Teachers in Technical Institutions reports that only two of the eleven long-established boards are able to provide data on changes in the proportion of women receiving training. Moreover, no board is making a positive effort to increase the range of jobs for women or to give special encouragement to firms to train them for new types of jobs. The ATTI concludes:

> The recommendations for training and further education so far published by the boards make no reference to any discrimination between men and women employees in the matter of grants or the nature of training, and boards tended to refer to this with some satisfaction in such terms as 'schemes are designed to improve quantity and quality of training by types of employment but not by sex' – a fairly clear indication that they did not so far see it as any part of their function to open up wider possibilities of training and promotion for women employees.[12]

The boards have reacted to this criticism by claiming that the manpower reports they have undertaken do not produce sufficient evidence to justify special consideration being given to women. Some are not even prepared to discuss the subject. The Distributive Industry Training Board, for instance, says it has 'no facts to indicate there is a special problem concerned with female training which needs immediate attention'. As if to emphasize the dismissive attitude of the ITBs, the 1973 Government consultative document, *Training for the*

Future, contains not a single proposal for improving the training programmes for women.

It is apparent from the evidence already discussed that it will take more than a national complaints' commission to establish sex equality in education and training. Various pressure groups have already put forward action programmes to support and supplement the legislative process. For instance, the ATTI suggests that the industrial training boards should make it a condition of a grant that firms allow the same proportion of girls as boys to participate in any job training and release for education and that there should be special grants for firms training girls and women for jobs outside the traditional female range.

The National Joint Committee of Working Women's Organizations goes a step further by proposing compulsory day-release for all young people at work below the age of eighteen.[13] This last idea may be over-ambitious as an immediate remedy, but there is nothing impracticable about the ATTI programme. Yet so far the Department of Employment has not acknowledged any defect in the structuring of training facilities and has even aroused suspicions of deliberately trying to disguise the extent of the problem by discontinuing the publication of separate figures on women's training.

On the principle that a successful action programme must start with the origins of discrimination, what is perhaps needed is a lead from the education establishment. But here again, obstruction is the rule. The House of Commons Select Committee, while noting 'a widespread feeling that discrimination between boys and girls exists', adds that the Department of Education and Science 'has been complacent in its reaction to these criticisms'.[14] To put on a real show of energy the DES needs to detect a threat to the *status quo*. When, for instance, the supporters of coeducation came close to persuading the Lords and the Commons to include in their anti-discrimination bills a clause outlawing single-sex schools and colleges, the DES hurriedly pointed out that this would clash with the 1944 Education Act, which requires the Secretary of State to give approval to any change in the character of a single-sex school or other educational establishment in the maintained sector. DES witnesses to the Select Committees of both Houses explained that in giving such approval the Secretary of State attached importance to there being sufficient single-sex schools for parents who wanted their children to attend them. The Lords Committee compromised by exempting from their

Bill existing single-sex schools and colleges but recommended a prohibition on their future establishment. The Commons Committee was more amenable to DES opinion and after quoting the Secretary of State as saying that 'as far as schools were concerned there was virtually no scope for anti-discriminatory legislation', they declared against any attempt to make existing or future single-sex schools illegal.[15]

There can be no doubt that this view will prevail when the government eventually announces the contents of its own anti-discrimination bill. But the question is raised, what happens if the new Equal Opportunities Commission supports a complaint against a school or local education authority which is practising some form of sex discrimination? The previous Secretary of State, Mrs Margaret Thatcher, admitted that if such an allegation was made it would be difficult to know how to deal with it.[16] There are powers under the 1944 Education Act which entitle the central administration to intervene if local authorities or governors of schools and colleges act 'unreasonably' in pursuit of their statutory duties. But so far these powers have not been tested in a case of sex discrimination and Mrs Thatcher told the Commons Select Committee that she doubted if they ever could be so used: 'I think . . . the powers are little short of what they would appear to the non-lawyer . . . the word "unreasonably" has a very specific meaning in legal terms, and it may be that the powers are not quite sufficient.'[17] The clear implication is that however strong a claim that discrimination exists in the schools, the DES neither has nor will have the power to remedy the grievance.

More encouraging are the prospects for dealing effectively with allegations of discrimination in the entry to higher education courses. The Commons Select Committee suggests either an extension of the Secretary of State's existing powers of direction or a statutory provision enforced by whatever machinery is eventually set up to deal with sex discrimination in general. Either proposal could help to correct an admission imbalance which otherwise is likely to fall even more heavily in favour of boys. The problem is tied to the future of the colleges of education which in recent years have constituted a major source of post-A-level studies for girls. In the academic year 1969–70, well over 15,000 girls were accepted by the colleges while only 13,000 went to the universities and another 3,000 or so to the polytechnics. For the boys the position was reversed, with about 4,000 going to the colleges, 24,000 to the universities and 6,000 to the polytechnics.

Teaching is traditionally an acceptable feminine occupation and with the huge expansion of education over the last quarter century there has been positive and strong encouragement for girls to enter the profession. In 1939 there were 83 colleges, most of them very small (64 had fewer than 150 students and 28 less than 100). Today there are 157 colleges catering for over 100,000 students. This quite rapid development has taken place despite a less than generous allocation of resources. The Robbins Committee calculated that while a student at a college of education cost the country £255 a year, a university student required an annual investment of £660. In these circumstances it is hardly surprising that the colleges have recently come in for a good deal of criticism. They have been labelled as second-class institutions which have not even managed to keep up with changes in educational priorities or improvements in teaching techniques.

One of the most serious indictments the colleges have to face is their apparent willingness to tolerate social isolation. One survey of young teachers suggests that in an average week forty per cent of their students came into contact only with fellow students.[18] But for all their defects, the colleges have the potential for making a distinctive contribution to higher education. The advent of the three-year teaching course and the introduction of the B.Ed. degree have improved their image while the James Report recommendation, now endorsed by the Department of Education and Science, that the colleges should offer a general academic qualification, the Diploma of Higher Education, which can lead on to careers other than teaching, may help them to become less introverted.

Against this there is the danger that the government may continue to link the development of the colleges to the demand for teachers. Since the declining birth rate has produced fears of a surplus of teachers in the years ahead, the present intention is to reduce the number of training places from 114,000 in 1971–2 to about 70,000 in 1981. This could have disastrous implications for the future of higher education for women. The DES projection of student numbers gives the clearest indication of the scope of the problem. In the period up to 1981 the number of school leavers gaining two or more GCE A levels is expected to increase from twelve per cent to twenty-three per cent for boys and from nine per cent to nineteen per cent for girls.

So even on the assumption that the colleges of education are restricted to their present intake, other things remaining equal the proportion of women in higher education could actually fall from thirty-nine per cent in 1967 to thirty-eight per cent in 1981.[19]

The need to raise the women's quota of admissions to higher education must be extended to take account of those who want to brush up on vocational or academic studies or learn new skills after devoting five or ten years to the kitchen and the nursery. Part-time facilities are an important characteristic of these training programmes which must also take account of the nervousness of students who are resuming work after a long break. They frequently lack confidence and have to be persuaded that traditional attitudes based on the assumption that mature people are unable to adapt to new ideas have been proved wrong. Every survey of married women shows a high proportion who are not working but would like to do so. Viola Klein has put the figure at forty-seven per cent,[20] while a British Federation of University Women report suggests that for graduates it is nearer sixty per cent.[21]

When in 1968 the BBC launched *Fresh Start*, a careers advice series for housewives, there was a cascade of letters asking for help and information. The programmes were linked to the Come Back to Teaching campaign organized by the Department of Education and Science to win back qualified teachers who had left the profession to become full-time housewives. The response was such that even in a period of teacher shortage it was not possible to find enough jobs for all the applicants.

Women are enthusiastic students. In local education authority evening classes they outnumber men two to one. Most of these courses are non-vocational but their popularity is an indication of the potential for increasing knowledge and skills. Most universities and polytechnics will accept mature students without A level qualifications if they can show their evidence of intelligence and a sense of purpose. In 1970 there were just under 2,500 mature (over twenty-five) women students at the universities, ten per cent more than in 1969. The Open University is another important source of qualifications for mature women who now represent over thirty-seven per cent of all applicants and twenty-seven per cent of the total number of graduates. The proportion of full-time housewives ranges from ten per cent in the West Midlands to sixteen per cent in the South.

But not everyone is able or wants to slot into the education system at degree level. What is required is a whole selection of opportunities covering all stages of adult education. Hillcroft is the country's only residential college of adult education exclusively for women. When it was established in Surbiton in 1920, it catered chiefly for working-class women who had left school early and wanted a chance to stretch their abilities. Hillcroft now takes in a mixed social group – but the basic aim is still the same, to help those who lack formal academic qualifications. Courses range from general studies (economics, history of art, language, psychology, modern maths and social administration), studied over one year to provide a broad education, to curricula specifically designed for a degree or teaching qualifications. Hillcroft is run by the Department of Education and Science. It has a better scholastic reputation than some university colleges and competition for places is tough despite the reluctance of many local education authorities to give student grants.

Non-residential courses on general subjects are more readily available at least for those living in the big urban areas. In London, for instance, the City Literary Institute, which is part of the ILEA complex of adult education, offers women Fresh Horizons, a full- or part-time course lasting three terms which takes in social studies, written and spoken English, new maths, English literature and speech and drama. Students are expected to devote about ten hours a week to homework. A more specifically vocational course is under way at Hatfield Polytechnic where a ten-week programme, New Opportunities for Women, is designed to help students – usually without formal academic qualifications – to decide what they want to do and whether they have the ability to do it. Aptitude tests and careers guidance are merged into a broad study of sociology. Then there is the Government Training Opportunities Scheme, which aims to increase employment opportunities by sponsoring six-month courses in fifty-four training centres and in colleges and employers establishments. In 1970 there were five hundred women in training, now the figure is close to five thousand but most of these are engaged on commercial and clerical studies.

The interest that these courses have aroused is evidence of the urgent need for an effective careers advisory service. It is difficult to assess how much effort currently goes into careers guidance for girls. On one hand, careers teachers and local authority youth employment officers claim they give proportionately more time to girls because it is less easy to advise them than it is the boys. But the critics argue that few attempts are made to encourage youngsters to break away from the traditional pattern of job allocation. Girls are expected and encouraged to take up careers like nursing which require what are thought to be essentially feminine traits such as gentleness and sensitivity. Boys are given the pick of the best opportunities in commerce and technology, a world in which 'male' determination and grittiness are counted as important qualifications.

What is true is that many schools still use careers guidance as an excuse to award a special responsibility allowance to a long-serving but otherwise ineffectual member of staff, who is unlikely to discover the crusading energy that should be a prerequisite. More evidence will be available when the DES survey of careers' education is completed, but one encouraging sign is the growing demand for an improvement of training facilities which at present consist chiefly of short, in-service courses. The Association of Careers Teachers want a minimum of one year's full-time training and the TUC suggests that careers advisers should have some direct experience of industry and commerce. A possibility for the future is a link-up between the work of careers teachers and schools' counsellors, who will be available to advise pupils on personal, educational and vocational matters.

Another hopeful development is the appearance of first-class careers literature, such as Ruth Miller's *Careers for Girls*,[22] which gives detailed information on over three hundred possible occupations. What is refreshing is Miss Miller's realistic assessment of some of the jobs that are blessed with the romantic image. For instance, she offers little encouragement to the young aspiring actress. 'Prospects,' she says, 'are poor except for the talented and lucky few.' At any given time almost a third of professional actresses are out of work and those who are lucky enough to be employed can expect to earn an average of less than £550 a year. As for modelling, only a minute percentage of models do really well and then only as long as they keep their looks and figures. The young ladies who intend gracing the hairdressing salons are warned that while the prospects are first-rate they will have to spend most of each day on their feet in the exclusive company of other women. And any girl should think twice before opting for one of those jobs to do with animal care, however strong her maternal feelings. The work of a kennel maid, for example, is 'hard and usually dirty, her day starts at 8 a.m. and usually ends at 5 p.m.; she must be prepared to stay up all night when puppies are about to be born' – and for all this she will earn 'very low pay'. On the credit side Ruth Miller puts such careers as public health, the police, quantity surveying and dozens of other jobs ranging from engineering to landscape architecture and from tax-inspecting to speech therapy.

But it is not enough simply to point out the educational and occupational opportunities. A report to the 1972 TUC Women's Conference referred to the immense social pressures on girls to obey convention, and called for a new concept of 'careers education' which should embrace a 'study of the pattern of women's working life' to prove to girls that if marriage is their immediate goal they will probably be looking out for interesting work when their children are no longer dependent on them. Even this proposal will have little effect on social attitudes unless it is matched with positive encouragement for girls to enter what are at present male-orientated occupations. But it is at this stage of the argument that careers advisers start worrying that if they show too much enthusiasm for sex equality they will be accused of offending the sacred principle of free choice. Thus the Institute of Careers Officers claims that it is not the job of any member to steer anybody anywhere, 'It is his job to provide the information, to help develop the decision-making abilities of the individual, to give him all the help possible, but not . . . to direct, rather to help people to make their own decisions.'[23]

The trouble with this policy of neutrality is that it actually re-inforces the *status quo* by implying that there is not very much wrong with prevailing restrictions and conventions. So careers advisers find themselves in the curious situation of saying that they want to broaden the employment opportunities for girls while flatly refusing to do anything positive to achieve their object. The paradox is not restricted to vocational guidance; it can be detected at every point in the education system.

Why, then, does the idea of promoting sex equality create such nervousness when public opinion seems to be shifting so strongly in its favour? First, it is important to distinguish equality from equality of opportunity. Most people agree, at least in theory, that if a girl seriously and determinedly wants to become, say, an engineer, she should be given the chance to apply her talent. In practice, of course, her parents might warn that engineering lacks a romantic image – for women, anyway – and the neighbours will be a little incredulous when they hear the news, but if that is really what she wants to do, well. . . . But there is a world of difference between this situation and one in which the power of education is used to promote the idea of a career in engineering to girls who might otherwise be content to become secretaries or teachers.

The general view is that while exceptional girls might freely choose jobs normally taken by men, the majority are physiologically, emotionally and mentally attuned to performing the traditional feminine roles. There is a strong feeling, for example, that girls are naturally submissive and are unlikely to assert themselves either in employment or in the family. Superficial but nonetheless widely respected academic support for this opinion comes from the behaviourist school of psychologists who, according to Arthur Koestler, 'convert by crude analogies' data derived from conditioning experiments on animals into 'confident assertions about the political, religious and ethical problems of man'.[24]

Consider, for example, this extract from J. A. Hadfield's *Childhood and Adolescence*:

> There are basic emotional differences between the sexes. In the main, male sexuality is aggressive (as witness the bull contrasted with the castrated bullock); female sexuality is receptive and seductive. The male wants to protect the female and the female wants to be protected while she protects the offspring. Another factor which affects the relationship of the sexes is that the stronger male, if sexually aroused, can force the female to gratify his passions, whereas the female can do nothing about it if the male refuses to be attracted. I have seen a heifer tenderly licking the neck of a bull for a long period, but he remained passive and couldn't have cared less! That is why the female adolescent is equipped with the will to seduce. Sexual play depending on this relationship is very common. You often see an adolescent boy bullying a girl and twisting her arm while she cries to him 'Stop!' But as soon as he stops she starts to provoke him again. He likes bullying to show his strength; she likes to be mastered. Both conform to their sexual natures.[25]

As Koestler points out, in the end the behaviourist line of enquiry is unproductive, since 'it is impossible to arrive at a diagnosis of man's predicament . . . by starting from a psychology which denies the existence of mind'.[26] The focus must then be shifted to enquiries that are directly related to the capacity of the sexes to behave in particular ways and to perform particular tasks. The intelligence testers have first claim to critical attention since one of their much published findings is that girls tend to achieve higher verbal scores than boys, but invariably do less well in assessments of arithmetic ability. The statistical variations are very small but they have led many psychologists and educationists to conclude that more sophisticated research techniques will detect other measurable differences in the mental processes of the sexes. At that point we might also be able finally to decide whether the differences in intellectual capacity are the product of biology or of the cultural environment. Meanwhile most parents and teachers seem to assume that boys and girls are intrinsically at odds in their academic abilities and interests. Yet so far the best evidence suggests that in bringing up children we perpetuate, often quite unconsciously, a loyalty to culturally inspired ideas of how boys and girls *ought* to perform in particular subjects. For instance, the apparent male superiority in the solution of arithmetic and scientific problems, the performance of mechanical tasks and the comprehension of mechanical relationships can be explained quite adequately by reference to environmental influences. Dr Paul Torrance, who is one of the pioneers in developing tests for creativity in children, has often tried the experiment of handing a youngster a toy and asking 'How could you change this to make it more fun to play with?' He finds that invariably girls have little to offer when it comes to dealing with science-based toys, objecting that they know nothing about them.[27]

By contrast, boys are encouraged by their fathers to exercise their talents for mathematics and science. The strongest evidence for this assertion is the result of an American survey of male undergraduates who were infants when their fathers were recruited into the army during the Second World War. It was found that these young men lacked the characteristic male bias towards mathematical reasoning. This deficit was particularly marked among those whose fathers had been away from home for the first two to three years of their lives.[28]

Conversely, girls who are brought into contact with the male enthusiasm for mathematics and science tend to do better in these subjects than others of their sex. Douglas Pidgeon, in his account of the influence of teachers' expectations on pupils' performance, points to three research studies which indicate that girls in coeducational schools achieve a greater success in mathematics than they do in single-sex schools.[29] Pidgeon comments: 'Other factors besides attitudes may be operating here, but this evidence is certainly suggestive that where girls are taught in an atmosphere where the traditional female suspicion of mathematics is less noticeable and where, perhaps, the teachers are less inclined to doubt their abilities in the subject, then they make greater strides than they would otherwise have done.'[30] Supporting evidence comes from the Soviet Union, where girls are expected to be as mathematically sophisticated as boys. The annual selection procedure to detect the most mathematically-able pupils for training at Alsademgorod recruits an increasing number of girls each year. At present more than a third of the most gifted pupils are girls.[31]

The bias against mathematics as an appropriate study for the sensitive minds of young ladies extends to science and technology. In the early 1960s the Industrial Fund, which was set up to improve the facilities for science teaching in direct grant and public schools, disposed of £3m. to 210 schools. Of these, 187 were boys' schools, 5 were coeducational and 18 were girls' schools. Serious note is still taken of the 1956 Ministry of Education Bulletin which recommended less laboratory space for girls' schools than for boys'. With discrimination on this scale it is scarcely surprising that of pupils leaving school in recent years with two or more A levels, only about twenty per cent of girls compared with fifty per cent of boys have specialized in science subjects. The 1970 figures for university attendance show that the science faculties cater for 43,250 men but only 13,270 women. In engineering and technology the contrast is between 35,475 men and 817 women. Even in the colleges of education where men are out-numbered nearly three to one, the only science in which women clearly predominate is biology. Yet a survey of seventeen schools and eight firms carried out by a research group at the London School of Economics discovered no evidence to show that girls lack aptitude for science subjects.[32]

Organizations like the Women's Engineering Society do their best to reverse the trend, but feel that the odds against them are too high to hope for any early improvement. When, recently, an official spent two days at a comprehensive school, she had only three career enquiries from girls. A few educational establishments make an effort to stimulate girls' interest in technology but with little success. Enfield College of Technology sponsored school talks on engineering until funds ran out and now organizes open days for sixth formers. Reading University has voiced strong opposition to the male monopoly of this profession and to the rough and tough image it has acquired, but so far the increase in the number of women candidates has been infinitesimal.

It is true that some schools – those that are committed to the idea of encouraging more creative work in science and technology – have succeeded in interesting girls in group projects of quite considerable complexity. But the emphasis is usually placed on domestic matters such as shrink-proofing and bleaching of woollen fabrics, strength and wear tests on artificial and natural fibres and the discovery of the nutritional value of certain foods. In one school a group of fourth-year girls who embarked on an electronic project produced a 'baby alarm'. Of broader significance is a Kingsway College of Education course linking chemistry, biology and physics, which enables girls to acquire scientific knowledge by studying the process of cosmetic manufacture. Mathematics, science and technology are the subjects in which girls most obviously suffer from 'poverty of aspiration', but the trait can be detected in every area of life where there is a possibility of conflict with the Victorian ideal that most women should look to marriage and the family as the dominant theme in their lives.

The chief conditioning agency is undoubtedly the family which specializes in the formation of identity. The extent to which parents intuitively influence children's interpretations of their sex roles is shown by an investigation by the Norwegian sociologist Sverre Brun-Gulbrandsen. He began by asking a group of mothers whether they thought that boys and girls should be brought up in as similar a manner as possible. More than ninety-five per cent answered yes. But when more concrete and specific questions were put the response was less emphatic. Nearly a quarter of the interviewees thought that boys should not be expected to help with the housework, but almost every mother agreed that 'parents ought to place great emphasis on teaching girls housework because this will be useful to them if they become housewives'. Moreover, about half the mothers thought that a good education was more important to a boy than to a girl.[33]

For most children the process of sex-role indoctrination begins from the moment of their first social contacts. Edmund Dahlström, whose survey, *The Changing Roles of Men and Women*, provides a wealth of evidence on this topic, comments:

> Books for girls concentrate on the home and love relationships, while books for boys deal with tales of conquest and experience in a world adventure. Girls are assumed to prefer company in pairs, with a best girl friend or boy friend, while boys form gangs and groups of friends. Girls are reared largely for intimate relations while boys are reared to deal with the wider society.[34]

The way in which school publications tend to reinforce family preconceptions of how children should behave can be judged by glancing along the shelves of any classroom. To take a recent example from the review pages of a national educational journal, teachers are currently being urged to buy such books as *101 Best Action Games for Boys* and *101 Best Games for Girls*. The contrast in these titles is totally justified by the contents of the books. According to the reviewer: 'Both start with "icebreakers" but after that different roles are considered appropriate for the sexes. Girls are offered one chapter of action games while the boys have a whole book of them. Boys have stunts and team relays whereas girls have singing and dramatic games and quiet games.'[35] The age range for these books is six to twelve.

Even at this early stage in their lives girls are encouraged to direct their steps along the bridal path. One teenager summed up the experience of many of her contemporaries when she complained: 'My father started giving me wedding pictures out of newspapers when I was six. When I was at school my mother used to tell me not to seem too smart in front of the boys or I wouldn't get dates.'[36]

In their survey of the progress of a group of secondary-school children, Douglas, Ross and Simpson point out:

> Between eleven and fifteen the boys become increasingly aware that what they learn at school will influence their future careers, the sort of employment for which they will be suited and the level of training that will be open to them on leaving school. In contrast, the girls see themselves as entering work that requires relatively little specialised training and will last only a few years before marriage.[37]

The propensity for teenage girls to drop out of education is, in some areas, so pronounced that local authorities use this as an argument for increasing the share of grammar-school places that are awarded to boys without apparently showing any awareness that in so doing they are helping to reinforce traditional attitudes. In *The Feminine Mystique*, Betty Friedan claims that in America the pressure on women to conform to the housewife stereotype has actually increased over the last few years. In women's colleges, for instance, the emphasis has shifted from career training to an orientation towards marriage and home-making. According to another authority the American girl 'tries to pass for more stupid than she is in order to please her boyfriend'. In one sample forty per cent of girls interviewed admitted to having concealed some of their qualifications from their boyfriends. [38] Then there are the comics and romantic magazines to confirm the lesson that a girl's chief aim is to secure a man. A popular theme in these publications, which are read regularly by at least two million girls, especially in the eight to thirteen age group, is the apparent need for potential housewives to get used to the idea that what is chiefly required of them is self-sacrifice. The weekly magazine *Fabulous* offers this comprehensive set of 'do's' and 'don'ts' for a girlfriend who wants to go to the top of her class:

Not wanting to go to the disco with your workmates anymore.

Spending your money on aftershave or a T-shirt for him instead of make-up and clothes for you.

Washing your hair on the night that he's at football.

Not wanting him to see you without your make-up.

Being nice to his family and putting up with his friends.

Getting used to the back seat of his scooter or his open top car.

Telling him he's wonderful – when he's happy and when he's down.

Such an extravagant display of loyalty is reminiscent of the stories published in the *Girls' Own Paper*. On one occasion the editors responded to a reader's request for an instance of perfect wifely duty by quoting an experience of Lady Beaconsfield. It was she who concealed the fact that her husband had crushed her finger in the carriage door till he had safely disappeared into the House of Commons lest it should distract his mind on the eve of one of his great speeches. The basic message has not changed very much. The big difference is that today it reaches a wider audience. Indeed, there is evidence to suggest that while the Victorian feminine ideal is somewhat loosening its grip on the middle class, its hold over girls from the working class is stronger now than it was one hundred or even fifty years ago when few of them had the option of experiencing the cosier side of the family ethic.

The Newsons, for instance, in their survey of infant care, point out that a middle-class wife expects to be an independent person in her own right, her working-class neighbour is more inclined to search for her main source of satisfaction within her family.[39] This view seems to be confirmed by Hannah Gavron's study of young married women which indicates that middle-class wives have a more positive and creative attitude to employment – regarding it 'as something more than a financial aid and a solution to loneliness'.[40]

But it would be unfair to suggest that it is merely because of their devotion to the Victorian feminine ideal that working-class girls are less than enthusiastic about their jobs and their career prospects. The Schools Council and Government Social Survey report on *Young School Leavers*, the great majority of whom are from working-class backgrounds, shows that parents and pupils attach tremendous importance to the vocational function of schools and that girls as much as boys expect to be taught subjects that will help them to obtain good jobs.

The trouble is that while families from the lower cultural strata may be ambitious for their children, they are unlikely to be aware of all the possible openings or to possess the self-confidence to push ahead when chances do occur. It is in the nature of contemporary society that working-class children – and particularly the girls – should have less than their fair share of the educational and training opportunities that lead to remunerative and interesting occupations. It is hardly surprising therefore that many girls should want to romanticize domestic life in the hope of finding a release from the dull routine of unskilled employment.

But to return to the main theme, assume for a moment that we agree that the differences in boys' and girls' educational achievement and social attitudes can be accounted for by reference to cultural influences. Can we then proceed to formulate a policy to demolish what remains of the Victorian feminine ideal? The immediate answer is no, because even if it is acknowledged that traditions and habits can be changed it does not follow that everyone wants them to be changed. The feminine ideal has never lacked defenders, although in recent years few have expounded their philosophy so clearly and boldly as Sir John Newsom. His opinions on girls' education have excited such controversy that he may have deterred others from wandering into what can plainly be hostile territory. Newsom first recorded his views in the late 1940s when he was Chief Education Officer of Hertfordshire. His object was to show that the schools should devote as much time to preparing youngsters for marriage and home-making as to giving them a grounding in the academic subjects, a policy which sounds encouraging until it is realized that he was referring exclusively to girls who, he believed, should be educated 'in terms of their main social function – which is to make for themselves, their children and their husbands a secure and suitable home, and to be mothers'. For men 'the equivalent dominant is to earn enough to support their wives and families'.[41] Inevitably his views irritated the feminists but Newsom was writing at a time when a war-weary public was in the mood for a 'back to home' philosophy and overall his ideas were given a sympathetic hearing. The reception was less friendly when, in the 1960s, the *Observer* invited him to restate his theories.

His critics, who in numbers alone disproved the popular libel that women are short of intellectual leaders, were unanimous in their disapproval of trying to relegate all girls to the status of trained home-makers. But so obsessed were they with the vision of a restoration of the Victorian family ethic that no thought was given to the idea that careful preparation is needed for practical co-existence within marriage and the family or that possibly many of Newsom's comments and recommendations make sense if they are applied to boys as well as to girls. 'Consider,' said Newsom, '. . . the qualities needed to be a successful home-maker' and then '. . . marvel at the conceit which places domestic efficiency on a lower level than salesmanship.' He was scornful of the type of school where 'the more intellectually able pupils take a second foreign language while the less able are allowed to take domestic science' and blamed education as a whole for failing in such matters as inculcating standards of discrimination in design and colour for the home. '. . . the subject is almost entirely ignored or relegated to an inferior position,' he complained, 'inferior at any rate to the study of arithmetic, history, geography or physical training.'[42]

The attributes Newsom associated with good home-making included a knowledge of cookery, the principles of nutrition and household economy; an ability to exercise informed taste in the choice of furniture, equipment and decoration; and an understanding of the needs of infants. Altogether it is a perfectly sensible basis for a course of study for all children, and is calculated to appeal with equal force to those who are in pursuit of sex equality as to those who want to hold on to what is best in the tradition of the Victorian feminine ideal. Even Newsom must have suspected that it was illogical to exclude boys totally from his plan. When challenged to explain why women should bear the entire burden of home-making he reluctantly conceded 'that men, too, should be competent at those tasks for which they are biologically suited – although there are dangers to domestic harmony should the male by chance excel the female in these skills'.[43]

The common view still seems to be that as long as girls are taught the rudiments of domestic science and boys learn how to fix mechanical gadgets, nature can be safely allowed to take its course. Proposals for broadening the scope of family-orientated education invariably exclude the boys altogether. For instance, the Crowther Report, while quite reasonably suggesting that 'girls should be encouraged to qualify before marriage in a greater number of professions or occupations which will provide opportunities for them in later years', goes on to emphasize that because 'boys' thoughts turn most often to a career, and only secondly to marriage and the family, and that the converse obtains with girls . . . there is a clear case for a curriculum which respects the different roles they play.'[44]

Recently, the better understanding of early environmental influences on children has strengthened the interest in education for motherhood. One proposal is that girls should have the chance to visit day nurseries, nursery schools and pre-school play groups where they can study such aspects of parenthood as the quality of relationships with children and play and language development. Such initial training, it is argued, might help the next generation of mothers to maximize the value of pre-school learning for their own children.[45]

But in all this there is no thought that the next generation of fathers might contribute more usefully to the upbringing of their families if they had some preparation for their future role. Predictably, Hannah Gavron found that in only half of the families she interviewed were the men enthusiastic helpers and then only while the children were young. Even the girls are frequently ill-equipped by the schools to enjoy marriage. Eighty-one per cent of Hannah Gavron's sample of middle-class wives had had no experience of any kind with babies when they came to have their first child, yet husbands and health visitors implied that they ought to know what to do. The working-class wives were somewhat better off – thirty-seven per cent had some experience – but this was only because they came from larger families and had closer contact with children of relatives.[46] It must be added that the Newsom Report, *Half Our Future*, which put great emphasis on the need for improved social education, awarded high praise for a school in which the barriers between the traditional girls' and boys' subjects had been removed: 'They followed a common course in metalwork and woodwork with a syllabus covering household repairs and "do-it-yourself" projects . . . [and] . . . courses in home-nursing, typewriting and commercial practice. . . . Physical education was also a mixed activity.' But this school was for pupils of 'very limited abilities' and the Report contained no suggestion that the pattern of study might usefully be adopted in other sectors of education.[47]

As a result of the Newsom Report's comments on social studies, some local authorities appointed special organizers who were made responsible for improving the domestic courses for girls. Ironically, several of these ladies now spend much of their time trying to break down the sex barriers in social education by organizing domestic courses for boys and girls. But there really needs to be much more than this if the schools are to make a serious contribution towards preparing young people for inevitable changes in the structure of marriage and the family. Whether we like it or not the more educated women are the more anxious they become to work and to devote themselves to a career. Even if the present educational inequalities remain it is still undeniable that the schools and colleges will turn out an increasing proportion of girls who are eager and qualified to take up responsible jobs. At the very least this involves a reassessment of women's responsibilities in the home. It may be that many household activities are no more than a part-time occupation but they can become unpleasantly arduous when combined with a full-time career.

It is thus depressing that apart from the efforts of a few local education authorities to encourage boys to take an interest in cooking, there remains a sharp division between girls' and boys' subjects. The Schools Council Enquiry into Young School Leavers found that woodwork, technical drawing, metalwork, engineering and workshop practice are learnt almost exclusively by boys while housecraft subjects such as mothercraft, hygiene, needlework and commercial subjects (typing and shorthand) are confined entirely to girls.[48] It is instructive to contrast this state of affairs with the situation in Sweden where they were debating the question of sex equality – and coming up with some answers – long before Kate Millet, Germaine Greer and the other contemporary stars of women's lib converted their opinions into best-sellers.

For some time now it has been the rule in Swedish comprehensive schools that all education be given equally to boys and girls. This applies to such subjects as domestic science and child care. Girls participate in handicraft courses and are encouraged to interest themselves in what were once thought to be exclusively masculine skills like carpentry and metalwork. School studies in Sweden are centrally-controlled, which is a big advantage when it comes to persuading a basically conservative profession to change the direction of teaching. The latest secondary-school curriculum which came into force in 1971 states unequivocally:

Schools should work for equality between men and women – in the family, on the labour market, and within society as a whole. They should give instruction on the sex role question and should stimulate pupils to debate and to question the existing conditions. Ideally, sex role issues should be discussed not only as a specific topic in social studies classes but in other subjects as diverse as history, biology, religious knowledge and geography.

Not many schools are quite so enthusiastic but most of the present generation of students will learn enough to realize that the social structure is at a critical point in its evolution.

All the Swedish political parties and the three largest employee associations have permanent bodies to draft publications and programmes aimed at speeding up the movement towards the equalization of the sexes. One of the organizations which is particularly active in this respect is the Joint Female Council, which was set up as a cooperative effort between the trade unions and the employers' federation. It was a member of the Council who persuaded a correspondence college that it was committing blatant discrimination by publishing two catalogues – one for boys and one for girls. Officials are for ever writing to job advertisers to point out the error of their prejudices – 'They ask for applications without mentioning sex but then publish a picture showing only one sex actually doing the job.' They have even been known to protest against Punch and Judy shows in schools because they think that Judy receives more than her fair share of violence.

In the past there have been complaints about books which depict girls as conscientious, dutiful, tidy and helpful, but at the same time passive and timorous, while boys are described as aggressive, disdainful of girls, untidy and forgetful but without any suggestion of reproach being made for these failings. Now, the emphasis is changing. A picture showing mother baking cakes would no longer receive official approval. The last time an illustration like this appeared in a Swedish text it was cut out and replaced by drawings, which included a kitchen scene with father helping to prepare the breakfast. One technique that is used to open up occupations that are either male or female dominated is the 'sex quota'. This means that if, for example, a boy wants a job as a nursery school teacher or a girl shows an interest in computer programming, they must be total duds to fail in their applications. The same effect could be achieved in this country by adopting the proposal from the Association of Teachers in Technical Institutions for special government grants to go to firms that train girls and women for jobs outside the traditional female range.

But possibly the boldest venture in the promotion of sex equality has been the lavish advertising campaign in the schools. One poster which appeared on many notice boards shows a girl smoking a cigar. The caption reads: 'Girls are not supposed to smoke cigars. What else is it that they are not supposed to do?' The answer is in smaller type: 'A girl is not supposed to think she is anything except a girl. A girl is not supposed to take charge of anything. A girl is not supposed to care about getting a lengthy education, because she will only want to get married and have children. A girl does not want a technical career, so she should study art, history or literature. These subjects are more ladylike.' And the punchline: 'The prejudices are many but it is possible to break them.'

An attempt to break the prejudices in British schools might usefully start with the reform of sex instruction, a subject which has been pioneered in the Swedish schools. One of the most irritating characteristics that identifies many writers on sex in this country is their patronizing assumption that girls should be treated differently from boys. A common theme is that every 'nice' girl should want little more than to become a wife and mother. This means that she must be respectable which, in turn, implies that she is not greatly interested in such sexual activities as making love despite the attentions of lustful men. On the other hand, once she has chosen her life partner, her sex life is miraculously transformed into a matter of immense significance, while for her unfortunate husband it can never be anything more than a passing thrill in the night.

This is still the popular interpretation of sex instruction in British schools, where the traditional social pattern requires that girls should be protected from social and psychological pressures until they are safely married. If a few white lies help to achieve this object then that is counted as sufficient justification.

Michael Schofield, whose research provides one of the few authoritative sources of information, estimates that just over half the boys and about four-fifths of the girls receive some kind of sex instruction. The fact that so many schools exclude the subject altogether would not be so serious if there was a reasonable assurance that the others were doing the job properly. But this is not the case. Schofield was 'left with the overall impression that there was a lack of frankness in the teaching. Sex education, when it occurred, seemed to concentrate on biological and physiological matters and seemed to be unrelated to human affairs except when it was wholly concerned with putting across a particular moral point of view.' For example, forty per cent of the schools that do give sex instruction make no mention of masturbation and ninety per cent give no information about methods of birth control.[49]

A recent, and for the initiated, hilarious survey of books that claim to introduce youngsters to the facts of life, reveals that most of these publications are 'inaccurate, misleading (in some cases deliberately deceitful) and almost invariably contain insidious moralising'.[50] Far from talking about facts these books deal more with the euphemisms of life. For instance, 'no normal boy thinks of making sex his life's work. He thinks of it as a spare-time interest, when he is not studying, playing games, mending a motor-cycle or arguing about politics.'[51] In 1972 there was a report in the *Times Educational Supplement* of a company producing what was described as 'realistic dolls' for sex education. It was noted that the boy doll was only a baby because 'in dealing with the very delicate subject of male reproduction it is so much easier to use the image of a baby having its nappy changed ... than to expose a maturer figure'.[52] If these examples are in any way representative, it is hardly surprising that children resort to fantasy and myth. Schofield concludes, 'going on the record of present sex education courses in schools today, nine out of ten boys and girls would fail an examination about the art of love and any examination about the symptoms of VD or birth control'.[53]

Since the opponents of sex instruction find it easier to talk in negatives, it might be useful if the liberals produce their own list of 'don'ts'. Hill and Lloyd-Jones suggest, reasonably enough, that sex education should not 'conceal facts; discourage the expression of affection and love; use the threat of disease or unwanted pregnancy to frighten the young for moralistic purposes; attempt to create guilt by claiming that sexual activity ought to occur only within marriage or imply that the only respectable life-aim for girls is to become wives and child-bearers'.[54] In their early years at school children want to know – and are entitled to know – how babies are created, how they develop before birth and how they are born. Before they reach their teens, youngsters should understand the structure and function of the sexual organs and be able to talk openly and sensibly about such topics as puberty, menstruation, masturbation, conception and pregnancy. Later, say between the ages of fourteen and sixteen, there should be discussions on social questions like contraception, venereal disease and abortion.

One vital consideration is that instruction should be given to mixed groups. Improved teaching standards are unlikely to help the cause of better understanding between the sexes, if boys and girls equipped with essential knowledge are unable to talk about it with each other. And unless more effort is made to bring this subject up to date the consequences will be serious, particularly for the 1,900,000 unmarried girls in Britain aged between twelve and eighteen, the great majority of whom are in the schools or colleges. These girls mature physically much faster than their nineteenth-century counterparts and experience the sex drive earlier in their teens, yet they are expected to conform to a system of public morality that relies on the double standard every bit as strongly as that evolved by the Victorians. Newspapers that condemn permissiveness are themselves among the leading commercializers of sex, the people who oppose advice to teenagers on birth control are invariably those who are most horrified when there is an increase in the abortion rate. Parents and teachers who claim to want their girls to be confident and unafraid are nevertheless eager to protect them from any contact with boys that might put at risk their virginal status. Hence, so many girls are confused by what they feel and what they are told about their feelings. They grow up timid and not a little frightened of relationships outside their immediate family. 'One of the most constant products of the English educational system,' writes Geoffrey Gorer, 'is shyness – the fear that one will be laughed at or rejected by strangers, particularly strangers of the opposite sex.'[55] For boys there are compensating ego-building activities which enable them to combat more easily their frustrations of insecurity. By contrast, shyness is often thought to be a positive virtue for girls, who are, after all, destined for a submissive and therefore inferior role. Honest and competent sex instruction would go a long way to correcting the balance but beyond this there is a need to broaden the entire scope of social studies. A step has been made in this direction with the Schools Council Humanities Curriculum Project and the Moral Education Project (Lifeline) based on the principle that providing teachers and their pupils with mixed materials – newspaper articles, tapes, book extracts, topic pamphlets, statistical tables – which contain evidence and opinion on such popular themes as relations between the sexes, is sufficient to stimulate wide-ranging and thought-provoking discussions. There is a clear implication that these student debates should help to create more liberal attitudes but the projects are really too much of a soft sell for this hope to be realized. The Humanities team, for instance, insists that the teacher should not attempt to be anything more than an independent chairman, while Lifeline aims simply to prepare boys and girls 'to choose to decide what in particular situations they will do so long as it is only consistent with taking the needs, interests and feelings of others into consideration as well as their own'.

The reluctance of social and moral educators to go much beyond the broadest declarations of belief derives from the strongly held opinion that questions of interpersonal relationships are better dealt with in the home environment than in the schools and colleges. Thus in a 1972 television discussion on equality between the sexes about a dozen senior teachers unanimously agreed that it is not their responsibility to try to speed up the process towards equality because they and their schools are merely a reflection of majority opinion within society at large. On the face of it this is an obtuse argument. Education is self-evidently a part of society and its participants have as much right as anyone else to express moral views. On the other hand, in strictly political terms it is not difficult to appreciate the dilemma of teachers, who, in a period of rapidly changing moral standards, prefer not to get involved in controversial issues that can bring them up against the opposition of parents and administrators.

But if the teachers' mood of disinterestedness is at least understandable it is difficult to imagine a situation in which it can be sustained indefinitely. Rising living standards, the new pattern of women's employment and the evolution of the family, must have repercussions in education as in every other area of society. Teachers are still in a position to choose whether they will help or oppose the movement towards sex equality. If they eventually decide against conservatism we will at last be able to stop thinking in terms of the education of boys or the education of girls and get on with the business of educating *children*.

References
1. Hansard, House of Lords, 14 March 1972.
2. Edmund Dahlström, *The Changing Roles of Men and Women* (Duckworth, 1967), p. 151.
3. Alva Myrdal and Viola Klein, *Women's Two Roles* (Routledge and Kegan Paul, 1968), p. 77.
4. Margherita Rendel *et al.*, *Equality for Women* (Fabian research series 268, 1968), p. 7.
5. Special Report from the Select Committee on the Anti-Discrimination (no. 2) Bill (HMSO, 1973).
6. Donald Hutchings and Judith Clowsley, 'Why Do Girls Settle for Less?', *Further Education*, Autumn 1970.
7. 'The A Level Stakes', *Where*, September 1969.

8. Pauline Pinder, *Women at Work* (PEP, 1969), p. 55.
9. Sixth Report from the House of Commons Expenditure Committee, *The Employment of Women* (HMSO, 1973), p. 22.
10. 'Training and Retraining for Women', *Ministry of Labour Gazette*, November 1966, p. 721.
11. *The Roots of Inequality*; A Report to the 1972 TUC Women's Conference.
12. *Education, Training and Employment of Women and Girls* (Association of Teachers in Technical Institutions, 1970).
13. National Joint Committee of Working Women's Organisations; Campaign Notes, 1972.
14. Special Report from the Select Committee on the Anti-Discrimination (no. 2) Bill (HMSO, 1973).
15. Ibid.
16. Ibid.
17. Ibid.
18. *The Future of Teacher Education* (NUT, 1969).
19. Student Numbers in Higher Education in England and Wales, Education Planning Paper No. 2 (HMSO, 1970).
20. Viola Klein, *Working Wives* (Institute of Personnel Management, 1958).
21. Constance E. Arregger (Ed.), *Graduate Women at Work* (Oriel Press, 1966).
22. Ruth Miller, *Careers for Girls* (Penguin, 1970).
23. *The Employment of Women*, p. 89.
24. Arthur Koestler, *The Ghost in the Machine* (Hutchinson, 1967; Pan edn, 1970), p. 24.
25. J. A. Hadfield, *Childhood and Adolescence* (Pelican, 1962), pp. 191, 192.
26. Koestler, op. cit., p. 33.
27. Paul E. Torrance, *Guiding Creative Talent* (Prentice-Hall, 1962).
28. Carlsmith, 'Effect of Early Father Absence on Scholastic Aptitude', *Harvard Educational Review*, 1964. Quoted in Liam Hudson, *Frames of Mind* (Methuen, 1962), p. 21.
29. J. C. Daniels, *Some Effects of Sex Segregation and Streaming on the Intellectual and Scholastic Development of Junior School Children* (Unpublished PhD Thesis, 1959, Nottingham University); R. R. Dale, 'An Analysis of Research on Comparative Attainment in Mathematics in Single-sex and Co-educational

Maintained Grammar Schools', *Educational Research*, Vol. 1, 1962, pp. 10–15; T. Huren (Ed.), *International Study of Achievement in Mathematics* (Wiley, 1967); Quoted in Douglas A. Pidgeon, *Expectation and Pupil Performance* (NFER, 1970), p. 33.

30. Ibid., p. 33.
31. Evelyne Sollerot, *Women, Society and Change* (Weidenfeld and Nicolson, 1971), p. 85.
32. Nancy Seear, Veronica Roberts and John Brock, *A Career for Women in Industry* (1964).
33. Sverre Brun-Gulbrandsen, 'Sex Roles and the Socialisation Process', in Dahlström, op. cit., pp. 63, 64.
34. Ibid., p. 43.
35. *The Teacher*, 15 October 1971.
36. *Guardian*, 30 April 1970.
37. J. W. B. Douglas, J. M. Ross and H. R. Simpson, *All Our Future* (Peter Davies, 1968; Panther Books, 1971), p. 44.
38. Sollerot, op. cit., p. 158.
39. J. and E. Newson, *Infant Care in an Urban Community* (Allen and Unwin, 1963).
40. Hannah Gavron, *The Captive Wife* (Routledge and Kegan Paul, 1966; Penguin, 1968), p. 113.
41. John Newsom, *The Education of Girls* (Faber and Faber, 1948), pp. 12, 25.
42. Ibid., pp. 24, 82, 104.
43. Ibid., p. 128.
44. 15 to 18, Report of the Central Advisory Council for Education, Vol. 1 (HMSO, 1959), pp. 33, 34.
45. Michael Stanton, 'Education for Motherhood', *Trends in Education*, October 1969.
46. Gavron, op. cit., pp. 70, 80.
47. *Half Our Future*, A Report of the Central Advisory Council for Education (HMSO, 1965), p. 38.
48. *Young School Leavers*, Schools Council Report (HMSO, 1968), p. 56.
49. Michael Schofield, *The Sexual Behaviour of Young People* (Longmans, 1965).
50. Maurice Hill and Michael Lloyd-Jones, *Sex Education – The Erroneous Zone* (National Secular Society, 1970), p. 2.

51. K. Barnes, *15 + The Facts of Life* (BMA, 1966); M. O. Lerrigo, *Sex Education Series* (Heinemann, 1958).
52. Quoted in the *New Statesman*, 30 June 1972.
53. Michael Schofield, *Sex Education now and then; the right of children to know* (Rights of Children, National Council of Civil Liberties, 1972), p. 16.
54. Hill and Lloyd-Jones, op. cit., p. 27.
55. Geoffrey Gorer, *Sex and Marriage in England Today* (Nelson, 1971), p. 23.

Index

Council of Macon, grants women a soul, 13

Crowther Report, and boy/girl roles, 214

curriculum, efforts to restructure, 7, 109, 147; concern with accomplishments, 26; in charity schools, 29–30, 37–8; distinctions between two sexes, 30, 183, 208–9; teacher-training colleges, 64–5, 67; boarding schools, 73–5, 76; relationship to fees, 122; place of science, 144–5; correlated schemes, 147; higher sector ,165, 169; secondary, 177–8; adult, 203

Dahlström, E., *Changing Roles of Men and Women*, 210

Dale, R. R., *Mixed or Single-Sex Schools*, 184, 185

Dalton, H., *Education of Girls*, 92

Davies, Emily, and equality of opportunity, 8, 97, 103–4; admissions to local university exams, 97–8, 99, 107–8, 165; educational philosophy, 168, 169

Department of Education and Science (DES), 201, 202, 204; and single-sex schools, 199–200; Hillcroft college, 203

Department of Employment, 199

discipline, 15–16, 30, 33, 166–7; assumed adjunct to learning, 77, 78–9

Disraeli, Benjamin, 91

domestic economy, prevalence in teacher-training, 64–5, 67, 96; courses for students, 146, 176; women instructors, 160; in girls' schools, 177–8, 213–16; absence in boys, 216

domestic servants, 153; Victorian plentifulness, 8; upper class functions, 39; creation of leisured classes, 82; decline in numbers, 179, 190

Edgeworth, Richard L., 26

education, 58; influence on social attitudes, 9, 180; religio/social concept, 28; and mass discontent, 37, 59; promotion by industrialization, 54–5; and women's rights movement, 91, 152, 154; class distinctions, 108–9; boy/girl value, 209; further, 197–8, 199; higher, 147, 165, 167–8, 175, 196, 201–2; rural, 160; secondary, 174–7, 183; vocational (medieval), 17

Education Department, 63, 64, 108; pupil-teacher scheme, 66, 67

Eliot, George, 43, 90

Elliott, Rev. Henry V., Brighton school, 76–7

Ellis, Sarah, *Wives of England*, 85

Employment of women, mass movement into new areas, 152–3; substitute for marriage, 154; economic depression, 170; in senior posts, 186; fall in age composition, 190; discrimination against, 190–1, 194–5; romanticized jobs, 204; working class disadvantages, 213; agriculture, 153, 160, 162, 196; civil service, 155–6; dressmaking, 158–9; engineering, 179, 193, 208; hairdressing, 198, 204; journalism, 156–7, 193; kennel maids, 204–5; missionaries, 153, 161–2, 173; *see also* Professions

Endowed Schools Commision, and girls, 108, 119

English Woman's Journal, The, 89

Equal Opportunities, Commission, 200

Erasmus, Desiderius, 20; and girls' education, 18–19

evening classes, 175, 202

examinations, 33; examiners' incompetence, 143; limited scope, 144; boy/girl inequality, 195–6; civil service, 155; GCE – A-level, 196, 201, O-level, 195; 'higher local', 167–8, 169; Oxford and Cambridge local, 97–8, 107–8; pupil-teacher, 66; University, 167, 196

factory system, 38, 54, 82, 153; influence on women's lives, 54–5, 61; women inspectors, 159

family, the, sacred emblem of Victorian society, 12, 84; and

feminine ideal, 82; changed pattern, 189–90, 215; influence on girls' identity, 209
Fawcett, Henry, 166
Fawcett, Millicent, 152
Female Instructor, The, 44–5
Female Middle Class Emigration Society, 161
Female Reform Societies, 54
feminist movement, 7, 89–90; new breed, 97, 189; conservative opposition, 151–2; contrasting philosophies, 167–8, 169; loss of enthusiasm, 178
Fénelon, François Salignac, *Education of Daughters*, 24–5
Fordyce, Dr James, *Sermons*, 50
Francis Holland C. of E. School, 121, 123–4, 128, 131, 143; drill lessons, 134
Friedan, B., *The Feminine Mystique*, 211
Froebel philosophy, 147
Fry, Elizabeth, Newgate school, 89
Fuller, Thomas, on convent schools, 16

games and sports, 11, 135–8, 148, 210
Garrett, Elizabeth, 171–2
Gavron, Hannah, *The Captive Wife*, 212, 215
girls, practice of boarding out, 21–2, 26; Tudor and Stuart, 22–3; pit employment, 62; absence of school facilities, 62–3; 19th C. working class, 82–108; feminine ideal, 82–7 (*see also* under women); sexual ignorance, 84; frustrated existence, 84–9; and boys' occupations, 148–9; single-sex and co-education schools, 184–5; 20th C. marriage patterns, 190; pressure to conform to feminine role, 205, 206; compared with boys, 206–7; and teacher expectation, 297–8; romanticised domestic life, 212; and motherhood, 214–15; sex instruction, 218, 219; girls' education, 7; theological influences, 12, 60–1; concern with accomplishments, 26, 39, 72, 87, 149; in the

home, 26, 68, 124; public attitudes, 103, 108–9, 175; condemned by inspectors, 104–7; disparity with boys, 109; reform movement, 110; era of expansion, 118 ff.; acquires a distinguishing ethos, 151; influence on employment market, 152; Girton v. Newnham philosophies, 167–8; cross-fertilizes boys' sector, 178; isolation from main stream, 180, 182; need for careers advice, 203–4; and a postmarriage return to work, 205; teenagers' view of their future, 210–11
Girls' Friendly Society, 162
Girls' Own Paper, 211–13; quoted, 68–9, 72, 83, 84, 121, 157–9, 162
Girls' Public Day School Company (GPDSC), 109, 111–13; fees, 122; prize day, 130; timetable, 133; domestic subjects, 145–6; training facilities, 174; staff salaries, 179
Gisborne, Rev. Thomas, *Duties of the Female Sex*, 47, 83–4, 87
Glasgow; Westbourne Gardens School, 120, 130, 131
Godwin, William, 51
Gorer, Geoffrey, *Sex and Marriage in England Today*, 220
governesses, 160; treatment, 68–71, 92–3; training for, 77, 93–4
Governesses' Benevolent Association, 92–3, 95
Gray, William, Bishop of Lincoln, 16
Greece, ancient, position of women, 18
Gregory the Great, Pope, on Pastoral Care, 12
Gregory, A., *A Father's Legacy to his Daughter*, 46, 50
Grey, Mrs Maria (née Shirreff), 109–10; and girls' education, 110–11, 174; training college, 111
Gurney, Mary, and GPDSC, 112

Hadfield, J. A., *Childhood and Adolescence*, 206
Hadow Report, 183
Hardwick, Bess of, 21; boarded out, 22
headmistresses, final arbiters, 130–1;

marriage, 42, 215; an escape from home, 16; social advancement by, 105; a girl's ambition, 150; influence of co-education, 186–7; younger age entry, 190; idea of self-sacrifice, 211–12

married women, financial dependence, 44, 88; diversity of home tasks, 44–5; factory work, 54; Victorian image, 85; duties to their husbands, 85, 88; and daughters, 86; male status symbols, 87; legal changes, 90, 178; increase in labour force, 190; and a return to work, 202, 205; continuing concept of 'feminine ideal', 213

Maurice, F. D., 93–4, 95

medical profession, 84, 85, 133

men, and clever women, 46, 48, 171; women's role and, 46–7, 81, 83, 87; student conditions, 65; reaction to suffragettes, 152; 'preserved' occupations, 156, 191; training for homemaking, 214–16

Merchant Taylors' School, 22; for girls, 119, 132

middle classes, upward mobility, 39; women writers, 43; emergence of leisured women, 82; political work, 91; private schools, 119–24; acceptable occupations, 153, 154–155; and co-education, 182; and feminine ideal, 212

Mill, J. S., 166; *Subjection of Women*, 91

Miller, Ruth, *Careers for Girls*, 204–5

monasticism, position of women, 12–13; Dissolution, 16

Montague, Mrs Elizabeth, 42

Moore, Mrs, *Cheap Repository*, 86

More, Hannah and Martha, 39, 40; *Strictures on Female Education*, 42–3

More, Sir Thomas, 18–19, 20

Morris, Rev., women's minds, 87–8

Mulcaster, Richard, 22–3

Murray, Hon. Amelia, and governesses, 93, 94

Myrdal, Alva and Klein, Viola, *Women's Two Roles*, 192–3

National Association for the Promotion of Social Science, 99

National Health Society, 159

National Joint Committee of Working Women's Organizations, 199

National Society, 93; Church schools, 56, 58–60; teacher training, 64–5, 66

National Union for Improving the Education of Women of all Classes, 111, 173

National Union of Women's Suffrage Societies, 152

Newcastle Report, on elementary education, 63–4

Newsom, Sir John, concept of feminine ideal, 213–14; *Education of Girls*, 213; *Half Our Future*, 215

Nightingale, Florence, 86, 87; on frustrated bright girls, 88–9

nonconformists, schools, 29, 38, 119; oppose state control, 59

North of England Council for Promoting Higher Education of Women, 165, 166, 167, 181

North London Collegiate school, 8, 102, 136; under Miss Buss, 101–3, 104; middle class ethos, 101, 102; expansion, 102–3, 121; fees, 122–3

Norton, Caroline, 90

Owen, Robert, free schools, 55

Pankhurst, Emmeline and Christabel, 152

parents, 55; and girls' education, 107, 109, 112–13, 128–9, 209, 210; and their employment, 162

Parkes, Bessie R., 89; *Education of Girls*, 91–2

Parliamentary Commissions: Education of Lower Orders, 58; of the Poorer Classes, 60; schools for middle class children, 103–4; Education of Girls (Taunton), 104–9, 110, 142, 175–6; on elementary education (Cross), 176; on the Anti-Discrimination Bill, 199–200

Paston, Elizabeth, harsh treatment, 15–16